Headway English A2

Teacher's Book | **Liz and John Soars**
Amanda Maris

with Teacher's Resource Disc

OXFORD
UNIVERSITY PRESS

Contents

TEACHER'S RESOURCE DISC (inside back cover)

Communicative activities
Tests with test audio
Grammar Reference with practice
Student's Book word lists
Class tapescripts
Video worksheets
CEFR mapping information

Introduction

Headway English A2

Headway English A2 is a course for students who already have some basic knowledge of the language. They may have recently completed a beginner course or they may be returning to language learning after a break and need to revise key language before being able to progress further.

New language is introduced systematically and at a steady pace, allowing students to increase their knowledge of the language and build their confidence. Listening material is provided on class CDs and as MP3 files on a disc supplied with the Student's Book. New vocabulary is introduced gradually and there are regular controlled practice activities, allowing students to activate the language in a supported way. There are also freer practice activities where students have the ability to start focusing on their fluency. In the *Everyday English* sections, useful chunks of language are presented, which students can use in several different social contexts.

Elements in the learners' L1 (e.g. learner strategies, bilingual word lists) give additional support. To reflect the CEFR (Common European Framework of Reference), unit goals are clearly stated at the start of each unit. At the end of the unit, learner strategies and can-do statements enable students to take control of their own learning.

Organization of the course

The organization of *Headway English A2* is similar to other levels of *Headway English*. Each unit has the following:

- Starter
- Presentation of new language
- Practice
- Skills work – always speaking, combined with listening or reading, with a writing section for each unit at the back of the book
- Vocabulary
- Everyday English

Each unit ends with two pages of *Extra practice* material, a page of *English for work* exercises with additional relevant vocabulary, and some *Video activities* for use alongside the student video DVD. The answer key for these exercises is included at the back of the Student's Book.

Starter

The *Starter* section is designed to be a warmer to the lesson and has a direct link with the unit to come.

Presentation of new language

New language items are presented through texts, often conversations, which students can read and listen to at the same time. This enables students to relate the spelling to the sounds of English, and helps with pronunciation, as well as form and use.

The main verb forms taught are:

- *to be*
- Present Simple
- *can/can't*
- *was/were/could*
- Past Simple
- *I'd like*
- *have got*
- Present Continuous
- *going to*
- Infinitive of purpose
- Present Perfect

There are *Grammar Spots* in the presentation sections. These aim to focus students' attention on the language of the unit. There are questions to answer, charts to complete, and short exercises. The *Grammar Spot* ends by cueing a section of the Grammar Reference at the back of the book.

Practice

This section contains a variety of controlled and freer practice exercises. The primary skills used are speaking and listening, but there is also some reading and writing.

There are information gap exercises, group discussions, information transfer listening exercises, pronunciation exercises, and a lot of personalized activities. There are exercises where the aim is overt analysis of the grammar, such as *Check it*.

Vocabulary

There is a strong lexical syllabus in *Headway English A2*. Vocabulary is introduced systematically and it is reviewed and recycled throughout the course. Lexical sets are chosen according to two criteria. They complement the grammatical input, for example, jobs and free-time activities with the Present Simple; or shopping items for count and uncount nouns. However, they are mainly chosen for their usefulness. Students at this level need to build on their vocabulary set and they primarily need words for everyday life. Students also work on word patterns in the form of collocations. Knowledge of common collocations can really help to improve a student's level of fluency. The course covers noun + noun combinations as well as verb + noun combinations, such as *drive a car*, *look after children*, *get married*, etc. Students also focus on other patterns throughout the course, such as opposite adjectives and adverbs.

Skills work

Listening

Regular unseen listening sections, in dialogue or monologue form, provide further practice of the language of the unit and help to develop students' ability to understand the main message of the text.

Reading

At the beginning of the course the reading texts are relatively short and are carefully graded to allow students to build on their previous knowledge and to increase their confidence as they start a new level. As students move through the course, the texts quickly become longer and more challenging, with students being exposed to increasing amounts of new lexis. This encourages them to start deducing meaning from context and enables them to engage with more complex reading texts.

Speaking

In the presentation sections, students have the opportunity to practise the pronunciation and intonation of new language. In the practice sections, less controlled exercises lead to freer speaking practice.

There are many speaking exercises based around the listening and reading activities, including regular roleplays. There are speaking opportunities before a text, to launch the topic and create interest; and there are speaking activities after a text, often in the form of discussion.

Writing

Writing is primarily practised in a separate section at the back of the Student's Book. This comprises 12 complete writing lessons cued from the unit, which can be used at the teacher's discretion. The writing syllabus provides models for students to analyse and imitate.

Everyday English

This is an important part of the syllabus of *Headway English A2*. Students have the opportunity to practise chunks of language used in formal and informal situations. Students learn phrases for requests and suitable responses, for use whilst shopping, when asking for directions, and for many other situations. Students also learn about appropriacy, as there is a focus on how to sound polite by choosing suitable phrases and using polite intonation.

Grammar Reference

This is at the back of the Student's Book, and it is intended for use at home. It can be used for revision or reference.

Revision

Regular revision of grammar and vocabulary is provided throughout the course. As well as the *Extra practice* pages at the end of each Student's Book unit, there is a photocopiable activity for each of the 12 units at the back of this Teacher's Book. These photocopiables also feature on the Teacher's Resource Disc, along with an additional 12 photocopiable *Communicative activities*. There are also 12 *Unit tests*, five *Skills tests*, three *Stop and check tests*, two *Progress tests*, and two *Exit tests* on the Disc.

Video

Video clips are available on the DVD that accompanies the Student's Book. There are 12 clips, one for each unit. The language and theme in each clip are linked to the relevant Student's Book unit. The majority of the clips follow a documentary style, and include native speaker interviews. Activities to use with the video clips are included on the last page of each unit in the Student's Book. Video worksheets are also included on the Teacher's Resource Disc.

Teacher's Book

The Teacher's Book offers the teacher full support both for lesson preparation and in the classroom. Each unit starts with a clear overview of the unit content from the Student's Book, along with a brief introduction to the main themes of the unit and a summary of additional materials that can be used. There are opportunities for additional activities with *Suggestions* and *Extra activities*. This allows for further work on key language or skills when appropriate.

Teacher's Resource Disc (TRD)

The Teacher's Resource Disc can be found inside the back cover of the Teacher's Book. It contains additional printable material to support the teacher with the course. There is a comprehensive range of testing materials, including *Placement tests*, *Unit tests*, *Stop and check tests*, *Progress tests*, *Exit tests*, and *Skills tests* with audio files. As well as the tests, it also has photocopiable *Communicative activities*, *Video worksheets*, *CEFR mapping information*, *Tapescripts*, *Word lists*, and Grammar Reference with related grammar exercises.

Finally!

The activities within *Headway English A2* are designed to enable students at this level to build on their knowledge of the language and to allow them to activate what they have learnt. There is also an emphasis on increasing confidence, so that students feel able to actively participate in short conversations and discussions. We hope that students will enjoy using the course and that it will give them a real sense of progression in their language learning.

1 You and me

am/is/are **•** ***my/your/his/her*** **• Verbs –** ***have/go/live/like*** **• Possessive** ***'s*** **• Word groups • Everyday conversations**

As you begin *Headway English A2*, you are probably starting a new course with a new group of students. The main aim of this first unit is that students get to know each other and you, and you get to know them. In addition to this focus on personal information, students also practise greetings and expressions from everyday conversations.

LANGUAGE INPUT

GRAMMAR	
am/is/are (SB p8, p13)	• Practising *be* in all persons (affirmative/negative/questions).
my/your/his/her (SB p8, p9, p13)	• Reviewing subject pronouns and possessive adjectives.
Verbs – *have/go/live/like* (SB p10)	• Recognizing and using basic verbs to talk about everyday life (*I* form).
Possessive *'s* (SB p10)	• Understanding *'s* for possession and as the short form of *is*.

VOCABULARY	
Opposite adjectives (SB p13)	• Focusing on key adjectives and their opposites in context.
The family (SB p14)	• Practising vocabulary to ask and answer about your family.

EVERYDAY ENGLISH	
Everyday conversations (SB p15)	• Using greetings and key expressions in everyday situations.

SKILLS DEVELOPMENT

READING	
A student's blog (SB p12)	• Reading about a student's experiences of school and family in England.

LISTENING	
Five conversations in a student's day (SB p13)	• Listening for key information in five short conversations and completing a chart. **T 1.13** (SB p168/TRD)

SPEAKING	
Talking about you (SB p9)	• Exchanging personal information.
The family (SB p14)	• Talking about your family.

WRITING	
You and your life (SB p11)	• Writing key information about yourself.
A blog – Keeping an online journal (SB p154)	• Completing gapped blog entries, then writing an entry to read aloud.

MORE MATERIALS

Photocopiable worksheets – Everyday conversations (TB p148/TRD), Adjectives pelmanism (TRD) **Test** (TRD) **Video** (DVD)

STARTER (SB p8)

SUGGESTION

Whatever your students' knowledge of the alphabet at the start of the course, remember that they will all need regular practice in the alphabet and spelling. This can easily be integrated into any lesson when teaching new vocabulary (*How do you think you spell … ?*), or when reviewing vocabulary (*How do you spell … ?*), and by the use of spelling games or cards.

At this early stage or with weaker classes, you may want to write the alphabet on the board and drill the letters in groups of five before moving on to exercise 1.

1 **T 1.1** **[CD 1: Track 2]** Say your own name – *I'm (Liz)* – and point to yourself to make the meaning clear. Write your name on the board and then spell it out, pointing to each letter in turn. Focus attention on the letters in exercise 1 and tell the students that they are going to listen to the alphabet. Play the recording and get students to just listen.

Say *A*, *B*, *C* and then invite students to continue. Encourage the class to help each other if students have problems with individual letters. Note down the letters students get wrong or don't know, paying particular attention to *a*, *e*, *g*, *i*, *j*, *q*, *r*, *u*, *w*, and *y*, which often cause problems for students. Drill the letters which students found difficult. Play the recording again as consolidation if necessary.

2 Invite a few students to say their first name. Check students understand 'alphabetical order' by putting letters a–g on the board in random order and asking students to reorder them alphabetically. Then ask students to stand up in alphabetical order and say their name. If appropriate, repeat this, getting progressively faster each time.

Encourage students to memorize as many names as they can. If appropriate, play a memory game by pointing to individual students and yourself, and getting the class to say the correct names. Encourage students in a multilingual class to pronounce each other's names (and your name!) as accurately as possible. If there are not too many students in the class, put their names on the board so that everyone can begin to learn them.

EXTRA ACTIVITY

Consolidate the alphabet by getting students to categorize the letters according to their sound:

/eɪ/	a h j k
/iː/	b c d e g p t v
/e/	f l m n s x z
/aɪ/	i y
/əʊ/	o
/uː/	q u w
/ɑː/	r

HELLO! (SB p8)

am/is/are – my/your

1 Write your own first name and surname on the board. Point to each name and say the appropriate word. Elicit some first names and surnames from the class. Pre-teach/check the question *How do you spell that?* and briefly review the alphabet from the *Starter* section.

T 1.2 **[CD 1: Track 3]** Play the recording once and get students to read and listen. Then ask them to point to Bill and the interviewer in the photo. Ask *Where are Bill and the interviewer?* (at a business conference).

Play the recording a second time. Students repeat as a class. Play the recording again then practise it in both open pairs (i.e. students ask and answer the questions across the room with the rest of the class listening) and closed pairs (i.e. the whole class working in pairs). Make sure students can accurately produce the contracted forms *name's*, *what's*, and *I'm*, and the falling intonation on the *Wh*-questions.

GRAMMAR SPOT (SB p8)

Focus attention on the contractions. Ask students to circle the contracted forms in exercise 1.

2 Focus attention on the example and then ask students to complete the conversation. Remind them to use contracted forms. Ask students to point to Carla and David in the photo.

T 1.3 **[CD 1: Track 4]** Play the recording and let students check their answers.

Answers and tapescript

C Hello. My name's Carla. What's **your** name?
D David.
C **Where** are you from, David?
D **I'm** from Bristol. Where **are** you from?
C **I'm from** Bristol, too!
D Oh! Nice to meet you!

Ask students to practise the conversation in open and closed pairs. If students sound a little flat, encourage a wide voice range, particularly on the last two lines of the conversation. Also highlight the contrastive stress in: *I'm from Bristol. Where are you from?*

3 This is a mingle activity. Demonstrate the conversation first in open pairs, and then get students to move around the class and talk to as many people as possible. Monitor and check for accurate pronunciation. Don't let this activity go on too long. If you have a large class, it will be impossible for all the students to talk to everyone.

PERSONAL INFORMATION (SB p9)

he/she – his/her

⚠ POSSIBLE PROBLEMS

- Note that in the negative of *be*, *Headway English A2* uses the contracted forms of *not*, not the contracted forms of the verb, i.e. *she isn't, they aren't, you aren't, we aren't*, rather than *she's not, they're not, you're not, we're not*. Try to stick to these forms when you speak to the class. The contraction ~~*I amn't*~~ isn't possible, and the correct form is shown in the Grammar Spot on SB p9.
- Where other languages will answer an inverted question with simply *yes* or *no*, English prefers to add a short answer. Without the short answer, the speaker can sound rather abrupt. Having been introduced to contracted forms, students are tempted to use them in short answers, for example, *Are you married?* ~~*Yes, I'm*~~, but this is not possible.
- The names of the characters are pronounced /bɪl freɪzə(r)/ and /səbiːnə gæns/.
- Lower-level students often have difficulty reading phone numbers and email addresses fluently. In English we give phone numbers using single figures 0–9, and 0 is pronounced 'oh'. Repeated numbers are usually expressed with *double* e.g. *44 = double four, 555 = five, double five*. Be prepared to give a lot of practice during this presentation and also in later lessons. It's a good idea to prepare a list of fictitious email addresses and phone numbers from a range of countries before the lesson to help students with this.

1 Point to the photo of Bill and ask *What's his name?* Then point to the photo of Sabine and say *This is Sabine*. Check comprehension of the key categories in the table and then give students time to read about Bill and Sabine.

Focus attention on the information about reading email addresses. Write a number of fictitious email addresses on the board and get students to practise reading them aloud.

2 **T 1.4** **[CD 1: Track 5]** Focus attention on the gapped questions and on the example. Play the recording through once and get students to complete the questions. Play the recording a second time if necessary. With weaker classes, you could complete the questions orally as a class first and then play the recording as consolidation.

Ask students to write the answers on the board to make sure they are using the short form *What's* and the full form *is* correctly. Point out that *isn't* is the negative, and that *n't* is the short form of *not*.

Answers and tapescript
1 What's his surname?
Frasier
2 **What's** his first name?
Bill
3 Where's he from?
Chicago
4 How old **is** he?
30
5 What's **his** phone number?
312 555 0749
6 **What's his** email address?
bfrasier@gmail.com
7 Is **he** married?
No, he isn't.

Review/check the way we read phone numbers (see *Possible problems* opposite). Before students practise the questions and answers in closed pairs, let them practise in open pairs. Highlight the voice range and intonation on the questions – questions with a question word start high and fall. With weaker classes, be prepared to drill the forms and spend less time on the intonation.

3 **T 1.5** **[CD 1: Track 6]** This exercise highlights the use of *she* and *her* to talk about women and girls. Focus attention on the gapped questions and on the example. Play the recording through once and get students to complete the questions. Play the recording a second time if necessary. With weaker classes, you could complete the questions orally as a class first and then play the recording as consolidation.

Answers and tapescript
1 What's her surname?
2 What's **her** first name?
3 Where's she from?
4 How old **is she**?
5 What's **her** phone number?
6 **What's her** email address?
7 **Is she** married?

Highlight the use of *he/his* to talk about Bill and *she/her* to talk about Sabine. Consolidate the difference by asking *What's his/her name?* and *Where's he/she from?* about the students in the class. With weaker classes, drill the questions with the whole class and correct any mistakes in the use of *he/she* and *his/her* carefully.

Get students to practise the questions and answers in open pairs before repeating in closed pairs. If necessary, highlight the voice range and intonation again. With weaker classes, be prepared to drill the forms and spend less time on the intonation.

GRAMMAR SPOT (SB p9)

1 Focus attention on the positive forms in the chart. Make sure students understand that there is a long form and a short form for each part of the verb.

Focus attention on the negative forms in the chart. Give some true negative examples to reinforce the meaning, e.g. *I'm not American. You aren't English.* Elicit the negative forms for *he* and *she* and drill the pronunciation if necessary.

Answers

Positive	Negative
I am = I'm	I'm not
you are = you're	you aren't
he is = he's	he **isn't**
she is = she's	she **isn't**

2 Highlight the use of the subject pronouns by pointing to yourself for *I* and students in the class for *you*, *he*, and *she*. Give students time to write the missing possessive adjectives and then check the answers.

Answers

Pronouns	Possessive adjectives
I	my
you	**your**
he	**his**
she	her

▶▶ Read Grammar Reference 1.1–1.2 on SB p184 together in class and/or ask students to read it at home. Encourage them to ask you questions about it.

Talking about you

⚠ POSSIBLE PROBLEMS

This section consolidates the *Wh*-questions and also includes a *Yes/No* question and short answers. Having focused on the short forms in positive sentences, students may be tempted to use a short form in positive short answers. The Caution box covers this and highlights that we can't say ~~*Yes, I'm.*~~ At this early stage, don't give a long explanation of what short answers are and how they operate. It is better to let students see them in context and use them in controlled exercises.

4 This is the students' first opportunity to personalize the language in this section, so try to make sure that they work with a partner that they don't know.

Ask the question *Are you married?* and elicit the answers *Yes, I am./No, I'm not.* Focus attention on the note about short answers and point out we can't say *Yes, I'm.*

With weaker classes, briefly review commonly confused letters of the alphabet *a*, *e*, *i*, *o*, *u*, *m* and *n*, *c* and *k*, etc. and how to read phone numbers. You could also elicit a range of answers to the questions across the class and drill the question forms, before students do the pairwork.

Students ask and answer the questions with a partner. Monitor and check for correct formation of questions and short answers, and for correct pronunciation and intonation.

EXTRA ACTIVITIES

- You can consolidate the use of *he/she* and *his/her* by asking students to work with a new classmate and tell him/her about their partner in exercise 4. Students can also tell the rest of the class about their partner in a short feedback activity.
- You can give regular practice of phone numbers (and numbers in general) and email addresses in dictation activities, either with you dictating or with the students working in pairs.

Teacher dictation: Dictate five or six phone numbers/email addresses, writing them down yourself so that you have a means of checking. Students write the numbers/addresses as you say them, and then write them on the board to check.

Pairs dictation: Students prepare a list of phone numbers/email addresses to dictate to their partner and then exchange lists to check.

RICK'S FAMILY (SB p10)

Verbs – *have/go/live/like*

NOTE

The purpose of this section is to introduce/review some high-frequency verbs to allow students to give everyday information about themselves. It is not intended to be a full presentation of the Present Simple and so students practise just the *I* form. Don't include any questions in the Present Simple about this section, as a complete review/presentation of the Present Simple is given in Units 2 and 3.

Some basic family words are included in the text and in the Practice section (*brother*, *sister*, *parents*, *mother*, *father*, *grandmother*). This vocabulary is reviewed and extended in *Vocabulary and speaking* on SB p14.

1 **T 1.6** **[CD 1: Track 7]** Pre-teach/check *salesman* and *girlfriend*. Focus attention on the photo and say *This is Rick Wilson.* Ask *How old is he? Where is he from?* Play the recording once and get students to follow in their books. With weaker students, you could get students to point to the correct photo as they read and listen. Elicit the answers to the pre-questions (He's 19. He's from London.)

2 Give students time to complete the sentences, using *have*, *live*, and *like*.

T 1.7 **[CD 1: Track 8]** Play the recording and let students check their answers.

Answers and tapescript

1 I **go** to Kingston University.
2 I **have** a brother and a sister.
3 I **live** with my parents in a house in West London.
4 My family really **like** Lily!

3 Elicit possible endings to the sentences, feeding in necessary vocabulary, e.g. *college*, *language school*, *husband*, *wife*, etc.

Put students in pairs to exchange their information. Monitor and help as necessary.

Possessive *'s*

⚠ POSSIBLE PROBLEMS

Students may well have problems distinguishing the contracted forms *he's/she's/it's* and the marker for possessive *'s*. The Grammar Spot for this section clarifies the usage, but be prepared to review this point regularly to help students in both speaking and writing.

4 Go through the Grammar Spot with the class.

GRAMMAR SPOT (SB p10)

Focus attention on the use of *'s* as the contraction of *is* and as an indicator of possession.
Refer students back to the text about Rick. In pairs, students underline examples of possessive *'s* and circle examples of *'s* as the contraction of *is*.

Answers
Possession
brother's name
sister's name
is
My name's Rick Wilson.
He's 16 and he's at school.
She's 23, and she's married.
Her name's Lily. She's lovely!

►► Read Grammar Reference 1.3 on SB p184 together in class, and/or ask students to read it at home. Encourage them to ask you questions about it.

5 Focus attention on the example. Get two strong students to model the example question and answer. Ask *Who's Rosie?* and elicit the answer (*She's Rick's sister.*)

Students ask and answer the questions in closed pairs. Monitor and check for correct use of the possessive *'s* and contracted forms of *be*. If students have problems, drill the questions and answers and get students to repeat in closed pairs.

Answers
2 Who's Rosie? She's Rick's sister.
Who's Peter? He's Rick's father.
Who's Helen? She's Rick's mother.
Who's Lily? She's Rick's girlfriend.
3 He's a salesman.
4 She's a teacher.

EXTRA ACTIVITY

Students will need regular reviews of the possessive *'s*. You can do this in a later lesson by asking ten or so students for a photo or other personal item. Put them all in the middle of the room. Students then have to point to a photo/an object and say *That's my sister. That's Maria's mobile*, etc.

PRACTICE (SB p11)

be – am, is, are

1 This exercise consolidates a range of forms of the verb *to be*, including questions and short answers. Get students to complete the sentences, working individually.

T 1.8 **[CD 1: Track 9]** Give students time to check their answers in pairs then play the recording for a final check.

Answers and tapescript
1 Where **are you** from?
2 '**Are** you from London?' 'Yes, I **am**.'
3 'How old **are** you?' '**I'm** 15.'
4 '**Are** your sisters married?' 'No, they **aren't**.'
5 I like you. You**'re** my friend.
6 Hans **isn't** from Germany, he's from Switzerland.
7 '**Is** your mother a doctor?' 'No, she **isn't**.'
8 **I'm not** Italian. I'm French.

2 This exercise gives further practice in distinguishing the meaning of *'s* – short form of *is* or possession.
Focus attention on the examples, then get students to complete the task, working individually. Elicit a range of answers from the class. If there is disagreement, write the sentences on the board for analysis with the whole class.

Answers
3 is 4 is 5 possession 6 possession

Pronunciation

3 **T 1.9** **[CD 1: Track 10]** This exercise tests students' ability to listen carefully and discriminate between similar words and phrases.

Play number 1 as an example and elicit the correct sentence (b). Play the rest of the recording. Students tick the sentences they hear. You can make this exercise productive by asking students to read the pairs of sentences aloud.

Answers and tapescript
1 **b** She's from Italy.
2 **a** What's his name?
3 **a** Your English is good.
4 **a** Where's she from?
5 **b** He's a teacher in England.
6 **b** We aren't English.

Spelling

4 Briefly review the alphabet, prioritizing letters that students have problems with, and the use of *double* for spelling (e.g. *Swiss* = *s, w, i, double s*). Point out that numbers 1–3 are names and that 4 and 5 are email addresses. Explain that students will hear the information in a short context but they should listen for just the missing letters and parts of the email addresses.

T 1.10 **[CD 1: Track 11]** Play number 1 as an example and elicit the missing letters, writing the complete name on the board.

Play the rest of the recording without stopping. If necessary, play the recording again to allow students to complete any missing answers. Don't keep repeating the recording, however, as students need to get used to isolating key information fairly quickly, as they would in real life.

Check the answers by getting students to write the answers on the board to make sure they have recorded the dots correctly in the email addresses.

Answers and tapescript
1 VANESSA
2 JOSEPH BOWEN
3 KATIE MATTHEWS
4 g.**hunt**8@yahoo.**com**
5 zac.**yates**@gmail.co.**uk**

T 1.10
1 My name's Vanessa. That's V - A - N - E - S - S - A. Vanessa.
2 My first name's Joseph. That's J - O - S - E - P - H. My surname's Bowen. That's B - O - W - E - N. Joseph Bowen.
3 My name's Katie Matthews. That's Katie, K - A - T - I - E, Matthews M - A - T - T - H - E - W - S.
4 My email address is g.hunt8@yahoo.com. That's G dot H - U - N - T eight at yahoo dot com.
5 My email address is zac.yates@gmail.co.uk. That's Zac Z - A - C, dot Yates, Y - A - T - E - S, at gmail dot co dot UK.

Talking about you

5 This exercise consolidates the verb *to be* in a range of persons, and allows students to make true sentences about themselves. Pre-teach/check *at home*, *at work*, and *café* by using pictures or simple explanations.

Answers
There can be no set answers for this exercise, but monitor and check students haven't made mistakes in the forms of *to be*.

Get students to compare their answers in pairs.

Writing

6 After quite a lot of oral class work, the silent, individual work in this exercise provides variety and balance.

Focus attention on the sentence starters and elicit a range of possible endings. The starter *I'm a ...* requires a job or the word *student*. In the sentences about family, point out that students can change the key word, e.g. *sister* → *brother*; *father* → *mother*.

Give students time to write about themselves, using the sentence starters. (If you are short of time, students can do this task for homework.)

Students read their description to the class, or to their classmates in small groups. Don't over-correct students if they make a lot of pronunciation mistakes; the aim is for students to show what they can do, and to say a little about themselves and their families. They can't do everything at once!

READING AND LISTENING (SB p12)

A student's blog

ABOUT THE TEXT

This is the first piece of extensive skills work in *Headway English A2*. The aim of this section is to recycle key language and expose students to new language in a relatively natural context. The choice of text type – a blog – will be familiar to the majority of students and reflects communication in the real world. This section also provides a link to the Writing section on SB p154.

After a lead-in and vocabulary work, students read and listen to the blog at the same time. This might be considered an unnatural activity, but this technique is used only in the early stages of the book to help build confidence. Learners at this level typically find reading easier than listening, because they can recognize cognates without the interference of different pronunciation. However, if they read the blog silently at their own speed, they could become distracted by unknown and unimportant vocabulary. Reading and following the recording allows them to follow the material in a more fluent way.

The places mentioned in the blog are:

Notting Hill – a fashionable area of West London, famous for its annual carnival

Covent Garden – an area of central London full of shops and places to eat, also the location of the Royal Opera House

National Gallery – a public art gallery, which contains a large collection of mostly European art

The following vocabulary items might be new:

– the adjectives in exercise 2 SB p12

– *blog* (a type of Internet diary), *speak fast*, *understand*, *in the centre* (of a city), *international*, *park* (n), *gallery*, *free*, *go by Underground* (the Metro system in London)

With weaker students, pre-teach/check the vocabulary or set it as homework prior to the lesson. However, if you feel your students don't need so much support, simply encourage them to use the context to help them understand the new vocabulary.

1 Introduce the topic by writing *London* on the board and letting students tell you anything they know. Refer them to the photos and elicit information about what's in the photos – Tower Bridge, Big Ben and the Houses of Parliament, Hyde Park, and Trafalgar Square (a large square in the heart of London). The National Gallery, mentioned in the text, is the building on the left side of Trafalgar Square in the bottom photo.

Elicit the names of any other places that students know in London.

2 With weaker students, you may want to pre-teach/check the adjectives if you didn't set them for homework (see *About the text* above). Check the pronunciation of the following adjectives, which can cause problems:

beautiful /'bjuːtɪfl/, interesting /'ɪntrəstɪŋ/, friendly /'frendli/.

Check students understand the idea of noun + adjective collocation. Write the following examples on the board and check the ones which are and aren't possible:

a friendly person ✓ / *language* ✗ / *place* ✓ / *book* ✗.

Also check students understand the use of *a/an* in sentences 1 and 4: *a* + adjective beginning with a consonant; *an* + adjective beginning with a vowel. Elicit two examples, e.g. *a beautiful city/an expensive city*.

Put the students into pairs to complete the sentences. Monitor and help as necessary.

Elicit a range of possible answers in a short feedback session. Ask students to justify their answers in simple English as best they can. Try not to let students give their reasons in L1!

Possible answers
Answers will depend on students' own opinions but these are possible collocations.
1 London is/isn't a/an big/small/nice/beautiful/expensive/interesting/friendly/cold/sunny city.
2 The people are/aren't nice/interesting/friendly.
3 The weather is/isn't cold/sunny.
4 English is/isn't a/an beautiful/interesting/difficult/easy language.

3 See the note about vocabulary in *About the text*. Refer students back to the text about Rick on SB p10 and ask what they can remember about him. Then focus attention on the photo of Annalisa. Explain that she is a student in London and that the Wilsons are her host family.

T 1.11 **[CD 1: Track 12]** Play the first two lines of the blog and get students to follow in their books. Focus attention on the examples. Play the rest of the recording and then get students to complete the true/false task. Give students time to compare their answers in pairs and correct the false sentences. Check the answers with the class.

Answers
3 True
4 False. She isn't in a small school. She's in a big school.
5 True
6 False. They aren't all from Europe. They're from Mexico, Japan and Egypt too.
7 False. She isn't Annalisa's teacher. She's Rick's sister.
8 False. It isn't expensive. It's free.
9 False. It isn't difficult. It's easy.
10 True

4 Students often have problems with the formation of questions, so this task provides further practice. Focus attention on the example and remind students to focus on the answers to help them form the questions.

Give students time to complete the questions, working individually. Then put students in pairs to ask and answer. Monitor and check for accurate question formation.

T 1.12 **[CD 1: Track 13]** Play the recording and let students check their answers. Students practise the questions and answers again. If necessary, drill the questions for pronunciation practice, encouraging accurate intonation.

Answers and tapescript
1 'Where's Annalisa from?' 'Italy.'
2 '**Where's** her school?' 'In the centre of London.'
3 'What's **her teacher's** name?' 'Charlotte.'
4 '**What's her family's** name?' 'Wilson.'
5 '**Where's** their **house**?' 'In Notting Hill, in West London.'
6 'How **old are** the two brothers?' 'Edward's 16 and Rick's 19.'
7 '**Is the weather** OK?' 'Yes, it is. It's cold and sunny.'

5 Give students a few minutes to discuss their answers in small groups. Elicit a range of answers from the class.

Answers
We can see the Wilson family and their house, her school, some students, and her teacher, and Trafalgar Square and the National Gallery in London.

Listening

6 This is the first listening task in *Headway English A2* without some written support. Reassure the students that the conversations are very short and they only have to listen for the key information to complete the chart. With weaker students, refer students back to Annalisa's blog on SB p13, briefly review the names of the people she knows and write them on the board.

T 1.13 **[CD 1: Track 14]** Tell students they are going to listen to Annalisa in five different situations. Play the first conversation, pausing the recording to elicit the answers (see *Answers* below).

Play the rest of the recording, pausing after each conversation to allow students to record their answers. Check answers with the class.

Answers and tapescript

Where's Annelisa?	Who is she with?
1 at home	Peter Wilson
2 at school/in class	her teacher, Charlotte
3 at school	another student
4 at the National Gallery	a gallery assistant
5 in a café	a waitress

T 1.13
1 **P** Goodbye, Annalisa! Have a good day at school!
A Thank you, Peter. And you have a good day at work!
2 **C** Good morning, Annalisa. Where's your homework?
A It's here, Charlotte.
3 **A** Hello, Cristo. Where are you from?
C I'm from Mexico.
4 **A** A ticket, please.
B The National Gallery is free.
A Oh, good! Thank you.
5 **A** A coffee, please.
B Certainly. Here you are.

If you have time, refer students to the tapescript on SB p168 and let them practise the conversations in pairs.

Vocabulary work

SUGGESTION
Students could use dictionaries to help them with the vocabulary work on adjectives and their opposites.

7 Focus attention on the example to check students understand the concept of opposites. Get students to work in pairs or small groups to pool their knowledge. With weaker students, write the missing opposites (see *Answers* below) on the board in random order for them to match.

Check the answers with the class, drilling the pronunciation of the adjectives as necessary. You could ask students to mark the stress on words with two syllables or more.

Answers
2 a **small** town
3 **cold** weather
4 a **lovely/fantastic** meal
5 an **expensive** restaurant
6 a **young** girl
7 a **fast** car
8 **difficult** homework

SUGGESTION

You could give students further practice with the adjectives in this section by giving the names of countries, cities, famous people, names of cars, etc. and eliciting possible descriptions, e.g. *a Ferrari – a fast car/ an expensive car.*

GRAMMAR SPOT (SB p13)

This section reviews and extends the positive forms of the verb *to be* and the possessive adjectives that students first met on SB p9.

1 Focus attention on the examples. Then get students to complete the chart, referring to Annalisa's blog if necessary. Make sure students provide the full forms, as in the examples. Check the answers.

Answers
I am
you **are**
he **is**
she **is**
it **is**
we are
they **are**

2 Focus attention on the examples. Then get students to complete the chart, again referring to Annalisa's blog if necessary. Check the answers.

Answers

I	my
you	**your**
he	**his**
she	**her**
we	**our**
they	their

►► Read Grammar Reference 1.1–1.2 on SB p184 together in class and/or ask students to read it at home. Encourage them to ask you questions about it.

ADDITIONAL MATERIAL

Teacher's Resource Disc
Communicative activity Unit 1 Adjectives pelmanism

WRITING (SB p154)

A blog

Keeping an online journal

NOTE

This is the first main writing activity in *Headway English A2*. Students are provided with a clear framework for each section of their writing, building on the format they saw in Annalisa's blog on SB p13. There is also a speaking stage in which students talk about their blog and read a section aloud to the class.

You may well get students to do the main writing task for homework, but it's worth spending some class time preparing students for the writing, particularly with weaker classes.

SUGGESTIONS

- If your students have access to a computer and the Internet, you can get them to write and upload their blogs for other classes to read. These can be updated as the students progress through the course.
- If you have access to video equipment, it's a good idea to record the students when they read their blog aloud. Students usually overcome any initial shyness and soon get used to being recorded. It can be interesting to repeat the same task at a later stage, using a different topic, and let students compare the two talks. This can provide a concrete indicator of progress and so add to students' overall motivation.

1 Ask the questions to the whole class. If any students write a blog, ask what they write about.

2 Ask students if they can remember the topics in Annalisa's blog (a welcome section with personal information, the first day at school, information on London).

Focus attention on the three sections in the blog on SB p154. Give students a few moments to read through the sections and think about possible information they can include. Elicit a range of possible answers from the class. Feed in any necessary vocabulary, checking both spelling and pronunciation. Students complete the blog individually.

3 Ask two confident students to demonstrate the activity. Remind the student who is talking not to read all of the text aloud but to use the notes to help him/her remember key information. The student who is listening should show interest and ask a few simple questions if possible. Divide the students into pairs to talk about their blog. Monitor but try not to interfere or over-correct as this is primarily a fluency activity.

4 Brainstorm possible topics for the blog, e.g. a favourite sport/food/city/possession. Remind students that they should choose topics that they can write about in the present tense, using *be* and *I like/love/go/have …* . Feed in any necessary vocabulary, checking both spelling and pronunciation.

If you set the writing task for homework, remind students to check their work when they have finished. If you do the task during class time, monitor students carefully and help as necessary.

Give students a few moments to read their blog to themselves and prepare to read it aloud. Monitor and help, checking for potential pronunciation problems.

Let students who feel confident read their blogs first. Insist that the rest of the class pay attention and avoid interrupting. Encourage them to note any questions they want to ask. There probably won't be time to hear every student in a single lesson, so set up a timetable of who will read their blog in the subsequent classes. Don't let the less confident students have to wait until the end!

If you collect in the writing for checking, mark it sympathetically, only highlighting major errors so as not to limit students' confidence.

VOCABULARY AND SPEAKING (SB p14)

The family

SUGGESTION

If possible, it's a nice idea to base family descriptions on real photos. Bring in photos of your family and ask students to do the same. If you have a small enough class, sit them around you and talk about the photos slowly but naturally and pass them around. Encourage students to ask questions, following the models in exercise 4 on SB p14.

This section reviews and extends the family words students met on SB p10. Introduce the topic by talking about your immediate family in a natural way but using the language students have met, e.g. *I have a …*, *My mother's name is …*, *She's (age)*, etc.

1 Focus attention on the diagram and the example. Elicit another example, e.g. *husband and wife*, to show that the words work in male and female pairs.

Students works in pairs to complete the diagram. Monitor and help as necessary.

Check the answers, drilling the pronunciation of the words as necessary. Students may need help with the word stress, vowel sounds, and silent letters in the following:

*grand*mother, *grand*father

niece /niːs/ nephew /ˈnefjuː/ aunt /ɑːnt/
daughter /ˈdɔːtə/

Answers
father and mother
husband and **wife**
son and daughter
brother and sister
grandfather and **grandmother**
uncle and **aunt**
nephew and **niece**
boyfriend and girlfriend

2 This exercise consolidates the vocabulary from exercise 1 and also introduces *cousins*, *children*, and *parents*. Focus attention on the example and then give students time to complete the sentences, working in pairs.

Check the answers, drilling the pronunciation of the words as necessary.

Answers
2 grandmother
3 aunt
4 uncle
5 nephew
6 niece
7 parents
8 children
9 cousins

3 This is another short listening task that students do without the support of the written text. Students have met all the language in the script and so should be able to match the names to the people in the family tree without too many difficulties.

Focus attention on the family tree. Ask *Who's Joseph?* and get students to point to the correct person in the family tree. Explain that students are going to hear Joseph talking about his family. Check the pronunciation of the names in the box, particularly *Andrea* /ˈændrɪə/ and *Odile* /əʊˈdiːl/.

T 1.14 **[CD 1: Track 15]** Now focus attention on Joseph and play the recording as far as … *he's 25*. Say *Andrea?* and get students to point to the correct person on the family tree (*Joseph's sister*). Repeat for Richard (*Joseph's brother*).

Play the rest of the recording to the end and give students time to check their answers in pairs. With weaker students, pause the recording after each piece of key information. Play the recording again if necessary to let students check/complete their answers. Then check with the class.

Answers and tapescript

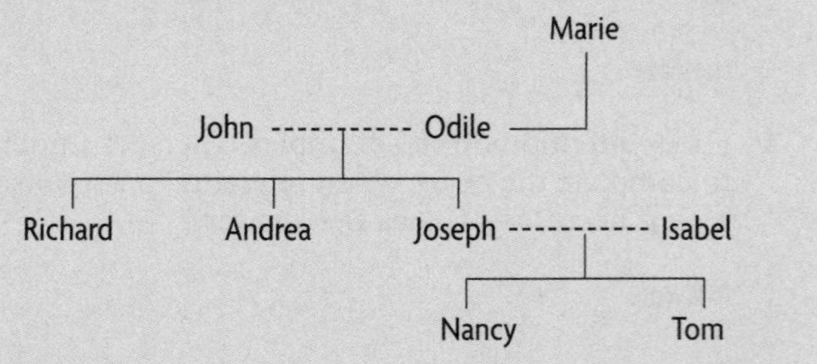

T 1.14
My family isn't very big. I have a sister, Andrea, she's 18, and a brother Richard, he's 25. They're not married. I'm married, erm, my wife's name is Isabel. We have two children, a daughter, Nancy, that's N - A - N - C - Y, she's 4, and a son, Tom, he's only six months old. We live near my parents. My dad's name is John and my mum's is Odile, that's O - D - I - L - E. She's French. My grandmother lives with them, her name's Marie. She's my mum's mum.

4 Demonstrate the activity by writing the names of your extended family on the board and talking about them. Give the information quite slowly but naturally and then ask a few questions to check understanding, e.g. *Who's this?*, *How old is she?*, etc.

Students write down the names of some of their relatives on a piece of paper. Model the example questions and answers in open pairs, encouraging the correct stress pattern. Students then exchange pieces of paper with a partner and ask and answer questions about each other's families.

Monitor and check for correct use of *be*, possessive *'s*, and possessive adjectives. Feed back on any common errors after the pairwork in a later lesson, but don't over-correct during the task.

SUGGESTION

With weaker students, or if students are having problems with the possessive *'s*, write the following on the board:

Who<u>'s</u> Joseph? *'s* = is

He's Andrea<u>'s</u> brother. *'s* = possessive, not *is*

Refer students to **T 1.14** on SB p168 as reinforcement. Get them to look at the examples of *'s* and check what they mean.

5 Demonstrate the activity with two strong students. Give students time to exchange information in pairs. Some students may try to ask follow-up questions that require the Present Simple, e.g. *Where do they live?* Just note this if it happens but don't give any correction/explanation if students make mistakes. The Present Simple is covered in Units 2 and 3 of the course.

EXTRA ACTIVITIES

- Get students to draw their own family tree as a mini-project (and have their family photos ready if relevant). Divide the class into new pairs and get students to ask about each other's family. Then ask a few students to choose someone in a family tree or in a photo and give a brief description of him/her. The person can be from their own or their partner's family.
- Give students further practice on families and possessive *'s* by referring to famous people. Draw the family tree of a famous family, e.g. the British or Spanish royal family and get students to ask and answer questions with *Who?* Alternatively, you can prepare true/false statements about the family relationships. You could also try a quiz based on famous people. Prepare questions based on relationships that your students will know, e.g. *Who's Joachim Sauer?* (*He's Angela Merkel's husband.*) Be prepared to modify the questions to suit the age and experience of individual groups.

EVERYDAY ENGLISH (SB p15)

Everyday conversations

This section introduces and practises expressions for short conversations in everyday situations.

1 This exercise revises the language used in greetings, both in informal and slightly more formal situations. Write on the board *Hi, Pete!* and *Good morning, Mr Simpson.* Ask *Which conversation is with a friend?* and elicit *Hi, Pete!* Explain that some of the expressions are for talking to friends (informal) and some are for talking to people you don't know very well (more formal).

Choose a confident student and elicit the following model:

T Hi, (*name of student*). How are you?
S Fine, thanks. And you?
T All right, thanks.

Elicit a more formal model, using two confident students.

Students continue building conversations, using the lines in the boxes. Monitor and check for appropriate use of the greetings and for pronunciation, particularly voice range. If students sound 'flat', use **T 1.15** as a model to help with intonation.

2 **T 1.15** **[CD 1: Track 16]** Tell students that there are four short conversations on the recording, each in a different situation. Play the recording, pausing after each conversation to ask *Friends or not?* (conversations 1 and 2 are friends; 3 and 4 aren't friends and are slightly more formal).

If students had problems with intonation, play the recording again as a model and get them to repeat chorally and individually.

Tapescript

1 **A** Hello, Sally. How are you?
B OK, thank you. And you?
A Fine, thanks.
2 **A** Hi, Pete. How are you?
B All right, thanks. And you?
A Not bad, thank you.
3 **A** Good morning, Mr Simpson. How are you?
B Very well, thank you. And you?
A Fine, thank you.
4 **A** Hello, Mrs Brown. How are you?
B Fine, thank you. And you?
A Not bad.

Students then practise making more conversations, using the expressions in exercise 1.

3 Focus attention on the photos. Ask *Who are the people? Where are they?* about each one. Focus attention on the example in conversation 1 and elicit the other missing words (see *Answers* below).

Students work in pairs and complete the conversations with the expressions given. Monitor and help as necessary.

T 1.16 **[CD 1: Track 17]** Play the recording and let students check their answers. If students query any of the grammar in the expressions, e.g. *Can I ...?*, refer the students back to the context and explain the use in relation to the situation. There's no need to go into a grammatical explanation of *can* at this stage.

Answers and tapescript

1 **A** Bye, Mum! It's time for school.
B Goodbye darling. Have **a good day**!
A Thanks. See you **later**.
2 **C** Good morning!
D **Good morning**! **Can** I have a coffee, an espresso, please?
C Yes, **of course**! Anything else?
D No, thank you.
3 **E** **Good afternoon**. Can I **help** you?
F No, thank you. We're **just** looking.
E That's OK.
4 **G** Frank. **This is** Gina. She's from our New York office.
H Hello, Gina. Nice **to meet** you.
I Hello, Frank. **Pleased** to meet you, too.
5 **J** Thank goodness it's Friday! **Bye**, Ian.
K Bye, Derek. Have **a good weekend**.
J Thanks. Same **to you**.
K See you on Monday!
6 **L** Good night! Sleep **well**.
M Good night! **See you** in the morning.

4 Students practise the conversations with a partner. Then ask them to learn two or three of the conversations by heart to act out for the rest of the class. Acting out conversations can improve students' pronunciation considerably. Remind them of the importance of voice range. If students have problems, play relevant conversations from **T 1.16** again and get students to repeat chorally and individually.

SUGGESTIONS

- Encourage students to use these expressions in class whenever appropriate, e.g. saying hello and goodbye at the start and end of class, introducing someone, asking for something with *Can I have …?* You could put key phrases on a classroom poster.
- Students can think of other situations when these expressions would be useful and write or act out parallel conversations.

Photocopiable Activity

UNIT 1 Everyday conversations TB p148/TRD

Note: This activity is best used in a later lesson as consolidation and not straight after finishing SB p15.

Materials: One copy of the worksheet cut up per pair of students; drawing pins or sticky tape.

Procedure: This is a running dictation race, in which students have to memorize and dictate key lines from four short conversations. The first pair of students to complete the conversations accurately wins. Alternatively, the activity can be done as a conventional dictation, with the students working face to face.

- Explain that students are going to do a dictation activity in the form of a race. Pin up all the Student A worksheets on one side of the room and all the Student B worksheets on the opposite wall.
- Pre-teach/check *How do you spell …? Can you repeat that, please?*, and basic punctuation: full stop, question mark, and comma.
- Divide the class into A/B pairs. Students write the headings *Conversation 1*, *2*, *3*, and *4* on a piece of paper on their desk. They then take it in turns to be a runner and a writer. Student A starts by running to their worksheet, memorizing the first line of Conversation 1, running back, and dictating the line to Student B, including the punctuation. Student B then runs to their worksheet, memorizes the next line, runs back and dictates the line to Student A.
- Students continue until they have written out all four conversations on their piece of paper. Check each pair's work for accuracy as they finish. The first pair to finish all four conversations correctly wins.

Don't forget!

Grammar Reference (SB p184 and Teacher's Resource Disc)
Unit 1

Word list (SB p204 and Teacher's Resource Disc)
Unit 1

Test (Teacher's Resource Disc)
Unit test 1A
Unit test 1B

Video (DVD)
Unit 1 London

2 A good job!

Present Simple (1) – *he/she/it* • Questions and negatives • Jobs • What time is it?

The themes of this unit are jobs and people's work routines. These themes lend themselves to the practice of the grammatical aim – the third person singular of the Present Simple. The skills work includes a reading text about an Indian teenager who is also a teacher, and listening and speaking activities to consolidate question and answer forms and the vocabulary of jobs.

LANGUAGE INPUT

GRAMMAR

Present Simple (1) – *he/she/it* (SB p20)	• Practising the third person singular positive form of the Present Simple.
Questions and negatives (SB p21)	• Practising the third person singular negative and question forms of the Present Simple.

VOCABULARY

Verbs (SB p21)	• Understanding and practising vocabulary to describe jobs.
Jobs (SB p26)	• Understanding and practising vocabulary to talk about a range of jobs.

EVERYDAY ENGLISH

What time is it? (SB p27)	• Understanding and practising expressions to tell the time.

SKILLS DEVELOPMENT

READING

A really good job (SB p24)	• Reading about a teenager from India who teaches younger children.

LISTENING

Five conversations about people (SB p23)	• Listening for key verbs in five short conversations. **T 2.10** (SB p169/TRD)
Five conversations about jobs (SB p26)	• Listening for key words in five short conversations. **T 2.15** (SB p169/TRD)

SPEAKING

Roleplay – An interview (SB p24)	• Roleplaying an interview between a journalist and a student.
Jobs (SB p26)	• Talking about friends and family and their jobs.

WRITING

Improving style – Using pronouns (SB p155)	• Understanding subject and object pronouns and possessive adjectives, then improving the pronoun use in a description.

MORE MATERIALS

Photocopiable worksheets – Say it! (TB p149/TRD), Present Simple dominoes (TRD) **Test** (TRD) **Video** (DVD)

STARTER (SB p20)

The *Starter* activity recycles the family vocabulary from Unit 1 and allows students to use some of the jobs vocabulary they already know. Give some examples of jobs of the people in your own family and then get students to continue the activity in pairs. If students ask for the names of individual jobs, give some examples that are common to the whole class, but do not let the *Starter* activity go on too long or reduce the usefulness of the *Vocabulary and listening* section on SB p26.

TWO OUTDOOR JOBS (SB p20)

Present Simple (1) – *he/she/it*

⚠ POSSIBLE PROBLEMS

The Present Simple is the most used tense in the English language. It is therefore important to introduce it early in the course. In *Headway English A2*, the introduction is staged over two units. In this unit only the third person singular (including questions and negatives) is presented and practised. All the other persons are introduced in Unit 3.

- The English language does not have many inflections. Unfortunately, this means the few that do exist cause a disproportionate amount of difficulty for foreign learners. The *-s* on the third person singular of the Present Simple is a classic example of this. Therefore we introduce it first in the hope that it will be more memorable and students will be less likely to omit it.
- The third person *-s* can be pronounced in three ways:

  /z/ comes /kʌmz/
  /s/ works /wɜːks/
  /ɪz/ teaches /ˈtiːtʃɪz/

  The difference between /s/ and /z/ endings is practised after the presentation texts on Andrew Johnson and Claudia Luke.
- The use of *does/doesn't* in the question and negative often seems strange to students, because of the absence of the auxiliary in the positive.

NOTE

For the first eight units of *Headway English A2*, the verb *have* is introduced and practised as a full verb with its *do/does* forms. *Have got* is introduced in Unit 9. This is for several reasons:

- By using the *do/does* forms, the verb *have* operates like any other verb in the Present Simple (with the exception of *has* in the third person singular).
- When students have just learnt the Present Simple and have been introduced to the auxiliary verbs *do/does*, it is very difficult and confusing for them when they come across the verb form *have got*, which operates differently.
- Although *have got* is common, especially in spoken language, the full verb *have* with its *do/does* forms covers all the uses in a way that *have got* doesn't. *Have got* expresses possession, but it cannot express a habitual action. So students can learn *How many children have you got?*, but then it is very confusing when they are introduced to *What time do you have lunch?* We cannot say **What time have you got lunch?*
- Finally, *have* with its *do/does* forms is becoming more common in spoken British English. It is the standard form in American English.

SUGGESTION

Before you start this unit, you could set the vocabulary homework below in preparation for the presentation texts. This will save a lot of classroom time checking vocabulary, and it will give you more time to focus on the grammar.

Homework prior to the lesson

Ask students to check the following words and learn them for the lesson. They can use a bilingual dictionary to look up words they don't know and write the translation if appropriate.

Verbs: *come, work, earn, go to the gym, play snooker, study, walk the dog*

Nouns: *engineer, oil rig, coast, holiday, free time, zoologist, snake, desert, song*

1 Focus attention on the photos of Andrew and Claudia and on the text headings. Check comprehension of *outdoor*. Elicit Andrew and Claudia's jobs (*He's an engineer. She's a zoologist.*)

Ask students *Where's he from?* and *Where's she from?* then ask them to look quickly at the texts to find the answers (*New Zealand* and *California*).

T 2.1 **[CD 1: Track 18]** Now play the recording and ask students to read and listen to the texts at the same time.

2 With weaker classes, you could deal with the texts one at a time, doing the underlining with the students for the first text and then asking them to repeat the process on their own for the second.

Tell students that they should only look for verbs in the positive form. Ask them to work on their own to underline the verbs and then check their answers with a partner before you conduct a full class feedback.

Answers

is comes lives works has earns goes plays teaches studies likes writes walks

Ask the whole class what the last letter is (*-s*) and point out that this is the ending for the third person singular – *he/she/it* – of the Present Simple. If students query why some verbs have *-es* or *-ies*, refer them to Grammar Reference 2.2 on SB p185.) Point out that the *have* is irregular in the *he/she/it* form – *has* and NOT **haves*.

Pronunciation

3 **T 2.2** **[CD 1: Track 19]** Say the sounds and verbs in the chart as examples. Tell students they need to listen for the pronunciation of the final *-s* in each verb. Play the recording. Students listen and write the verbs in the correct place in the chart. Check answers with the class.

Answers and tapescript

/s/	likes	works	writes	walks
/z/	comes	goes	earns	plays
/ɪz/	teaches			

Play the recording again. Students listen and repeat chorally and individually.

SUGGESTION

You can provide more pronunciation practice by getting students to take it in turns to read the texts on SB pp20–1 aloud in pairs. Monitor for correct pronunciation. If appropriate, ask one or two students to read a text aloud to the whole class.

4 Give students time to complete the sentences, working individually. Make it clear that each gap represents a word and that students sometimes need a verb in the Present Simple and sometimes the correct form of *be*. The last gap requires a negative.

T 2.3 **[CD 1: Track 20]** Students listen and check.

Answers and tapescript

1 Andrew is an engineer. Claudia **is** a zoologist.
2 She comes from the US. He **comes** from New Zealand.
3 He lives in Scotland. She **lives** in California.
4 She works in the desert. He **works** on an oil rig.
5 He earns £200 a day. She **earns** $60,000 a year.
6 She likes her job, and he **likes** his job, too.
7 He **goes** to the gym in his free time. She **walks** her dog. Her dog's name **is** Brewer.
8 She's married. Her husband's **name** is Jim. Andrew **isn't** married.

Ask students in pairs to read the sentences aloud. Monitor to check that students are producing the *-s* ending. If necessary, play the recording again and get students to repeat.

5 This activity gets students to transfer the key information about Andrew and Claudia into note form, to help them prepare for the freer practice in exercise 6. Check comprehension of the categories in the chart. Elicit Andrew and Claudia's surnames as an example, also checking the spelling.

Students complete the chart, working in pairs. Check the answers, dealing with any pronunciation problems as you go.

Answers

	Andrew	Claudia
surname	Johnson	Luke
age	30	41
country	New Zealand	the USA
job	engineer	zoologist
salary	£200 a day	$60,000 a year
free time	goes to the gym/ plays snooker	writes songs/ walks her dog
married?	no	yes

6 The aim of this activity is to give students the chance not just to produce single sentences, but to speak at more length to describe Andrew and Claudia. It is both useful and satisfying for low-level students to use language for 'display' purposes in this way and not always engage in the more 'natural' question-and-answer activities.

Give students a few moments to look back at the chart in exercise 5. They then take turns to close their books and talk about Andrew and Claudia. Encourage them to prompt each other with the categories in the chart. With weaker students, you could write a few word prompts on the board.

Monitor and check for correct use of the Present Simple third person. Point out any errors in the third person *-s* ending and major problems with pronunciation, but also allow students to self-correct and encourage peer correction from the other students as much as possible.

WHAT DOES HE DO? (SB p21)

Questions and negatives

⚠ POSSIBLE PROBLEMS

Be prepared for some students to make mistakes in the use of *does/doesn't* to form questions and negatives. Try to review these forms as often as necessary. In the Present Simple and Past Simple tenses, where there is no auxiliary in the positive, the use of the auxiliary verbs can seem very strange. Many students feel that it would be much more logical to say:

- Lives he in Paris?
- Where lives she?
- She not lives in London.

The short answers *Yes, he does./No, he doesn't.* and common mistakes of form like **he doesn't comes* also cause problems and need to be pointed out to students.

1 To signal that you are going to introduce the question form, you could draw a large question mark on the board.

T 2.4 **[CD 1: Track 21]** Play number 1 as an example and elicit the answer. Make sure students understand that *What does he/she do?* means the same as *What's his/her job?*, but that *What does he/she do?* is the more common question. Play the rest of the recording and get students to read and listen, and complete the answers.

Answers and tapescript

What does Andrew do? He's an **engineer**.
Where does he come from? New **Zealand**.
Does he live in Scotland? **Yes**, he does.
Does he live in New Zealand? **No**, he doesn't.
He **isn't** married. He doesn't have any children.

Play the recording again and get students to repeat both chorally and individually. Then get them to ask and answer in open pairs across the class.

NOTE

Encourage good pronunciation at all times. Highlight the pronunciation of *does* and *doesn't*, getting students to repeat the weak and strong forms in isolation, and as part of the question and short answers.

Where does he come from? /weə dəz hɪ kʌm frɒm/

Does he live in Scotland? /dəz hɪ lɪv ɪn 'skɒtlənd/

Yes, he does. /jes hɪ dʌz/

GRAMMAR SPOT (SB p21)

1 Ask students to complete the sentences using the verb *live*.

Answers

Positive

He **lives** in Scotland.

Negative

He **doesn't live** in New Zealand.

Question

Where **does** he **live**? In Scotland.

Point out that the *-s* isn't used on the main verb in the negative and question, but appears in *does*.

2 **T 2.5** [CD 1: Track 22] This exercise serves to further reinforce the weak and strong forms of *does* when unstressed, i.e. in positive sentences, the form is weak: /dəz/. However, when stressed, i.e. in a short answer or the negative, it is strong: /dʌz/, /'dʌznt/.

Play the recording. Students listen for the weak and strong forms of *does/doesn't*, then listen again and practise saying them. Drill the forms as necessary.

►► Read Grammar Reference 2.1–2.2 on SB p185 together in class, and/or ask students to read it at home. Encourage them to ask you questions about it.

2 **T 2.6** **[CD 1: Track 23]** Students complete the sentences, then check with a partner. Play the recording and get them to listen and check. Students ask and answer in pairs. Monitor and check for correct stress and pronunciation. If students have problems, play the recording again and drill the questions and answers chorally and individually.

Answers and tapescript

1 Where does Andrew work?
On an oil rig.

2 **Does** he work hard?
Yes, he **does**.

3 How much **does** he earn?
£200 a day.

4 What **does** he do in his free time?
He **goes to the gym** and he **plays snooker**.

5 **Does** he like his job?
Yes, he **does**.

6 **Does** he have a dog?
No, he **doesn't**.

3 Focus attention on the examples. Ask two confident students to ask and answer about Claudia across the class. Students continue in closed pairs. With weaker students, give them time to write out the questions before starting the pairwork. Monitor and check for correct use of third person *-s*, and correct stress and pronunciation. Feed back on any common errors carefully.

Possible questions and answers

Where does she live? In California.
Does she work with her husband? Yes, she does.
Does she like her job? Yes, she does.
Does she have a dog? Yes, she does.
What does she do in her free time? She writes songs and walks her dog.
How much does she earn? $60,000 a year.

PRACTICE (SB p22)

The dancer and the DJ

1 Focus attention on the photos of Darcey Bussell and David Guetta. Check the pronunciation of their names and of *DJ* /'diːdʒeɪ/ (short for *disc jockey*, a person who plays music in a club or on the radio). Elicit any information that students know about them.

2 Give students time to read about Darcey and David. Deal with any vocabulary queries and check the pronunciation of the names of people and places *Phoebe* /'fiːbɪ/, *Zoe* /'zəʊɪ/, *Ibiza* /aɪ'biːθə/, *Miami* /maɪ'jæmi/, *Mauritius* /mə'rɪʃəs/, *Senegal* /senɪ'gɔːl/.

Focus attention on the example. Elicit where Darcey comes from, then elicit a little information about David as a further example. Divide the class into pairs. Students describe Darcey or David to their partner. Monitor, helping as necessary. Check for correct use of *be*, *she/he*, *his/her*, and third person *-s* on the Present Simple forms. Note down any common errors to feed back on after the activity. Round off the activity by bringing the whole class together again, and asking one or two students to tell the others about Darcey and David.

Asking questions

3 Divide the class into pairs and ask each pair to choose either Darcey or David. Focus attention on the example question. Students work individually and write the rest of the questions about their character. Monitor and help as necessary. Check the questions quickly round the class, getting students to read them aloud. Be prepared to drill the pronunciation as necessary.

Answers
Where does she/he come from?
Where does she/he live now?
Where does she/he work?
Does she/he speak French?
How many children does she/he have?
What are his/her children's names?
What does she/he do in her/his free time?

Focus attention on the example question and answer about Darcey. Elicit the same question and answer about David. Students work in pairs and take it in turns to ask and answer questions about their character. Monitor and check for accurate question formation, use of *he/she* and *his/her*.

Students who finish early can ask about the other character but don't make the activity go on too long by insisting they ask every question about both characters.

Round off the activity by eliciting a few questions and answers in open pairs. Feed back on any common errors.

Stress and intonation

4 Demonstrate the activity by writing the following examples on the board. Drill the contrastive stress as marked below:

Darcey's Scottish. No, she isn't. She's English.

She has three children. No, she doesn't. She has two children.

She's married. Yes, that's right.

With weaker students, highlight the use of *is* in the sentence with *be* and *does* in the sentence with Present Simple.

T 2.7 **[CD 1: Track 24]** Play the recording of the examples in the Student's Book. Get students to complete the second example, then listen and repeat. Encourage them to reproduce the contrastive stress accurately in the sentences where the information is corrected.

Play the recording of the rest of the sentences (3–8 below) and get the class and individual students to respond. This should be quick and fun to do, so don't insist on the full correct answer if it slows down the activity – *No, he/she doesn't*, etc. is enough, especially with weaker classes.

Tapescript
1 Darcey comes from London.
2 She lives in England.
3 She has two children.
4 She plays tennis a lot.
5 David's English.
6 He works in Paris.
7 His wife comes from Miami.
8 He writes songs in his free time.

T 2.8 **[CD 1: Track 25]** Play the recording, pausing after each pair of sentences to give students time to listen to focus on the responses.

Tapescript
1 **A** Darcey comes from London.
B Yes, that's right.
2 **A** She lives in England.
B No, she doesn't. She lives in Australia.
3 **A** She has two sons.
B No, she doesn't. She has two daughters.
4 **A** She writes stories for children.
B Yes, that's right.
5 **A** David's English.
B No, he isn't. He's French.
6 **A** He works all over the world.
B Yes, that's right.
7 **A** His wife comes from Miami.
B No, she doesn't. She comes from Senegal.
8 **A** He writes songs in his free time.
B Yes, that's right.

T 2.7 **[CD 1: Track 24]** Play the cue sentences again and get students to respond. They should be able to do so more quickly and confidently this time, but with weaker classes be prepared to drill key sentences as a class.

Talking about family and friends

5 This exercise consolidates the third person *-s* on verbs in the Present Simple, Focus attention on the example. Students complete the sentences, working individually. Check the answers with the class, making sure students remember the *-es* ending on *watches* in number 6 and the pronunciation /ˈwɒtʃɪz/. If you want to give further pronunciation practice, get students to read the complete sentences aloud, focusing on the /s/ /z/ /ɪz/ endings.

Answers
1 comes
2 lives
3 loves
4 travels
5 speaks; wants
6 watches
7 writes

6 Ask two students to read out the example in exercise 5 and the example response in this exercise. Students continue the matching task, working in pairs.

7 **T 2.9** **[CD 1: Track 26]** Explain that students are going to check their answers against the recording and also listen for a third line in each conversation. Play conversation 1 as an example and elicit the reply *From the capital, Brussels*. Play the rest of the recording, pausing at the end of each one. Let students check their answers and elicit the reply each time. With weaker classes, you may need to play some of the conversations again.

Refer students to **T 2.9** on SB p169. Divide the students into pairs and get them to practise the dialogues. Encourage an animated delivery. If students sound 'flat', play the recording again as a model and get students to repeat. If necessary, model some of the lines yourself, exaggerating the voice range to help students improve their intonation.

Answers and tapescript

1 **A** My husband comes from Belgium.
B Where exactly in Belgium?
A From the capital, Brussels.
2 **A** My grandmother lives in the next town.
B Does she visit you often?
A Yes, she does. Every Sunday.
3 **A** My mother loves reading.
B What does she read?
A Detective stories.
4 **A** My father travels a lot in his job.
B Where does he go?
A He's in Berlin this week.
5 **A** My sister speaks Spanish very well. She wants to learn French too.
B Does she want to be an interpreter?
A No, she doesn't. She wants to be a teacher.
6 **A** My little brother watches TV a lot.
B What does he like watching?
A Sport, sport, sport and er- football!
7 **A** My friend, Tom writes a blog on the Internet.
B What does he write about?
A Everything and everybody!

Listening

8 **T 2.10** [**CD 1: Track 27**] This listening task consists of five short conversations. Play the recording and elicit the subject of each conversation. Check the answers.

Answers and tapescript

1 speaker B's sister and her studies
2 Peter's job
3 a dog
4 speaker B's friend and her level of English
5 speaker B's grandfather and his free time

T 2.10

1 **A** What does your sister do?
B She's a student. She wants to be a doctor so she studies a lot.
2 **A** Does Peter like his new job?
B No, he doesn't. He works very hard and he doesn't earn a lot of money.
3 **A** Is that your dog?
B No, he isn't. He's my mother's. He goes with her everywhere. She loves him a lot. His name's Boris.
4 **A** Your friend Ella speaks English very well.
B Yes, she does. She goes to England every summer.
5 **A** What does your grandfather do all the time?
B Well, he watches TV a lot, but on Saturdays he plays golf with friends, and on Sundays he visits us.

9 **T 2.10** [**CD 1: Track 27**] During the second listening, students have to focus on the key verbs. Explain that these are all in the Present Simple and don't include forms of *be*.

Play conversation 1 as an example. Elicit the missing verbs (*wants*, *studies*). Play the rest of the recording and get students to record the missing verbs. With weaker students, pause the recording after each conversation to give them time to write their answers. If necessary, play selected conversations a second time if students missed any of the answers. Check with the class, getting students to spell their answers and so review the alphabet.

Answers

1 wants, studies
2 like, works, earn
3 goes, loves
4 speaks, goes
5 do, watches, plays, visits

10 Focus attention on the example questions in the SB. Write the name of a friend or relative on the board. Elicit a range of questions about this person from the class. Give students a moment to choose a friend or relative and write their name down. Feed in any necessary vocabulary, e.g. *best friend*, *neighbour*, *(sister)-in-law*, etc.

Put students in new pairs to do the task, getting them to work with someone they don't know well. With weaker students, write prompts on the board to help students with the questions they can ask, e.g. *work*, *country/city*, *place of work*, *family*, *pets*, *free time*, *languages*.

Monitor and check as students do the activity, checking for question formation and third person *-s*. Don't interrupt or over-correct as this is a fluency activity. Make a note of any common errors in the main areas of grammar and feed back on them after the pairwork. Round off the activity by asking one or two students to tell the class about their or their partner's relative.

11 **T 2.11** [**CD 1: Track 28**] This is another discrimination activity. Play sentence 1 as an example. Then play the rest of the recording and ask students to tick the sentences they hear. You can make this exercise productive by asking students to read the pairs of sentences aloud.

Answers and tapescript

1 **a** He likes his job.
2 **b** She loves working.
3 **b** He isn't married.
4 **b** Does he have three children?
5 **b** Where does he go?

WRITING (SB p155)

Improving style

Using pronouns

This unit of the writing syllabus reviews subject pronouns and possessive adjectives, and also introduces object pronouns. Knowing how to use pronouns is an essential skill in fluent writing and it helps students understand how a text fits together.

1 Get students to complete the charts, working individually before checking with the whole class.

Answers

Subject pronouns	Object pronouns	Possessive adjectives
I	me	my
you	you	**your**
he	him	his
she	her	**her**
it	it	its
we	us	**our**
they	them	their

2 Write the following sentence on the board and get students to identify the subject pronoun, object pronoun, and possessive adjective:

I lend him my car every week.

Look at sentence 1 and the example as a class. Elicit the pronouns and other possessive adjectives in the sentence (pronouns: *I*, *him*; possessive adjective: *my*). In pairs, students continue to underline the pronouns and circle the possessive adjectives in sentences 2 and 3. Check the answers as a class.

Answers
1 pronouns: I, him; possessive adjectives: her, my
2 pronouns: She, it; possessive adjective: our
3 pronouns: They, he, them; possessive adjective: their

Refer students to Grammar Reference 2.3 on SB p185.

3 Focus attention on the example and get students to say what *she* and *me* refer back to (*girlfriend* and *I*). Look through the names in the sentences quickly and check students know if they refer to a man or a woman. Get students to complete the sentences, working individually. Give them time to check in pairs before checking with the whole class.

Answers
2 He; them
3 it
4 him
5 We; us
6 us
7 her
8 He; it
9 me
10 She; them

4 Ask students what they can remember about David Guetta (the DJ from SB p22). Check comprehension of *YouTube hits* (visits by computer users to a video website). Ask students to read the text quickly and find the answers to the questions. Elicit who is in the photo with him (*his wife*).

Answers
He's a DJ.
He works with pop stars.
He wants to work with Lady Gaga.
David's wife comes from Senegal. She's a businesswoman and an actress.
He has 70 million hits.

5 Read the first sentence of the text aloud and get students to say what is wrong with it (the repetition of *David* makes it sound unnatural). Focus attention on the example rewriting of the text and then get students to continue the task. With weaker classes, elicit a longer section of the text as a whole-class activity and write the answers on the board before students complete the task individually.

Check the answers either orally or by collecting in the students' written task.

T 2.12 **[CD 1: Track 29]** Play the recording and let students check their answers.

Answers and tapescript
David Guetta – The superstar with 70 million hits on YouTube!
David Guetta is French. He lives in Paris, but he works all over the world. He's a very famous DJ. He's number three in the 'Top 100 DJs' poll. He works with a lot of pop stars, such as Britney Spears, Celine Dion, and Madonna. He sometimes writes songs for them. He really likes Lady Gaga, and he wants to work with her. His job's very exciting, and he likes it a lot. He's married to Cathy. She comes from Senegal. She's a businesswoman and an actress. They often go to Ibiza.
Every year, they have parties there. People love their parties. Cathy and David have two young children, and they love to spend time with them.

EXTRA ACTIVITY

Give students additional practice by asking them to write a short description of a friend or relative, or a short profile of a famous person that they admire. This can be done as a mini-project, with the students then presenting their descriptions in the form of a short talk. If you have access to a computer network, students can type their description and then upload it for other students to read. If not, you can create an area for students' written work in the classroom and display it on the walls. With weaker classes, write prompts on the board to help students plan the type of information to include, e.g. *work*, *country/city*, *place of work*, *family*, *free time*, etc.

READING AND SPEAKING (SB p24)

A really good job

ABOUT THE TEXT

This activity brings together, in one text, much of the grammar students have studied so far. It should be motivating for them to read a piece of continuous prose of this length. The section also acts as a preview of the daily routine topic in Unit 3.

The text is based on a real young Indian man but the information has been carefully simplified and graded for students at this level. West Bengal /ben'gɔːl/ is a state in eastern India, which stretches from the Himalayas in the north to the Bay of Bengal in the south.

Encourage students to use the context in reading texts as much as possible to help them with new words. They can also pool their knowledge of vocabulary when working in groups, or, if appropriate, use a dictionary.

Students may need help with the words below in terms of meaning and/or pronunciation. You may want to pre-teach/check (some of) the following:

village, to be lucky, private school, rupee /ruː'piː/, *bamboo hut, housework, ambition, poor.*

1 Lead in to the topic by asking students: *What does a head teacher do? How old are most head teachers?* Focus attention on the map and the photos on SB pp24–5. Point to Babur /'bæbʊə/ Ali and read out the main heading. Ask students to tell you a little about what and who they can see in the pictures, and to predict a little about Babur Ali's life. Do not insist on accuracy at this stage – use this as an opportunity for students to get into the topic and predict what they might read in the text.

Put students into pairs to talk about the information in sentences 1–8. Don't let them refer to the text at this stage.

2 Ask students to read the first paragraph quite quickly. This helps them focus on the main information and not worry about words they don't recognize. Ask students to locate Babur's region on the map on SB p24.

With weaker students, you could ask and answer some of the questions in open pairs first. Students take it in turns to ask and answer the questions about Babur, working in closed pairs. Check the answers by getting students to ask and answer across the class. Decide according to the speed and ability of your students whether you want quick, short answers or fuller answers (see brackets).

Answers
1 West Bengal in India. (He comes from West Bengal in India.)
2 In the small village of Bhabta. (He lives in the small village of Bhabta.)
3 No, it doesn't.
4 Because he goes to a private school. (He's lucky because he goes to a private school.)
5 1,000 rupees a year. (It costs 1,000 rupees a year.)
6 Everything that he learns. (He teaches them everything that he learns.)
7 No, they aren't.
8 Anand Shiksha Niketan School. Yes, it is. (His school's name is Anand Shiksha Niketan School.)

If appropriate, ask students for their reaction to the first part of the text. Ask if they know anyone who is young and who has a job.

3 Write the times 5 a.m. and 4 p.m. on the board and elicit the expressions *five o'clock* and *four o'clock*. Do not cover other expressions, as students will revise telling the time more fully in the *Everyday English* section at the end of this unit.

Give students time to read the second paragraph. Then get two students to ask and answer the questions using the example in the Student's Book. With weaker classes, you could write the key verbs on the board as prompts: *get up, go to school, travel back to his village, begin classes, stop teaching.*

Students continue to ask and answer questions. Monitor and check. Then check the answers with the class.

Answers

What time does he get up?	At five o'clock.
What time does he go to school?	At eight o'clock.
What time does he travel back to his village?	At four o'clock.
What time does he begin classes?	At five o'clock.
What time does he stop teaching?	At eight o'clock.

4 Give students time to read the last paragraph. Focus attention on the example and elicit the correction. Write the sentences on the board and highlight the contrastive stress:

It doesn't have sixty students. It has six hundred and fifty.

Students works in pairs to correct sentences 2–4. Monitor and check. Then check the answers with the class.

Answers
1 It doesn't have sixty students. It has six hundred and fifty.
2 It doesn't have five teachers. It has ten teachers.
3 Babur doesn't want to stop teaching. He always wants to teach poor children.
4 He doesn't want to be a doctor. He wants to study at university.

5 Ask students to look back at their answers in exercise 1. Students check if their ideas were correct.

Answers

1 5 a.m.	4 4 p.m.	7 speaks
2 mother in the house	5 the classes	8 wants
3 bus	6 likes	

Roleplay – An interview

6 This activity consolidates question formation and also gives students the opportunity to roleplay characters from the reading text.

Ask students to imagine that a journalist is visiting Babur's school and that he/she wants to interview one of the students. Elicit a few possible questions that the journalist might ask. Focus attention on the question prompts. Elicit the first question as an example (*How many students does your school have? / How many teachers are in your school?*)

Divide the class into pairs to complete the rest of the questions. Monitor and help as necessary, checking for correct question formation. With weaker students, you could do the question formation as a whole class stage, drilling the forms as necessary.

Check the answers, accepting any suitable wording for the questions.

Answers
1 How many students does your school have? / How many students are in your school?
2 How many teachers does your school have? / How many teachers are in your school?
3 What time do your classes start? What time do your classes finish?
4 How much do your classes cost? / How much does your school cost?
5 What's your teacher's name?
6 Is he a good teacher?
7 What does he teach?
8 Does he work hard?

Divide the students into A/B pairs and assign the role of journalist to the As and one of Babur's students to the Bs. Remind students to use the questions as prompts but also to make the conversation between the journalist and students as natural as possible. Encourage the B students to give additional information in their answers. They can imagine extra details based on what they know from the text. Encourage the A students to react to the information given by the students and to sound interested.

Choose two confident students to demonstrate the beginning of the roleplay. Students then continue in closed pairs. Monitor and check for correct question formation and for good intonation. If students sound 'flat', model some of the roleplay yourself, highlighting a wide voice range, then get students to repeat.

T 2.13 **[CD 1: Track 30]** Play the recording and let students compare their conversation with the tapescript. Weaker students can follow **T 2.13** on SB p169.

Tapescript
I = Interviewer S = Student
I Can I ask you some questions about your school?
S Yes, of course.
I How many students are in your school?
S There are 650 now.
I That's quite a lot. And how many teachers?
S Ten teachers.
I And what time do your classes start?
S Five o'clock every day.
I How much does it cost?
S Oh, the school is free.
I Very good! And your teacher, what's your teacher's name?
S Babur Ali. He's only sixteen.
I Sixteen! That's amazing. Is he a good teacher?
S He is very good indeed.
I What does he teach?
S He teaches English, Bengali, history, and maths.
I That's a lot of subjects. Does he work hard?
S Oh, yes, very hard. He studies all day and he teaches us every evening. He's the best teacher in the world!

SUGGESTION

Asking students to act really seems to help their pronunciation, particularly stress and intonation. You could ask pairs of students to learn their conversation by heart to act out to the class. More confident students could improvise other conversations, e.g. between Babur and the journalist, Babur and another teacher, two of Babur's students.

VOCABULARY AND LISTENING (SB p26)

⚠ POSSIBLE PROBLEMS

In many languages, you don't need an article (*a*/*an*) when stating a person's job. This may lead to mistakes in English **I'm hairdresser*, etc. Exercise 2 provides the article in context, but students may make mistakes in freer practice, so be prepared to highlight the correct the use of *a*/*an* + job.

Jobs

1 Focus attention on the pictures and elicit the names of the jobs that students already know. Elicit the correct job in picture a (*nurse*). In pairs, students match the rest of the pictures with the words. If possible, students check any new words in their dictionaries.

Check the answers and drill the words both chorally and individually as you go, taking care with the stress. Also check students reproduce the correct vowel sounds (see *Answers* below). With weaker classes, you could keep revising the words by saying *Tell me again! What's picture a? What's picture d?* etc.

Answers

a nurse /'nɜːs/	f hairdresser
b journalist /'dʒɜːnəlɪst/	g dentist
c pilot /'paɪlət/	h receptionist
d architect /'ɑːkɪtekt/	i taxi driver
e lawyer	j accountant /ə'kaʊntənt/

2 Elicit the answer to sentence 1 (*hairdresser*) as an example. Students work in pairs to complete the rest of the sentences. Allow students to continue to use their dictionaries, or if you have a monolingual class, you could give quick translations of any words they ask about.

T 2.14 **[CD 1: Track 31]** Students listen and check their answers.

Answers and tapescript
1 She's a **hairdresser**. She cuts hair.
2 He's a **pilot**. He flies from Heathrow airport.
3 She's a **receptionist**. She works in a hotel.
4 He's an **architect**. He designs buildings.
5 She's a **lawyer**. She works for a family law firm.
6 He's a **taxi driver**. He knows all the streets of London.
7 She's a **journalist**. She writes news stories.
8 He's a **dentist**. He looks after people's teeth.
9 She's a **nurse**. She works in the City Hospital.
10 He's an **accountant**. He likes working with money.

3 **T 2.15** **[CD 1: Track 32]** Play conversation 1 and elicit the job (*journalist*) as an example. Play the rest of the recording and let students complete conversations 2–5. Check the answers.

Put the students in pairs to practise the conversations. Be prepared to drill selected lines if students have pronunciation difficulties.

Answers and tapescript

1 **A** What does your brother do?
B He's a **journalist**. He writes for *The Times* newspaper.
A Oh, that's a good job.
2 **C** What does your father do?
D He's an **accountant**. He works for a big firm in the city.
C And your mother? What does she do?
D She's a **teacher**. She teaches French and Spanish.
3 **E** Does your sister work in the centre of town?
F Yes, she does. She's a **receptionist**. She works in the Ritz Hotel.
E Oh, that's near where I work.
4 **G** Are you a **doctor**?
H No, I'm not. I'm a **nurse**.
G Oh, but I want to see a **doctor**.
5 **J** I want to be a **pilot** when I'm big.
K I want to be a **lawyer**. They earn lots of money.
J **Pilots** earn a lot too, *and* they travel the world.

EXTRA ACTIVITIES

- Students write their own short conversations containing jobs based on the model in exercise 3.
- Students play 'Twenty questions' in small groups to revise the vocabulary of jobs and the Present Simple. One student thinks of a job but doesn't say what it is. The rest of the class ask *Yes/No* questions to try and find out what it is. The student answering has to say a full short answer, e.g. *Yes, it is/No, it isn't., Yes, he does./No, he doesn't.* The person who guesses in fewer than 20 questions has the next turn. If the group cannot guess, the same student has another go.

Speaking

4 Focus attention on the examples in the Student's Book. Elicit more questions from the class about one of your friends or relatives. Students work in pairs to ask and answer questions about the jobs. If appropriate, you could set this up as a roleplay with students pretending to be delegates as a conference and discussing people's jobs.

Monitor and check, helping as necessary. Check for accurate use of *be*, *his/her*, third person Present Simple forms, and *a/an* + job. Don't interrupt students during the pairwork but feed back on any common errors at a later stage.

EVERYDAY ENGLISH (SB p27)

What time is it?

SUGGESTION

It is useful to have a toy or cardboard clock with movable hands for this lesson and for subsequent revision of telling the time. If you don't already have one in your school, then it is quite easy to make a cardboard one.

Introduce the subject of telling the time by asking *What time is it?* and *What time does the lesson start?* Initially you can accept answers in the hour + minutes form, e.g. *five thirty*, but explain that the system used in *Headway English A2* uses *past* and *to*.

NOTE

To help students learn the time in English the clocks in exercise 1 are arranged in four groups: *o'clock/half past*; *quarter past/to*; *minutes past*; *minutes to*. Each example has a similar time alongside to help students write the correct answers.

1 Focus attention on the first pair of clocks and elicit the missing time (*It's eight o'clock.*) Ask students to work in pairs, look carefully at the clocks and the examples provided, and write in the times.

T 2.16 **[CD 1: Track 33]** Play the recording for students to check their answers.

Answers and tapescript

It's five o'clock.	**It's eight o'clock.**
It's half past five.	**It's half past eleven.**
It's quarter past five.	**It's quarter past two.**
It's quarter to six.	**It's quarter to nine.**
It's five past five.	**It's ten past five.**
It's twenty past five.	**It's twenty-five past five.**
It's twenty-five to six.	**It's twenty to six.**
It's ten to six.	**It's five to six.**

Play the recording again. Encourage students to follow closely the stress pattern as they practise saying the times. Elicit the time of the end of the lesson.

If possible, bring a toy or cardboard clock with moveable hands to the lesson as an easy way of giving further practice. First, you can change the times on the clock, and then your students can also have turns, coming to the front of the class, moving the hands, and asking *What time is it?* Alternatively, draw clocks showing different times on the board. Continue to encourage students to use accurate stress patterns.

2 This exercise introduces useful expressions for times just before or after an exact division of the clock, and for an approximate time. Focus attention on the clocks and the times.

T 2.17 **[CD 1: Track 34]** Play the recording for students to listen and repeat.

Tapescript

1 It's nearly three o'clock.
2 It's just after five o'clock.
3 It's about half past two.

Practise these expressions with appropriate times shown on the toy or cardboard clock, or by drawing further examples on the board. Check pronunciation and sentence stress carefully.

3 Focus attention on the examples. Ask *Which conversation is with a friend?* (the one with the question *What time is it?*). *Where are the people in the other conversation?* (*in the street/in a public place*). Drill the pronunciation chorally and individually.

Ask students to draw three or more clocks on a piece of paper. Remind them to use the expressions in exercise 2. Students practise the conversations in pairs. Monitor and check for correct pronunciation. Drill the examples again if necessary and get students to repeat the pairwork.

4 **T 2.18** **[CD 1: Track 35]** With weaker classes, give students time to read through the conversations first. Play conversation 1, pausing at the end, and elicit the missing words. Play the rest of the conversations without stopping. Give students time to check their answers in pairs. Play the recording again for students to check/complete their answers.

Answers and tapescript

1 **A** Excuse me. Can you tell me the **time**, please?
B Yes, of course. It's **just** after **six** o'clock.
A Thank you **very** much.
2 **C** **Excuse** me. Can you **tell** me the time, please?
D I'm **sorry**. I don't have a watch.
C Never mind.
3 **E** Excuse me. What time does the bus leave?
F At **ten past** ten.
E Thank you. What time is it now?
F It's **about** five past.
E Five past ten?!
F No, no, five past **nine**. You're OK. No need to hurry.
4 **G** When does this lesson **end**?
H At four o'clock.
G Oh dear! It's only **quarter** past three!

Tell students (in L1 if appropriate) to imagine that they are stopping a stranger in the street in conversations 1–3 and that they must try to sound polite. Ask two confident students to practise one of the conversations across the class. Students continue in closed pairs. If students sound 'flat' or a little abrupt, play the recording as a model and drill chorally and individually. Really encourage a good imitation of the recording to help the students sound very polite.

Students can act out one or two of the conversations for the class. Keep the activity light-hearted and fun.

SUGGESTION

Try to integrate the language of telling the time into all of your lessons in a natural way. Ask students for a time check at various points in the lesson, ask about the times of their favourite TV programmes, and the times of local transport.

Photocopiable Activity

UNIT 2 Say it! TB p149/TRD

Materials: One copy of the worksheet for each group of three of four students; dice and counters for each group.

Procedure: Explain that students are going to play a board game to practise the language from Unit 2 and review some of the language from Unit 1. Pre-teach/check *It's my/your turn, I'm/You're next, That's right/wrong, I/you go back/forward.*

- Put students into groups and hand out copies of the board game, and the dice and counters. Explain that there are different types of square in the game – on a *Make a question* square students have to make a question from a prompt, e.g. *Your teacher = married?* and they should then answer that question. On a *What's the job?* square they should give the correct job. On an *Opposites* square they should give the correct opposite adjective. On an *About you* square students have to talk about themselves.
- Explain the rules: if a student gives a correct sentence from a prompt/definition, they stay on that square, if not, they move back one. If a student asks and answers the prompt on a *Make a question* square correctly, they move forward 2 squares. The first student to reach *Finish* is the winner.
- Students put their counters on *Start* and take turns to throw the dice and move around the board. Monitor and help as necessary. Try to encourage students to check each other's answers, but be prepared to be the final judge if there are any disputes.

ADDITIONAL MATERIAL

Teacher's Resource Disc
Communicative activity Unit 2 Present Simple dominoes

Don't forget!

Grammar Reference (SB p185 and Teacher's Resource Disc)
Unit 2

Word list (SB p206 and Teacher's Resource Disc)
Unit 2

Test (Teacher's Resource Disc)
Unit test 2A
Unit test 2B

Video (DVD)
Unit 2 A day in the life

3 Work hard, play hard!

Present Simple (2) – *I/you/we/they* • In my free time • Social expressions (1)

This unit builds on the theme of routines from Unit 2 but with the focus on free time and leisure activities. This creates opportunities for both controlled and personalized practice of the main grammatical aim – all other persons (those without the -*s*!) of the Present Simple. The skills work includes listening and reading tasks on what people do in their free time, and on different weekend routines, and speaking and listening tasks on work–life balance. This provides the opportunity to bring together and revise all persons of the Present Simple.

LANGUAGE INPUT

GRAMMAR

Present Simple (2) – *I/you/we/they* (SB p32)	• Practising the *I/you/we/they* form of the Present Simple.
Questions and negatives (SB p33)	• Practising the *I/you/we/they* negative and question forms of the Present Simple.
Frequency adverbs (SB p33)	• Expressing frequency with common adverbs.

VOCABULARY

Free time activities (SB p34)	• Understanding and practising vocabulary to talk about free time.
Verb + noun/adverb collocations (SB p36)	• Matching and using common collocations.

EVERYDAY ENGLISH

Social expressions (1) (SB p39)	• Understanding and practising expressions in everyday situations.

SKILLS DEVELOPMENT

READING

Town and country weekends (SB p36)	• A jigsaw reading about how two people spend the perfect weekend.

LISTENING

Five conversations about free time (SB p35)	• Listening for key information in five short conversations. **T 3.6** (SB p170/TRD)
A talk about work–life balance (SB p38)	• Listening for the main ideas in a talk. **T 3.9** (SB p171/TRD)

SPEAKING

Roleplay (SB p33)	• Roleplaying an interview between a journalist and someone with two jobs.
Questionnaire (SB p38)	• Talking about work–life balance.

WRITING

Form filling – An application form (SB p156)	• Understanding the conventions of form filling, then comparing the information in two forms.

MORE MATERIALS

Photocopiable worksheets – How often …? (TB p150/TRD), Language race (TRD) **Test** (TRD) **Video** (DVD)

SUGGESTIONS

- You could bring a calendar to the lesson to help with the presentation/review of the days of the week in the *Starter* section. (You can also use it to review/present months of the year in the *Vocabulary and listening* section on SB p34.)
- Setting some vocabulary for homework before you start this unit will give you more time to focus on the grammar. It is worthwhile to get students used to taking some responsibility for the learning of vocabulary. Encourage them to enter the new words in their vocabulary notebooks.

Homework prior to the lesson

1 Ask students to revise/learn the days of the week in English. You could give them a handout with the phonetic script such as this:

Monday /'mʌndeɪ/ Tuesday /'ʧuːzdeɪ/
Wednesday /'wenzdeɪ/ Thursday /'θɜːzdeɪ/
Friday /'fraɪdeɪ/ Saturday /'sætədeɪ/
Sunday /'sʌndeɪ/

2 Ask students to review/check the following words and learn them for the lesson. They can use a bilingual dictionary to look up words they don't know and write the translation if appropriate.

Verbs: *stay late, sing, go to bed, eat in a restaurant, cook*

Nouns: *bookstore, singer, nightclub, apartment, band* (= music group)

Adjectives: *happy, tired*

⚠ POSSIBLE PROBLEMS

Take particular care with the pronunciation of *Tuesday* /'ʧuːzdeɪ/ and *Thursday* /'θɜːzdeɪ/ which students can easily confuse because they sound quite similar. Also the pronunciation of *Wednesday* /'wenzdeɪ/ can be a problem because of the spelling, and the consonant cluster /nzd/ that results from it being pronounced as two syllables, not three.

STARTER (SB p32)

1 If you didn't ask your students to revise/learn the days of the week for homework, use a calendar to present the days. (Alternatively, write the days on the board in abbreviated form, e.g. *Mon*, *Tues*, etc.) Ask *What day is it today?* Go through the days of the week with the whole class, getting students to repeat chorally and individually. Then get one student after another to say the days in order very quickly round the class until students can say them correctly without hesitation.

To give further practice, ask one or two students to go through the whole week and also to spell some of the days, to revise the alphabet. This will take less time if you have set the above for homework.

2 Elicit the weekend days and ask students which days of the week they are busy. Ask students to give reasons.

I LIVE AND WORK IN NEW YORK (SB p32)

Present Simple (2) – *I/you/we/they*

See the notes on *Homework prior to the lesson* in *Suggestions* opposite. Getting students to preview vocabulary will help maintain a lively pace in the grammar presentation.

This section introduces the first person singular of the Present Simple. This should present few problems for students, as they have already seen the *he/she/it* form in Unit 2.

1 **T 3.1** **[CD 1: Track 36]** Focus attention on the photos and the heading of the text. Elicit basic information: *What's her name? (Lisa). Where is she in the photos? (in a bookstore and in a nightclub).* Focus attention on the questions in exercise 1. Ask students to close their books, then play the recording through once and elicit the answers to the gist questions.

Answers
She lives in New York.
She's 24.
She works in a bookstore and she's a singer.

2 Students open their books. Focus attention on the example in the text about Lisa. Elicit which verbs in the box are negatives (*don't do, don't go*). Students complete the rest of the text with the verbs.

T 3.1 **[CD 1: Track 36]** Give students time to compare their answers in pairs, before playing the recording as a final check.

Reading aloud is a way of consolidating new language in a way that all students find accessible. Ask a confident student to read out the first paragraph. Put students in pairs to read aloud alternate paragraphs. Monitor and check for accurate pronunciation. Be prepared to drill selected lines either from the recording or by modelling the sentences yourself.

Answers and tapescript
Lisa's two jobs
'Hi, I'm Lisa Parsons. I'm 24 years old and I live in New York City. I'm always very busy but I'm very happy. From Monday to Friday I **work** in a bookstore, the Strand Bookstore in Manhattan. Then on Saturdays I **have** another job – I'm a singer with a band. It's great because I love books and I **love** singing.
On weekdays I usually **finish** work at 6 o'clock, but sometimes I **stay** late, until 9 or 10 o'clock at night. On Saturday evenings, I **sing** in nightclubs in all parts of the city. I **don't go** to bed until 3 or 4 o'clock in the morning. On Sundays I **don't do** much at all. I often **eat** in a little restaurant near my apartment. I never **cook** on a Sunday. I'm too tired.'

Questions and negatives

3 You could signal that you are going to focus on questions by drawing a large question mark on the board.

T 3.2 **[CD 1: Track 37]** Play number 1 as an example. Play the rest of the recording and get students to complete Lisa's answers.

Answers and tapescript
1 Where do you live?
In New York.
2 Do you like your job?
Yes, I **do**.
3 Do you relax at weekends?
No, I **don't**.
4 Why don't you relax at weekends?
Because I **sing** in nightclubs.

Play the recording again or model the questions and answers yourself. Practise the questions and answers in open pairs across the class to correct any mistakes. Take particular care with these aspects of pronunciation:

Sounds
weak vowel sound /djə/ in the question
strong vowel sound /duː/ in the short answer

Do you like your job?	*Yes, I do.*
/djə laɪk jə dʒɒb/	/jes aɪ duː/

Stress and intonation
The intonation rises at the end of *Yes/No* questions and falls at the end of short answers and *Wh*-questions.

Do you like your job? *Yes, I do.*

Where do you live?

SUGGESTION
With weaker students or if students ask why *do* and not *does* is used in questions with *you*, go though the Grammar Spot with the class before students do the Roleplay section.

Roleplay

SUGGESTION
If you have access to video equipment, you could record students doing the interview.

4 Set up this task as an interview, rather than just straight question and answer practice. If possible, move the desks to create a more relaxed setting and get students to use a classroom object as a microphone prop. Pre-teach/check the language of greeting and thanking: *Nice to meet you. Thank you very much. A pleasure.* /ˈpleʒə/ and the use of *because* in replying to *why* questions.

Tell students to read the text on SB p32 quickly, but then to cover it and try to remember the information about Lisa's life. This will help the roleplay sound more natural. With weaker students, go through the questions as a class first and elicit the full form of each question.

Demonstrate the activity by getting two students to ask and answer the first two questions across the class. Students then work in closed pairs and roleplay the interview. Give students time to change roles so that everyone practises the question formation. Go round and check for correct question formation and correct use of strong and weak forms in the pronunciation of *do*.

T 3.3 **[CD 1: Track 38]** Play the recording and let students compare their answers. You could refer students to **T 3.3** and highlight the use of frequency adverbs (*often*, *usually*, *sometimes*, *always*, *never*) in the conversation, before students look at the Grammar Spot as consolidation.

Tapescript
I = interviewer L = Lisa
I Hi, Lisa. Nice to meet you.
L Nice to meet you too.
I Now, I hear you often sing in nightclubs here in New York.
L That's right. I love singing.
I And how old are you, Lisa?
L I'm 24.
I And do you live in New York?
L Yes, I do. I live downtown near the river.
I And where do you work?
L I work in a bookstore. The Strand Bookstore in Manhattan.
I What time do you finish work?
L Well, I usually finish at 6 o'clock but sometimes I stay late, until 9 or 10 o'clock, but I always finish at 6 on Saturdays because I sing in the evening.
I How many jobs do you have?
L Just two! The bookstore and singing.
I And do you like your jobs?
L Oh, yes! I love them both.
I Why do you like them?
L Because I love singing and I love books. I'm lucky. I love my work.
I What do you do on Sundays?
L I don't do much at all. I often eat in a little restaurant near my apartment.
I Do you sometimes cook on Sundays?
L Never! I'm too tired.
I I understand that! Thank you very much for your time, Lisa.
L My pleasure.

GRAMMAR SPOT (SB p33)

1 Ask students to complete the chart with the positive and negative forms. Check the answers.

Answers

Present Simple	**Positive**	**Negative**
I/you	work	don't work
he/she/it	**works**	**doesn't work**
we/they	**work**	**don't work**

Ask students to focus on the positive forms in the table. Ask them which have a different form (*he/she/it*) and how they are different (they end in *-s*).

Ask students to focus on the negative forms in the table. Ask them how the *I/you/we/they* forms are different from the positive forms (they use the auxiliary *don't*). Ask students to focus on the *he/she/it* forms and ask them how they are different from the other negative forms (they use the auxiliary *doesn't*).

2 Ask students to complete the questions and answers. Check the answers.

Answers
Where **do** you work?
Where **does** she work?
Do you work in London? Yes, I **do**.
Does he work in London? No, he **doesn't**.

Ask students which auxiliary verb is used in questions with *I/you/we/they* (*do*) and which with *he/she/it* (*does*). Remind students that questions can begin with a question word, or have no question word and the answer *Yes/No*. Ask students to give you examples of each type of question from the table.

SUGGESTION

Ask a few questions to revise the third person:
Where does Lisa live? (In New York.)
How old is she? (Twenty-four.)
What does she do? (She works in a bookstore and she's a singer.)
Does she like her jobs? (Yes, she does.)
What time does she finish work? (She usually finishes work at six o'clock.)

3 Students find the adverbs of frequency in the text about Lisa. To consolidate the meaning, refer students to the 'percentage' chart in Grammar Reference 3.2 on SB p186.

Answers
I'm **always** very busy …
On weekdays I **usually** finish work at 6 o'clock …
… but **sometimes** I stay late …
I **often** eat in a little restaurant …
I **never** cook on a Sunday.

▶▶ Read Grammar Reference 3.1–3.2 on SB p185–6 together in class, and/or ask students to read it at home. Encourage them to ask you questions about it.

EXTRA ACTIVITIES

- Student A describes their routine as if they do a certain job and the rest of the class has to guess what the job is. They can ask *Yes/No* questions.
- Student A describes their routine as if they were a famous person (politician, actor, singer, etc.) and the rest of the class has to guess who they are pretending to be. They can ask *Yes/No* questions. (You could provide role cards of people who are often in the news.)

Listening and pronunciation

5 **T 3.4** **[CD 1: Track 39]** Play number 1 as an example. Play the rest of the recording and students tick the sentences they hear. Play the recording again. Pause after each sentence and ask students to discuss the answer with a partner before you establish the correct one. You can make this exercise productive by asking students to read the pairs of sentences aloud.

Answers and tapescript
1 **a** Lisa, why do you like your job?
2 **b** Where do you live in New York?
3 **a** What do you do on Tuesday evenings?
4 **b** She really loves singing.
5 **b** She eats a lot.
6 **b** What does she do on Sundays?

PRACTICE (SB p34)

Talking about you

1 Focus attention on the example. Then ask students to match the rest of the questions and answers, working individually. Students who finish early can then check their answers with a partner.

T 3.5 **[CD 1: Track 40]** Play the recording and let students check their answers. As preparation for the next activity, ask students to listen and repeat the questions and answers chorally and individually. Take particular care with intonation.

Answers and tapescript
1d What time do you get up?
At about 7 o'clock on weekdays.
2b Where do you go on holiday?
To Turkey or Egypt.
3e What do you do on Sundays?
I always relax.
4c When do you do your homework?
When I get home.
5a Who do you live with?
My mother and brothers.
6h Why do you like your job?
Because it's interesting.
7f How do you travel to school?
Usually by bus.
8g Do you go out on Friday evenings?
Yes, I do sometimes.

2 This activity gives practice of the first and second persons only. Demonstrate the activity by getting a pair of students to ask and answer the first question across the class. Remind students to have the whole question ready before they speak.

Students work in pairs to ask and answer the questions in exercise 1. Go round and check as students do the activity, listening for correct intonation. Students who finish early can be encouraged to ask similar questions but with different days or question words, e.g. *Do you go out on Saturday evenings? Where do you do your homework?*

3 This activity practises the third person singular alongside the other persons. It also pulls the class together after the pairwork. Focus attention on the examples in the Student's Book. Then ask a few individuals to tell the rest of the class about themselves and their partner. If necessary, remind students they need to use the third person *-s* when talking about their partner. (Unless you have a small class, it would take too long to give everyone a turn.)

Positives and negatives

4 This exercise revises the verb *to be* alongside other verbs in the Present Simple. The exercise could be set for homework, but it can be quite fun if done orally and at a brisk pace with the whole class. Focus attention on the examples and then get students to complete the exercise orally. They could then write their answers as consolidation.

Answers

3 She speaks Spanish.
4 They don't want to learn English.
5 We aren't tired and we don't want to go to bed.
6 Roberto doesn't like watching football on TV, but he likes playing it.
7 I don't work at home because I don't have a computer.
8 Amelia is happy because she has a new car.
9 I don't smoke, I don't drink, and I go to bed early.
10 He smokes, he drinks, and he doesn't go to bed early.

5 Focus attention on the examples. Then write two false sentences, one about yourself and one about a student, for the class to correct. Give students time to write their sentences. Students read out their sentences for the rest of the class to complete. With larger classes, get students to work in small groups. If necessary, highlight the use of contrastive stress when correcting information:

I'm a doctor. *You aren't a doctor. You're a nurse.*

Yuko has two children.
She doesn't have two children. She has three children.

VOCABULARY AND LISTENING (SB p34)

In my free time

SUGGESTIONS

- You could bring a calendar to the lesson to help with the presentation/review of the months of the year in exercise 1.
- If you have access to a class set of dictionaries, bring them to this class to help students with the vocabulary work.
- It would save time in the lesson if you could ask your students to review/check the names of seasons and months for homework before the lesson. You could give them a handout with the phonetic script such as this:

Seasons

spring /sprɪŋ/	autumn /'ɔːtəm/
summer /'sʌmə/	winter /'wɪntə/

Months

January /'dʒænjəri/	July /dʒuː'laɪ/
February /'februəri/	August /'ɔːgəst/
March /mɑːtʃ/	September /sep'tembə/
April /'eɪprɪl/	October /ɒk'təʊbə/
May /meɪ/	November /nəʊ'vembə/
June /dʒuːn/	December /dɪ'sembə/

⚠ POSSIBLE PROBLEMS

Students often confuse the months *March* and *May*, and *June* and *July*. They are likely to need help with the vowel sounds and word stress in the months and seasons, particularly: *January* /'dʒænjəri/, *February* /'februəri/, *April* /'eɪprɪl/, *August* /'ɔːgəst/, and *autumn* /'ɔːtəm/. Be prepared to drill the months and seasons as a class, repeating as often as necessary until students feel confident using the words.

Students have already seen *like/don't like* + *-ing* and practised it in simple contexts. This section extends the vocabulary of free time activities and gives a reminder of the form in the Caution Box on SB p35.

1 Ask students to look at the pictures and see if they can identify the seasons. Ask students to work in pairs and answer the questions in exercise 1. They will obviously find this easier if you set the seasons and months for homework (see *Suggestions* above). Monitor, noting any problems with pronunciation and confusion with the months of the year.

If your students had no difficulties with the questions in exercise 1, briefly go through the answers as class feedback, highlighting any specific problems you noted earlier. If necessary, do further spot checks by asking: *What's before/after September?* etc. *When's your birthday?* (Make sure that students give only the month in their answers not the actual date.)

If your students had problems with the questions in exercise 1, use a calendar or write abbreviations of the months on the board to present the key language again. Go through the seasons and months. Say them first yourself and ask students to repeat each one in order both chorally and individually. Repeat the months and seasons a few times, making it fast and fun if you can. Then ask students the questions in exercise 1 again, checking for accurate pronunciation.

2 In pairs or small groups, students look at the photos and match as many as they can with the names of the activities. If possible, students check any new words in their dictionaries. Encourage them to enter any new words in their vocabulary notebooks.

Check the answers with the class, dealing with any pronunciation problems as you go.

Answers
m playing golf
d going to the cinema
c listening to music
e swimming
b watching TV
l going to the gym
q windsurfing
h playing computer games
n cooking
k playing tennis
a playing cards
p skiing
f dancing
i sailing
o running
g reading
j cycling

Ask the questions about seasons and activities, focusing on the example sentences. Students work in pairs or small groups to compare their ideas.

Possible answers
Summer activities: golf, swimming, windsurfing, tennis, sailing, cycling
Winter activities: skiing
More than one season: dancing, watching TV, going to the gym, cooking, playing cards, listening to music, running, reading, going to the cinema, playing computer games

Listening

Focus attention on the note about *like* + *-ing*. Write *I like …* and *I don't like …* and elicit a few true sentences from the class, making sure students use an *-ing* verb form rather than a noun.

Read Grammar Reference 3.3 on SB p186 together in class, and/or ask students to read it at home. Encourage them to ask you questions about it.

3 **T 3.6** **[CD 1: Track 41]** Tell students that they are going to listen to five conversations about what people like doing in their free time. This script includes the key language from this section and recycles vocabulary that students have already met, so students should not have problems completing the task. Point out that some of the speakers talk about more than one activity but may not say when they do each one. The information for *When do they do it?* can be seasons, months, days or parts of a day. With weaker students, remind them that they don't need to understand every word, just to pick out the key information to complete the chart.

Play conversation 1 as an example. They play the rest of the recording and let students complete the chart. Students compare their answers in pairs. Play the recording again to let students complete/check their answers. Check with the class, making sure students use *like* + *-ing* correctly.

Answers

	What do they like doing?	When do they do it?
Andy	playing tennis	usually summer, spring and autumn if sunny
Roger	skiing	January or February
Linda	going to the gym, swimming	every morning
Ben & Josh	windsurfing	every summer
	playing golf and football	–
	watching sport on TV	–
	playing computer games	after school
Sandra	watching TV	winter
	playing cards	summer, on holiday
Brian	watching TV	–
	playing cards	winter

Tapescript
I = Interviewer

1 **Andy**
A I play tennis a lot. I'm no good but I like playing.
I When do you play?
A Oh, summer usually but sometimes in spring and autumn if it's sunny.

2 **Roger**
R My favourite sport is skiing. I go skiing with my family every year. We all love it.
I When do you go?
R Always in January or February, after Christmas. We go to France.
I And are you a good skier?
R I'm OK. My wife's good, the kids are really good – but I'm just OK.

3 **Linda**
I Do you go to the gym every day?
L Yes, I do, every day, every morning before work.
I And do you go swimming there?
L Yes. I swim every morning too. Do you go to the gym?
I Well -er, no, I don't. I like my bed in the morning!

4 **Ben & Josh**
I You like a lot of sports, don't you?
B&J Oh yeah, my favourite is windsurfing. Me and my brother go to surf school every summer and … and we play golf and football of course.
I All outdoor sports?
B&J Er- no, we watch sport a lot on TV, and we play computer games after school.
I Not a lot of time for homework then?
B&J Well …

5 **Sandra & Brian**
S In winter we love evenings at home.
B What do you do? Watch TV?
S Well, yes, sometimes. We like all the cookery programmes. I love cooking.
B Oh, we love those programmes too, but we often play cards on winter evenings.
S We like cards too, but we only play when we're on holiday in summer. It's a 'holiday thing' in our family.
B What do you play?
S Well, usually we play …

If you have time, you could play the recording again and get students to tell you any other information they have understood. This can help to build confidence.

4 Choose a student and give examples of what you think he/she likes doing. Focus attention on the examples in the Student's Book. Then ask students what they think you like doing. Elicit one or two examples but don't confirm or deny at this stage.

Ask students to continue in groups, making a list of activities. Students can choose activities from the Student's Book and also ask you for other vocabulary as necessary.

Students ask you questions to find out if they were correct about what you like, following the example in the Student's Book. (Students are often interested to find out about their teacher, but keep this fairly short to allow time for the personalized stage.) Be prepared to drill key sentences if students have problems with stress and intonation.

Talking about you

5 First build a dialogue with two students, using the example in the Student's Book and the possible follow-up questions. Then tell the students some true things about yourself, encouraging them to respond to your likes and dislikes as in the example.

Students continue in pairs or small groups. Monitor and help as necessary. Check students are using the *-ing* form correctly.

Finally, ask a few students in the class to report back on themselves and their partners. This gives further practice in different persons of the Present Simple.

EXTRA ACTIVITIES

- Ask students to do some independent vocabulary research by looking for other activities which are not in the Student's Book. They can look them up in a bilingual dictionary, or on the Internet, as well as pooling their knowledge in groups. Students can then exchange the new vocabulary in a later lesson, including both spelling or punctuation. They can use mime or simple descriptions to help with meaning.
- Students interview each other to find out when the best month/season is for a certain activity in their country: *When's the best month for* (*skiing, walking, sunbathing, shopping, visiting your city*, etc.)?
- Students write a description of how their home area changes from season to season. Get them to include information on the weather, the activities people do, and the number of visitors.

WRITING (SB p156)

Form filling

An application form

The writing syllabus continues with a focus on filling in forms. The context is an application form for a sports and leisure centre and students review the language of talking about what you like doing.

Lead in to the topic by asking *What types of form do people fill in?* (applications for a job/course/bank account/organisation or society; booking forms for hotels/holidays; tax/voting/medical forms; feedback on objects/services, etc.) Ask *How often do you fill in a form? What for? Do you usually fill in a paper form or do the application online?* Elicit a range of answers from the class.

1 Focus attention on the categories on the form. Students met a lot of the personal information categories in Unit 1, but you may need to check the following: *title, dd/mm/yy* = *day/month/year, zip code* = American English for *post code*. Check *spa* and *exercise classes* from the *Health and fitness* section.

Ask a few check questions about Lena, e.g. *What nationality is she?* (Australian) *Where does she live?* (Sheffield) *How do you spell her first name?* (L - E - N - A) *Does she have a mobile phone?* (Yes, she does.), etc.

Focus attention on the sentence starters in the box. Elicit one or two examples of complete sentences. Then let students continue in pairs. Monitor and check for correct use of *to be*, third person singular of the Present Simple, and *like* + *-ing*. Feed back on any common errors.

2 Give students time to complete the form. Monitor and help as necessary. Then put students in new pairs. Try to get students to work with someone they don't know very well.

Focus attention on the example. Elicit one or two further examples from the class. Highlight the stress patterns if necessary, e.g.

I like swimming, but Natalia doesn't.

We both like going to the gym.

Give students time to continue in their pairs. Monitor and help as necessary, but don't interrupt to correct students. Feed back on any common errors after the pairwork.

3 Discuss as a whole class which activities are popular.

EXTRA ACTIVITY

Ask students to find examples of forms in English, either printed or on the Internet. Students can use them to consolidate the language of personal information by roleplaying new characters in different situations, e.g. booking a holiday, joining a club, giving feedback on an object, etc.

Photocopiable Activity

UNIT 3 How often …? TB p150/TRD

Materials: One copy of the worksheet for each student.

Procedure: You can consolidate the Present Simple and leisure activities from this unit, and also review frequency adverbs with the photocopiable activity on TB p150.

- Hand out the questionnaires and get students to complete the questions, using their own ideas for questions 9 and 10.
- Divide the class into pairs and get students to interview each other, recording their partner's answers.
- Then put two pairs of students together and get them to compare answers and find the relevant activities.
- Students report back to the class in a short feedback session.

READING AND SPEAKING (SB p36)

Town and country weekends

ABOUT THE TEXT

This is the first 'jigsaw' reading in the course and so will need careful setting up. The 'jigsaw' technique integrates reading and speaking skills by getting students to read one of two texts and then working in groups to exchange information in a speaking phase. It's important to remind students to read only their text and to get information about the other text via speaking. If necessary and possible, give the instructions for the jigsaw reading in L1.

The theme of the section is 'My perfect weekend' and the texts describe the weekend routines of a musician and an actress.

Jamie Cullum /'dʒeɪmi 'kʌləm/ is an English jazz pianist and songwriter. Although primarily a pianist, he also plays guitar and drums. He has released a number of successful CDs and has won several awards for his music. (There is an extract from one of his songs in exercise 7 of this section.) He is married to food writer and former model, Sophie Dahl, whose grandfather was the children's writer, Roald Dahl. In his text, he mentions Portobello Market, an antiques market in West London.

Shilpa Shetty /'ʃilpə 'ʃeti/ is an Indian actress and model. She has appeared in about 40 films and she is a star of Bollywood – the Hindi-language film industry of India, centered in Mumbai (formerly Bombay). She has won a number of awards for her acting and is also involved in charity work. She is married to businessman, Raj Kundra. In her text, she mentions Jamie Oliver, a popular TV chef.

These texts have been written to consolidate the grammar taught in this and previous units (Present Simple for routines, frequency adverbs, and *like* + *-ing*).

Encourage students to use the context to help them with new vocabulary and to pool knowledge with other students. With weaker classes or if you are short of time, ask students to check some of following vocabulary before the lesson:

Homework prior to the lesson

Jamie Cullum: *song-writer, pianist, model, cookery writer, market, to make breakfast, kitchen, postcards, foreign films, play poker, roast chicken, nan* (informal for *grandmother*)

Shilpa Shetti: *takeaway pizza, garden centre, countryside, green tea, to have a bath, to walk barefoot on the grass, to go to a pub, pudding, gardening, boutiques, lily, spa hotel, massage.*

1 **T 3.7** **[CD 1: Track 42]** This exercise reviews and extends common verb + noun/adverb collocations. Focus attention on the example, then get students to complete the task, working in pairs. Point out that some of the verbs have more than one answer.

Play the recording and get students to check their answers. Elicit the wording of the complete sentences, checking pronunciation as necessary.

Answers and tapescript

1 I often **watch TV**.
2 I sometimes **watch French films**.
3 I always **listen to music** in the car.
4 I don't **play the piano**.
5 I sometimes **play cards** with friends.
6 I **go dancing** a lot.
7 I **go shopping** every Saturday.
8 I **get up late** on Sundays.
9 I often **cook dinner** for my friends.

2 Focus attention on the photos. Check pronunciation of the names (see *About the text* above). Ask students if they recognize the people and elicit any information they know about each character. Give students a minute to read the introduction to each text. Elicit the answers to the questions.

Answers

Jamie Cullum is a song-writer and jazz pianist. He enjoys going to markets, French films, and playing cards at weekends.
Shilpa Shetty is a film actress and model. She enjoys takeaway pizza, going to garden centres, and playing cards at weekends.

3 Put students into two groups, A and B. (With larger classes, you may need to have multiple sets of the two groups.) Assign a text to each group and remind students to read only their text:

Group A – Jamie Cullum

Group B – Shilpa Shetty

Get students to read their text quite quickly, asking others in their group for help with vocabulary if you didn't pre-teach the items listed in *About the text*. Monitor and help with any queries.

4 Give students time to read the questions and deal with any queries. Get them to work in their groups and answer the questions about their text, noting down the answers to each one. Monitor and help as necessary. The answers for each group are provided below for reference but don't check the answers with the whole class at this stage.

Answers
Jamie Cullum
1 He stays in London/in the town.
2 He likes to be with his wife and his brother.
3 He goes dancing/to a club.
4 He likes getting up late, making breakfast, and playing the piano.
5 He goes shopping in Portobello Market.
6 He sleeps late, cooks Sunday dinner, and calls his parents and his nan.
7 Yes, he does.
8 Yes, he does.

Shilpa Shetty
1 She stays in the countryside.
2 She likes to be with her husband.
3 She usually watches TV, but she sometimes play cards. She gets takeaway pizza and drinks green tea.
4 She likes getting up late, having a long bath, walking barefoot on the grass, going to the pub for lunch.
5 She goes shopping in small boutiques and garden centres.
6 She loves shopping, gardening, and visiting garden centres. She sometimes eats out or goes to a spa hotel for a swim and a massage.
7 Yes, she does.
8 Yes, she does.

SUGGESTION
You might want to feed in the language students can use for the information exchange, e.g.
Do you want to start?
You next.
Sorry, I don't understand.
Can you repeat that, please?

5 Re-group the students, making sure there is an A and a B student in each pair. Demonstrate the activity by getting a pair of students to talk about the person in their text. Students continue talking about the answers to the questions in exercise 4 and exchanging the information about their person. Monitor and help. Also check for correct use of the Present Simple, frequency adverbs, and *like + -ing*. Note down any common errors but feed back on them at a later stage. Bring the whole class together to conduct the feedback. Encourage students to expand on their answers where applicable.

Answers
Both Jamie and Shilpa like being with their family and friends. They both like getting up late on Sundays and they like playing poker, shopping, and cooking.
Jamie likes spending the weekend in London but Shilpa enjoys being in the countryside. Jamie goes dancing on Friday nights but Shilpa stays at home. Jamie cooks at weekends but Shilpa doesn't. Jamie plays his piano but Shilpa listens to music. Shilpa likes watching TV but Jamie likes watching foreign films. On Sundays Shilpa sometimes goes to a spa hotel for a swim and massage, but Jamie doesn't.

Speaking

6 This is a simple guessing game to give further practice in talking about free time activities. Write down two things you like doing on a small piece of paper but don't tell students your choice. Students write down their activities, also keeping them a secret from the rest of the class. Remind them *not* to write their name anywhere on the paper.

Collect in the papers and then hand them out to different students at random. Focus attention on the example in the Student's Book. Students read out the activities on their paper to the class and they try to guess the name of the student. With larger classes, students can play in groups.

Bring the students back together to decide on the most popular weekend activities in the class.

7 **T 3.8** **[CD 1: Track 43]** This is an extract from a song by Jamie Cullum called *Twentysomething*. Play the recording and let students just listen. Play the recording again if necessary. Then elicit a range of reactions to the song and to Jamie Cullum's music in general.

SPEAKING AND LISTENING (SB p38)

Your work–life balance

This section focuses on one of the much-debated questions of modern life: how to achieve a balance between career and home life. Students read and complete a questionnaire on work–life balance, and then discuss their answers. Students then listen to a talk by an expert on work–life balance, and the section finishes with a short Writing section in which students write about their partner.

1 Introduce the topic by writing the name of the questionnaire on the board *Do you live to work or work to live?* Check comprehension: *Is your work the most important thing to you? Or do you work just to earn money to live?* Ask students which category they think they belong to.

Check comprehension of *relax at weekends* and *have trouble sleeping*. Focus attention on the questionnaire. Check students understand the convention of ticks (✓) and crosses (✗) – (tick = *yes* and cross = *no*). Students answer the questions and complete the *Me* column about themselves. Then get them to calculate their score and read the answer key. Elicit who thinks they have a good work–life balance and why.

2 Focus attention on the examples in the Student's Book. Get students to practise the questions and answers across the class. Then get individual students to ask you the questions so that they can complete the T section of the questionnaire. With weaker classes, be prepared to drill some of the questions with the class to ensure good pronunciation. Get students to work out your score. You can say whether you agree with it or not.

Ask all the class to stand up and mingle to do the next part of the activity (if there is enough space to do so!). Tell them to take it in turns with two other students to ask and answer the questions.

3 Divide the students into small groups, and get them to compare their scores before reporting back to the class. Elicit a range of scores from the class to establish which students have a good work–life balance.

4 **T 3.9** **[CD 1: Track 44]** Tell students they are going to hear a medical doctor talk about work–life balance. The recording is in the form of a talk, so Dr Hall's voice is the only one they will hear. Pre-teach/check: *structure*, *everyday life*, *balanced*, *bad for your health*. Give students time to read the questions, then play the recording through once. Give students time to exchange the information they understood and compare their answers. Play the recording again so that students can listen for any information they missed.

Check answers with the class.

Answers and tapescript

1 Work gives us money to live, and it gives structure to our everyday lives.
2 'Play' is important for a happy, balanced life. It's important to find time to relax with friends and family. It's not good to think about work all the time.
3 If you take your work home, you also take your problems home, so you never relax.
4 Do a job that you love doing.

T 3.9

Of course, work is important for us all, it gives us money to live, it gives structure to our everyday lives. But for a happy, balanced life it's also important to 'play' sometimes. It's important to find time to relax with friends and family. It's not good to think about work all the time. I know from my work as a doctor that it's sometimes difficult not to take your work problems home – but if you take your problems home you never relax, and it's difficult for your family and bad for your health. Don't live to work, work to live! Life is more than work.

What do you think?

The aim of this activity is to encourage some free speaking. Don't worry if the activity turns out to be quite short. Ask the questions to the whole class. Encourage students to join in the discussion and talk about their experiences and opinions.

Writing

5 This part of the activity is designed to revise the third person singular again alongside the other persons. (It could be set for homework or in class.)

Focus attention on the examples in the Student's Book. Also highlight the use of the auxiliary *does* to avoid repeating the main verb, e.g. *I don't relax at weekends but Leyla does.* Point out that we don't say **I don't often take work home but Sofia takes*, or … **Sofia yes*.

Students use the information they have collected to write and compare themselves with another student. Then ask one or two students to read what they have written aloud for the others to comment on.

EXTRA ACTIVITIES

- You can 'test' how much students can remember about each other's lives by using the ideas in the *Do you live to work or work to live?* questionnaire. Collect the questionnaires in and read out students' answers in turn. Ask the class to guess who is being referred to.
- Students imagine they have a very extravagant and luxurious lifestyle and interview each other, practising *Wh-* and *Yes/No* questions, e.g.

Where do you work?	*I don't work!*
What time do you get up?	*About 11 o'clock.*
Where do you live?	*In a very big house in Paris.*
Do you like cooking?	*No, I never cook. I have a chef.*
Do you have a busy life?	*Of course! I go shopping every day and I go to parties every night!*

EVERYDAY ENGLISH (SB p39)

Social expressions (1)

This is the first of two sections that focus on social expressions. The second is in Unit 10. The conversations introduce and practise expressions for day-to-day conversational exchanges.

1 Focus attention on the photos and ask the questions in open class. Encourage students to speculate about where he is and who the other people are.

2 Focus attention on the first lines of the conversations. Ask students who the speakers are. Ask students to relate each of the conversations to the correct picture.

Answers

1 his host family
2 Hakan
3 his teacher
4 Hakan
5 Hakan
6 the woman who works in the coffee bar
7 Hakan
8 another student
9 his host family

3 **T 3.10** **[CD 1: Track 45]** Focus attention on the example. Ask students to work in pairs and match the second lines of the conversations with the lines in exercise 2.

Then play the recording for students to check their answers.

Answers and tapescript

1 **A** Bye! Have a nice day!
H **Thanks. Same to you. See you later.**
2 **H** I'm sorry I'm late. The traffic's very bad this morning.
B **Never mind. Come and sit down.**
3 **B** What's the matter, Hakan? Do you have a problem?
H **Yes, I don't understand this exercise.**
4 **H** Can I open the window? It's really warm in here.
B **Sure. Good idea. It is hot in here, isn't it?**

5 **H** Can you help me? What does *bilingual* mean?
B **It means *in two languages*.**
6 **C** Do you want a macchiato?
H **Pardon? Can you say that again?**
7 **H** Excuse me? Is this seat free?
D **Yes, it is. Do sit down if you want.**
8 **F** *Parlez-vous français?*
H **I'm sorry. I don't speak French.**
9 **A** Hi, Hakan. How was your day?
H **Good, thanks. Really interesting. How about you?**

4 Focus attention on the example conversation. Ask two students to read it aloud across the class. Put students in pairs to practise the conversations. With larger classes, you may need to allocate just two different conversations to each pair so that the activity doesn't go on too long. Monitor and help as necessary. If students have pronunciation problems, play sections of the recording again. Students listen and repeat, paying special attention to stress patterns and intonation, following the model as closely as possible.

Students practise the conversations with a partner then try to continue them. With weaker students, you could brainstorm ideas as a class and write key lines on the board. Remind students to try to use the appropriate stress and intonation.

T 3.11 **[CD 1: Track 46]** Play the recording, pausing at the end of each conversation to give students time to compare their version.

If you have time, students can learn one of the conversations by heart to act out for the rest of the class. Acting out dialogues can improve their pronunciation considerably.

Tapescript
1 **A** Bye! Have a nice day.
B Thanks. Same to you. See you later.
A Right. At about four o'clock?
B Well, er … school doesn't finish till four.
A Oh, OK! See you about 4.30, then!
2 **B** I'm sorry I'm late. The traffic's very bad this morning.
C Never mind. Come and sit down.
B Thanks.
C We're on page 28.
3 **C** What's the matter, Hakan? Do you have a problem?
B Yes, I don't understand this exercise.
C Don't worry. I'll help you with it.
B Oh, thank you very much.
4 **B** Can I open the window? It's really warm in here.
C Sure. Good idea. It is hot in here, isn't it?
B Very. Thanks a lot.
C That's all right. I think we all need some fresh air.
5 **B** Can you help me? What does *bilingual* mean?
C It means *in two languages*.
B Oh, right, of course. I need to buy a bilingual dictionary!
C Yeah, that's a very good idea!
6 **D** Do you want a macchiato?
H Pardon? Can you say that again?
D A macchiato. Do you want a macchiato?
H Sorry. What is a macchiato?
D It's a strong white coffee.
H Er – yes, OK. Fine. I'll try one. Thank you!
7 **H** Excuse me! Is this seat free?
D Yes, it is. Do sit down if you want.
H Thanks very much. That's very kind.
D Not at all. Are you a new student?
H Yes, I am.
D Are you having a good time?
H Yes. It's getting better, thanks.
8 **E** *Parlez-vous français?*
H I'm sorry. I don't speak French.
E Oh! It's OK. It doesn't matter.
H Can I help you?
E No. Don't worry. I need some help with my homework, but I can do it.
H All right.
9 **A** Hi, Hakan. How was your day?
H Good, thanks. Really interesting. How about you?
A Oh, not bad. Just another day at work.
H Well, tomorrow's the weekend.
A Yes, thank goodness!

SUGGESTIONS
- Students can think of other situations when these expressions would be useful and write or act out parallel conversations.
- Encourage students to use these expressions in class whenever appropriate, e.g. apologizing for being late, asking to open the window, checking what a new word means, etc. You could put key phrases on a classroom poster.

ADDITIONAL MATERIAL

Teacher's Resource Disc
Communicative activity Unit 3 Language race

Don't forget!

Grammar Reference (SB p185 and Teacher's Resource Disc)
Unit 3

Word list (SB p207 and Teacher's Resource Disc)
Unit 3

Test (Teacher's Resource Disc)
Unit test 3A
Unit test 3B

Video (DVD)
Unit 3 Jobs

4 Somewhere to live

There is/are • _some/any/a lot of_ • _this/that/these/those_ • Adjectives • Numbers and prices

The theme of this unit is places. Students describe their own home, a famous building in their country, and where they live. There is a reading text about the White House, the US President's home and workplace. This text consolidates the language of the unit and hopefully students will be interested to find out about the place. There is a *Vocabulary and listening* section to extend students' range of adjectives and adverbs.

LANGUAGE INPUT

GRAMMAR

There is/are (SB p44) *some/any/a lot of* (SB p46) *this/that/these/those* (SB p46)	• Practising there *is/are* to describe places and facilities. • Practising *some/any/a lot of* to talk about indefinite quantity. • Practising *this/that/these/those* to identify objects.

VOCABULARY

Adjectives for *good* and *bad* (SB p50) Adverb + adjective (SB p50)	• Understanding and practising adjectives with positive and negative meanings. • Using adverbs to make adjectives stronger/not so strong.

EVERYDAY ENGLISH

Numbers (SB p51) Prices (SB p51)	• Understanding and practising the language of numbers and prices.

SKILLS DEVELOPMENT

READING

America's most famous address (SB p48)	• Reading about the home and office of the US President.

LISTENING

What's in your bag? (SB p47) Five conversations giving descriptions (SB p50)	• Listening for key words in a short monologue. **T 4.8** (SB p172/TRD) • Listening for key information in five short conversations. **T 4.12** (SB p172/TRD)

SPEAKING

What's in your picture? (SB p45)	• Exchanging information to describe a flat.

WRITING

Describing your home – Linking words *and, so, but, because* (SB p157)	• Understanding linking words, then writing a description of your home.

MORE MATERIALS

Photocopiable worksheets – Numbers and prices (TB p151/TRD), Houses board game (TRD) **Tests** (TRD) **Video** (DVD)

STARTER (SB p44)

⚠ POSSIBLE PROBLEMS

- Students may need help with pronunciation of some of the key words in this section: *sofa* /ˈsəʊfə/, *DVD* /diːviːˈdiː/, *chemist's* /ˈkemɪsts/, *bookshelves* /ˈbʊkʃelvz/, *pavement* /ˈpeɪvmənt/, *traffic lights* /ˈtræfɪk laɪts/, *fridge* /frɪdʒ/, *oven* /ˈʌvn/.

  You will also need to highlight the stress on the compound words: *washing machine*

  Note that students may also need help with the stress patterns of the words in the vocabulary box in *Starter*. If you think students will be unfamiliar with the idea of word stress, you can use international words such as *computer*, *Internet*, *telephone* to show students how words have both stressed and unstressed syllables.
- Students often confuse *cook* and *cooker*, believing that *cooker* should be a person and not a thing. Be prepared to explain the difference here.
- Students may query the use of *'s* in *chemist's*. Explain that this means 'the chemist's shop' but we don't need to say the word *shop*.

SUGGESTION

Homework prior to the lesson

Ask students to look up the following words in their dictionary, and put them in their vocabulary notebook.

sofa DVD player chemist's cooker bookshelves post office pavement traffic lights fridge oven mirror living room shower carpet dining room

1 Focus attention on the vocabulary and ask students to give two or three examples of correct words to go in the *living room* column. Students continue categorizing the vocabulary in pairs.

2 **T 4.1** [**CD 1: Track 47**] Play the recording and get students to check their answers. (Note that these are the most usual answers but other combinations may be possible, e.g. a table in the living room.)

Drill the pronunciation of the words chorally and individually, using the recording or modelling the words yourself. Check pronunciation of the words in *Possible problems* above in particular.

Answers and tapescript

living room	kitchen	street
sofa	cooker	bus stop
DVD player	fridge	post office
armchair	table	café
bookshelves	oven	pavement
mirror	washing machine	chemist's
		traffic lights

A FLAT TO RENT (SB p44)

There is/are – prepositions

⚠ POSSIBLE PROBLEMS

Students often confuse *It's a …* with *There's a …* . The difference is that *It's a …* defines something and gives it a name. *There's a …* expresses what exists. This is quite a subtle area, and we don't suggest that you explore it with students unless absolutely necessary, using translation as a support. Using *there is/are* in context is often the best way to help students understand the concept.

Learners sometimes confuse *there* and *their*. For such a short structural item, there are also a lot of pronunciation problems:

- Many nationalities have difficulty with the sound /ð/.
- In *There's*, the *r* is often silent. In *There are* and the question forms, the *r* is pronounced as a linking sound when the following word begins with a vowel.
- Students may need help with the intonation in questions. Encourage students to start 'high' and fall, ending with a rise in inverted questions.

It is worth working on these pronunciation areas, but not to the point of exhaustion!

1 **T 4.2** [**CD 1: Track 48**] Focus attention on the photo of Josie and Emily. Ask *Where are they?* (in a café). Read the instruction for exercise 1 as a class. Check the situation by asking *Who's Josie?* (the woman with the laptop) and *Who's Emily?* (the woman with the coffee). If necessary, you could briefly revise/check the names of the main rooms/parts of a house or flat: *living room*, *bedroom*, *kitchen*, *bathroom*, and *garden*.

Focus attention on the examples. Give students time to read the rest of the conversation through. Check comprehension of *It doesn't matter* (= it isn't a problem). Play the recording once without stopping. Play the recording again if necessary to let students complete/check their answers.

Ask students *Is Josie interested in the flat?* (Yes, she is.) *What does Emily say about it?* (It sounds great.)

Put students in pairs to practise the conversation. If students have problems with the pronunciation, highlight the linking in *there is* and *there are*:

There's‿a/an …

There‿are …

Answers and tapescript

J = **Josie** **E** = **Emily**

J Here's a flat in Queen's Road!
E Is it nice?
J There's a big living room.
E Mmm!
J And there are two bedrooms.
E Great! What about the kitchen?
J **There's** a new kitchen.
E Wow! How many bathrooms **are there**?
J Er … **there's** just one bathroom.
E **Is there** a garden?
J No, **there isn't** a garden.
E It doesn't matter. It sounds great!

GRAMMAR SPOT (SB p45)

Focus attention on the chart and on the examples of *there is/are* in exercise 1. Get students to complete the chart, using contracted forms where they can. Check the answers with the whole class. In a monolingual class, you might want to ask for a translation of *There's* and *There are*.

If students query the use of *any*, explain that it is used with plural negative sentences, but do not go into a long grammatical explanation at this stage. (*Some/any* is covered in the next presentation *A new flat*.)

Answers

Positive	There is a shower. There **are** two bedrooms
Negative	There **isn't** a garden. There aren't any carpets.
Question	**Is there** a dining room? How many bathrooms **are there**?

▶▶ Read Grammar Reference 4.1 and 4.2 on SB p186 together in class, and/or ask students to read it at home. Encourage them to ask you questions about it.

2 Call out the following words and get students to point to the objects in the photo of the living room on Queen's Road: *sofa, footstool, armchair, bookshelves, window, plant.*

Read the example sentences as a class. Check students understand the use of singular and plural. Ask *Why 'There's'?* (singular) and *Why 'There are'?* (plural).

Drill the sentences, checking for accurate linking between *There's a/an* … and *There are* … . Point out that with plural nouns students need to state the exact number.

Students then work in pairs to produce more sentences. Monitor and check for correct use of *there is/are.*

Bring the whole class together again to check the answers. Correct mistakes carefully.

Possible answers
There's a sofa. There's a footstool. There's a plant. There are two armchairs. There are two windows. There are five bookshelves.

3 **T 4.3** **[CD 1: Track 49]** You can signal that you are going to introduce the question forms by drawing a large question mark on the board.

Focus attention on the gapped questions and sets of prompt words. Make sure students realize that the first set is singular and the second and third sets are plural.

Get a pair of students to ask and answer the example question in open pairs. Elicit an example from the other sets of prompts, e.g. *How many bedrooms are there? Are there any pictures?*

Drill the questions and answers. Then get students to work in closed pairs to ask and answer the questions. Monitor and help as necessary. Check for accurate pronunciation (sounds, linking, and stress).

Play the recording and get students to check their answers. If students had problems with pronunciation during the pairwork, play the recording again and get them to repeat. Drill key sentences to ensure accurate pronunciation. Students then practise the questions and answers again.

Answers and tapescript
Is there a shower?
Yes, there is.
Is there a fridge?
Yes, there is.
Is there a dining room?
No, there isn't.
How many bedrooms are there?
Two.
How many bathrooms are there?
One.
How many armchairs are there?
Two.
Are there any pictures?
No, there aren't.
Are there any bookshelves?
Yes, there are.
Are there any carpets?
No, there aren't.

Prepositions

4 **T 4.4** **[CD 1: Track 50]** This exercise practises/revises prepositions. If you think the prepositions will be new to your class, you will need to present them first. Do this very simply, perhaps using classroom objects, such as a book or chair (*The book is on the desk*), or the students themselves (*Juan is next to Maria*), etc. Highlight the difference between *next to*, *opposite*, and *under* by using gestures.

Refer students to the picture of Queen's Road. Pre-teach/check *first floor* and *bench*. Ask students to work in pairs to put a preposition into each gap.

Play the recording and check the answers. You could practise the prepositions further by using your classroom layout and/or the area near your school.

Answers and tapescript
1 The flat's in Queen's Road.
2 It's **on** the first floor.
3 It's **above** a chemist's.
4 The chemist's is **next to** a clothes shop.
5 There's a mobile phone shop **opposite** the clothes shop.
6 There's a post office **near** the flat.
7 The bus stop is **outside** the café.
8 There's a bench **under** a tree.

PRACTICE (SB p45)

Location, location, location

1 Read the instructions as a class. Divide the students into A/B pairs. Make sure they understand that they each have a different advert for a flat and that they need to ask and answer questions to find out about the flats. Remind students not to look at each other's information.

Teach/check the meaning of *floor* (*on the first floor*, *second floor*, etc.) Focus attention on the examples and demonstrate the activity with a pair of students. Allow students enough time to complete the information exchange.

When students have finished, get them to compare their adverts and see how well they transferred the key information. Ask students which flat they would like to rent and why. Elicit a range of responses.

2 **T 4.5** **[CD 1: Track 51]** Ask students to look at the advert on SB p193. Read the instructions as a class. Pre-teach/check *town centre*, *view*, and *fire*. Focus attention on the example and highlight the contrastive stress used when correcting mistakes:

There aren't four bedrooms! There are only three!

Play the recording. Students listen and shout 'Stop!' when they hear a mistake.

Answers and tapescript

These are the mistakes:

1 There are only three bedrooms.
2 It has only one bathroom.
3 The kitchen is small.
4 There isn't a dining room.
5 The flat is on the third floor.
6 There is only one sofa.
7 There aren't any pictures on the wall.
8 There isn't a TV.
9 There isn't a DVD player.

T 4.5

The flat's near the centre of town. It has four bedrooms, a lovely living room with views over the town, and two bathrooms. The kitchen is very big, and there's a dining room next to it.
The flat's on the second floor. In the living room there are two sofas and an armchair. There are a lot of pictures on the wall. There's a carpet in front of the fire, and there's a TV and a DVD player. There is a table in front of the sofa.

3 Demonstrate the activity by drawing a simple plan of your home on the board. Describe what's in your home. Do this in as natural a way as possible, but do not give too much extra detail like size, colour, etc., as the main focus here is the core lexis of furniture and appliances, and the prepositions.

Give students time to draw their plan. Divide the class into pairs and get students to continue the activity working in pairs. Monitor and help as necessary. Check for correct use of *there is/are* and the prepositions of place, and note down any common errors. Don't interrupt or over-correct grammar mistakes, as the emphasis here is on fluency. You can feed back on corrections at a later stage.

Bring the class back together and ask for any interesting examples that students exchanged.

A NEW FLAT (SB p46)

some/any/a lot of

In this section, *some* and *any* are presented with mainly count nouns (*plates*, *glasses*, *clothes*, etc). In Unit 8, they are presented with both count and uncount nouns. Students also practise *a lot of* with count nouns.

⚠ POSSIBLE PROBLEMS

Some as a concept has a tangible meaning, i.e. a certain, unspecified number of (something). The same cannot be said of *any*. It is a determiner used often (but not exclusively) in questions and negatives. We suggest you do not go into the deeper areas of *any* expressing fundamentally negative ideas. This is unnecessary, and difficult for students at this level.

Some also presents problems of pronunciation with its weak form /səm/.

In affirmative sentences, we usually use *a lot of* rather than *much* or *many*, e.g. *She's got a lot of CDs.* (NOT **She's got many CDs.*) *She's got a lot of homework.* (NOT **She's got much homework.*) Students may need help with this usage, and with the weak forms and linking in the pronunciation /ə ˈlɒt‿əv/.

1 **T 4.6** **[CD 1: Track 52]** Refer students back to the photo on SB p44 and ask students to point to Josie. Ask *What does she want?* (a new flat). Refer students to the photo with exercise 1 and tell them this is Josie's new flat.

Use the photos on SB pp46–7 to pre-teach/check the key vocabulary: *clothes*, *mugs*, *towels* /ˈtaʊəlz/, *kettle* /ˈketl/, *lamp*.

Focus attention on the examples. Check students understand the use of crosses and ticks to cue the answers (two ticks = *some*; four or five ticks = *a lot of*; cross = *not any*). Drill the sentences chorally and individually. Don't go into an explanation of *some/any* and *a lot of* at this stage, but with weaker classes, you could copy the ticks and crosses onto the board and drill more examples of *She has some/a lot of* … and *She doesn't have any* … .

Put students in pairs to continue the activity. Monitor and check for correct use of *have got*, *some/any*, and *a lot of*, and for accurate pronunciation.

Play the recording as a check. If necessary, play selected sentences again, drilling chorally and individually.

Answers and tapescript

1 She has some plates.
2 She has a lot of clothes.
3 She doesn't have any glasses.
4 She has some pictures.
5 She has a lot of CDs.
6 She doesn't have any mugs.
7 She has a lot of shoes.
8 She doesn't have any towels.
9 She has some cups.

GRAMMAR SPOT (SB p46)

1 Look at Grammar Spot question 1 as a class. Allow students time to think before checking the answer.

2 Get students to work in pairs to answer question 2. Check the answers with the whole class.

Answers
1 *Five plates* gives us the exact number. *Some plates* doesn't give us the exact number. *A lot of* means 'a big number of'.
2 We use *some* in positive sentences. We use *any* in negative sentences and questions.

►► Read Grammar Reference 4.3–4.4 on SB p186 together in class, and/or ask students to read it at home. Encourage them to ask you questions about it.

this/that/these/those

2 Focus attention on the *Things to buy* list. Check students understand these are things Josie doesn't have in her flat. Elicit examples of what she still needs to buy. Check for the accurate use of *some*.

Answers
She needs some glasses and some towels.
She needs a lamp, a kettle, and some mugs.

3 **T 4.7** **[CD 1: Track 53]** Explain that Josie and Emily are shopping for things for Josie's new flat. Point to the man in photos 1 and 3. Ask *Who's he?* (the shop assistant).

Students listen to the conversations and fill in the gaps. Let them check in pairs, then play the recording again if necessary. Check the answers.

Put students in pairs to practise the conversations. Encourage a lively intonation and enthusiastic delivery. If students sound 'flat', play selected conversations again and get students to repeat.

Answers and tapescript
J = **Josie** **A** = **Shop assistant** **E** = **Emily**
1 **J** How much is **this** lamp, please?
A It's £45.
2 **J** I like that **picture**.
E Yes, it's lovely!
3 **J** How much are these **glasses**?
A They're £15.
4 **J** I love those **towels**!
E They're fabulous!
5 **J** Look at **those flowers**.
E They're beautiful!
6 **J** Do you like **this kettle**?
E Yeah, it's a great colour!
7 **J** How much are **these mugs**?
A Five pounds each.
8 **J** Look at **that coat**!
E You don't need any more clothes!

Read the chart with the class. Elicit further nouns that can go with each of the words.

Read Grammar Reference 4.5 on SB p186 together in class, and/or ask students to read it at home. Encourage them to ask you questions about it.

SUGGESTION
If students have difficulty with the use of *this/that/these/those*, use the classroom environment to consolidate the language. Choose objects near to you to demonstrate *this/these*, e.g. *This is my desk. I like these posters* and objects that you have to point to demonstrate *that/those*, e.g. *That CD player is new. We use those books.* Give students objects to hold, or point to objects and get students to say sentences using *this/that/these/those*.

PRACTICE (SB p47)

In our classroom

Note that there are a couple of examples of *some/any* with uncount nouns, but there's no need to go into an explanation of uncount nouns at this stage.

1 Focus attention on the example. Students work in pairs or small groups to fill in the gaps.

Check the answers by getting students to read out the complete sentences.

Answers
1 I have a dictionary and some books on my table.
2 There aren't **any** Chinese students in our class.
3 Do we have **any** homework tonight?
4 I need **some** help with this exercise.
5 Is there **a** test next week?
6 There are **some** difficult exercises in this book, but we have **a** very good teacher.

SUGGESTION
If your students need more practice with *some/any*, you could get them to write more true sentences about their own classroom.

2 Focus attention on the examples. Get students to work in pairs/small groups and describe the classroom. If necessary, write word prompts on the board to help generate a range of forms, e.g. *television*, *DVD player*, *flowers*, *photos*, etc.

What's in your bag?

3 **T 4.8** **[CD 1: Track 54]** Focus attention on the photo of Christina. Get students to say how old they think she is and what her job is.

Read the instructions as a class. Give students time to read the list of items and deal with any vocabulary queries.

Play the recording. Students record their answers with ticks (✓) and crosses (✗).

Answers and tapescript

✓	a phone	✗	photos
✓	a diary	✗	an iPod
✓	a lipstick	✗	stamps
✗	an address book	✓	keys
✓	pens	✓	a purse

T 4.8

What's in my bag? Well, there's my phone, and my purse, of course. I have some pens. I always have some pens. A blue one, and a red one. And there's my diary. I need to know what appointments I have. And I have a lipstick ... Oh, and keys, I have some keys, my house keys and my car keys. And that's all!

4 Put students into pairs to say what Christina has and doesn't have. Monitor for correct use of *some* and *any*. Be prepared to go over the difference between them again if necessary.

5 Focus attention on the examples and check comprehension of *wallet*.

With weaker students, brainstorm items that people often carry before students start the pairwork, e.g. *an umbrella*, *tissues*, *brush*, *comb* /kəʊm/, *driving licence*, *ID card*, etc.

Get students to practise the questions in open pairs, highlighting the stress to ensure good rhythm. Students then continue working in closed pairs. Monitor and help as necessary, feeding in any vocabulary students may need.

Ask one or two students to say what is in their or their partner's bag. Try not to be over-curious, as some students may consider it too personal.

Check it

6 Elicit the answer to number 1 as an example. Students work in pairs and complete the exercise.

Answers

1 Do you have a dictionary?
2 Here are some photos of my children.
3 I have a lot of books.
4 Pete, this is Dave. Dave, this is Pete.
5 I don't have any money.
6 Look at those people over there.

READING AND SPEAKING (SB p48)

America's most famous address

NOTE

At the end of this section, there is a speaking activity on a famous building in the students' own country. If you think your students may not have the knowledge to do this task without preparation, get them to research a building for homework. They can also note down any useful vocabulary they may need to describe the building.

ABOUT THE TEXT

The text gives a description of the White House, both in terms of the building and its function as the US President's home and workplace. The White House is located in the US capital, Washington DC. (This stands for 'District of Colombia' and means that Washington is a special area that is not contained in any of the 50 US states.) It was named after George Washington (1732–1799), the first President of the US.

People/Places mentioned in the text are:

- Queen Victoria (1819–1901), British queen from 1837 until her death, a reign of 64 years; President Reagan /'reɪɡən/ (1911–2004), US President from 1981 to 1989; the First Lady, the title given to the wife of the US President.
- the West Wing, where the staff offices are located, including the Oval /'əʊvəl/ Office, the official office of the President; the East Wing, where offices of the First Lady and her staff are located; the Press Room for dealings with the media.
- the Queen's Bedroom, the Lincoln /'lɪnkən/ Bedroom, where special guests stay; the East Room, where the President meets special guests; the State Dining Room, used for receptions and entertaining.

There are examples of American usage: *elevator* (UK = *lift*), and *movie theater*. Encourage students to use the context to help them with new vocabulary and to pool knowledge with other students. With weaker classes or if you are short of time, ask students to check some of following vocabulary before the lesson: *private home*, *birthday party*, *wedding*, *built*, *to govern*, *guest*, *staff*, *fireplace*, *curtains*, *furniture* /'fɜːnɪtʃə/, *gift*, *elevator*, *jogging track*, *billiard room*, *bowling alley*, *library*.

1 Focus attention on the photos and elicit examples of what is shown.

Answers

The outside of the building and park area round it, visitors queuing to see the White House, an old image of the White House from the 19th century, the President's office/Oval Office

2 This activity helps students think about what they know about the topic of the text and serves as a prediction exercise.

Pre-teach/check *government offices* and *open to the public*. Focus attention on the example. Ask students to work in pairs and decide on their answers to the rest of the questions.

3 Set a time limit of about three minutes to encourage students to read quickly. Tell them not to worry about words they do not recognize and just to focus on finding the answers.

Check the answers with the class. You could get students to correct the false answers. Ask students if they found any of the answers surprising.

Answers
1 True 2 False 3 False 4 True 5 True 6 True

4 Give students time to read through the questions. Deal with any vocabulary queries. Elicit the answer to question 1, then get students to complete the task, working in pairs.

Check the answers with the whole class. Decide according to the speed and ability of your students whether to accept short answers or whether you want fuller answers (given in brackets).

Answers
1 Where the US President works and also his private home. (The White House is the place where the US President works and also his private home.)
2 On the third and second floors. (The President lives on the second and third floors.)
3 In the Oval Office. (He works in the Oval Office.)
4 In the Queen's Bedroom or the Lincoln Bedroom. (They stay in Queen's Bedroom or the Lincoln Bedroom.)
5 Three large windows (behind the President's desk) and a fireplace (at the other end). (There are three large windows (behind the President's desk) and a fireplace (at the other end).)
6 Curtains, furniture, and a carpet. (Each new president chooses new curtains, new furniture, and a special new carpet.)
7 Nothing/It's free.
8 250 (150 people work for the President and the First Lady and another 100 look after the building day and night.)
9 Play tennis, go jogging, go swimming, watch a film/movie, play billiards, go bowling, and read. (The President can play tennis, go jogging, go swimming, watch a film/movie, play billiards, go bowling, and read.)

5 This is a referencing task. Briefly review how to say the numbers in the box. Focus attention on the example and then get students to continue the task, working in pairs.

Check the answers.

Answers

50	there are fifty states in the US.
304 million	the number of people in the US/the population of the US
6,000	the number of people who visit the White House each day
132	the number of rooms in the White House
35	the number of bathrooms in the White House
five	the number of kitchens in the White House
six	the number of floors in the White House
140	the number of guests that can go in the State Dining Room

Language work

6 This activity consolidates the use of *Is/Are there …?* and short answers. Focus attention on the examples. With weaker students, briefly review the use of *is* for singular objects (*cinema*) and *are* for plural (*offices*).

Students ask and answer the examples in open and closed pairs. Check students can reproduce the correct stress patterns. Drill the pronunciation of the list of things students have to ask about.

Students continue to ask and answer about the things in the list. Monitor and check for accurate use of *Is/Are there …?* and that students use *a lot*, not *a lot of* in short answers, e.g. **Yes, there are a lot of.* Check the answers with the whole class, feeding back on any common errors.

Answers

Is there a cinema?	Yes, there is.
Are there many offices?	Yes, there are a lot.
Are there many bathrooms?	Yes, there are (thirty-five).
Is there a swimming pool?	Yes, there is.
Is there a library?	Yes, there is.
Are there any elevators?	Yes, there are (three).
Is there a tennis court?	Yes, there is.
Is there a vegetable garden?	Yes, there is.

7 Get students to brainstorm a few rooms in a house and write a list on the board. Elicit possible actions for each room, e.g. *make dinner – kitchen.*

Focus attention on exercise 7 and get students to match the verbs and the places. Check the answers.

If appropriate, elicit other true sentences for each of the rooms, e.g. *We listen to music in the living room.*

Answers
cook – kitchen sleep – bedroom have a shower – bathroom
relax – living room eat – dining room work – office
read – library grow vegetables – garden

Project

See *Note* at the start of this section. Give an example of a building from your own country. Try to do this as naturally as possibly, using some of the following language:

The (building) is in/near/in the centre of …

It is a museum/cathedral/church/mosque/palace/ government building/station/office block.

People go there to meet their friends/take photos/relax/ look at the architecture/pray/get married.

I like/don't like it because …

With weaker students, write some of the above language on the board as prompts.

Divide the class into small groups to talk about their chosen building. Monitor and help as necessary. The aim here is for students to personalize the topic, so do not interrupt or over-correct.

EXTRA ACTIVITY

Students turn their work on famous buildings into a mini-project. If you have access to computers, this can be produced with researched photos and uploaded onto the class/school network. Alternatively, get students to produce their work on paper and display it on the classroom wall/noticeboard.

WRITING (SB p157)

Describing your home

Linking words *and*, *so*, *but*, *because*

Being able to link ideas is an essential skill for students. It's important to give a good grounding in understanding and using linkers, and so the writing syllabus continues with a focus on key linking words for students at this level.

1 Focus attention on the chart and elicit an example with *and*: *I love my new flat and I like your flat too*. Students continue making sentences. Check the answers.

Answers
I love my new flat and I like your flat too.
I love my new flat, so please come and see it soon.
I love my new flat, but unfortunately there isn't a garden.
I love my new flat because it's very beautiful.

2 Give examples based on where you live, e.g. *I like my flat and I love the park near it/so I want to stay there/but it's very expensive/because it's got a lot of space.*

Students write similar sentences about where they live. You could ask one or two students to read their sentences to the class.

3 Focus attention on the example and then get students to complete the sentences, working individually. Give them time to check in pairs before checking with the class.

Answers
1 because 2 but 3 because 4 so 5 because 6 but
7 and 8 so

4 **T 4.9** **[CD 1: Track 55]** Focus attention on the photo and elicit basic information (*Her name's Megan. She has a new flat.*) Pre-teach/check *to face south*. Elicit the first linking word in the text (*so*) and then get students to continue the task.

Play the recording and get students to check their answers.

Answers and tapescript

1 so	7 but
2 but	8 because
3 and	9 but
4 because	10 so
5 and	11 but
6 so	12 because

T 4.9
My new flat is near the centre of town, so I often walk to work. It's not very big, but it's very comfortable! There's just one bedroom, a living room, and quite a big kitchen with a table in the centre. This is good because I love cooking, and I can invite my friends to dinner. The living room has one big window. It faces south so it's always very sunny. I have two comfortable, old armchairs, but I don't have a sofa because the room is quite small.

There isn't a garden, but there's a small balcony in my bedroom. I want to put a chair there so I can sit in the sun on summer evenings.

I love my new flat for many reasons: the big kitchen, the sunny living room, but most of all I love it because it's my first home!

5 Set up the activity by answering the questions in exercise 5 about where you live. Then give students time to write notes about their home, using the questions as prompts. Divide the class into pairs and get students to exchange information about their homes, using the questions in the exercise and their notes.

Draw up a paragraph plan from the questions in exercise 5 for students to follow when they write their own description:

Paragraph 1: Where is it?
Is it old or new?
How many rooms are there?
Is there a garden?

Paragraph 2: Who do you live with?

Paragraph 3: Do you like it? Why?
What is the best thing?

With weaker classes, go back to the model text in exercise 4 and get students to underline the key structures they will need to use, e.g. *My (flat) is …, there's …*, etc.

6 Give students time to write their descriptions in class or set it for homework. Students read their descriptions to each other. Encourage students to ask each other questions.

When you check the students' descriptions, point out errors but allow students to correct them themselves. Try to limit correction to major problems to avoid demoralizing students. If possible, display the students' descriptions on the classroom wall or noticeboard.

VOCABULARY AND LISTENING (SB p50)

Adjectives for *good* and *bad*

This section is designed to extend students' vocabulary range. It's common for students at this level to rely on a small bank of early-learnt adjectives, such as *good*, *bad*, and *nice*. It is important for them to be encouraged to understand and use a wider range of vocabulary, particularly in the language of giving opinions.

SUGGESTION

It is worth checking from time to time how students are progressing with their vocabulary notebooks. Are they still adding to them? Have they started a new one? Do they try to revise regularly? Have they thought of new ways of organizing their notebooks?

⚠ POSSIBLE PROBLEMS

Students shouldn't have too many problems with the meaning of the adjectives, as many of them are similar in other European languages. However, be prepared to help with the word stress and vowel sounds in some of the words:

awful /'ɔːfl/
amazing /ə'meɪzɪŋ/
wonderful /'wʌndəfl/
fantastic /fæn'tæstɪk/
fabulous /'fæbjələs/
horrible /'hɒrəbl/
terrible /'terəbl/

1 Write *good* and *bad* on the board and elicit any words of similar meaning that students know. Focus attention on exercise 1 and on the example. Give students time to categorize the words, working individually.

Check the answers, drilling any words students have problems with.

Answers

good	bad
excellent amazing lovely great fabulous wonderful fantastic	terrible horrible awful

2 **T 4.10** **[CD 1: Track 56]** Focus attention on the examples. Remind students of the system of highlighting the word stress. Use the examples to point out that the stress can fall on different parts of different words and that it's a good idea for students to mark the stress when they record new words in their vocabulary notebooks.

Focus attention on the arrows. Remind students that these indicate the rise and fall of the voice across the sentences.

Play the recording. Reinforce the intonation by drawing the pattern in the air with your hand.

Play the recording again. Get students to repeat, paying special attention to the intonation. If students sound 'flat', exaggerate the intonation pattern, then get students to repeat the sentences again.

Model pronunciation of the sentences again, replacing the adjectives with others from exercise 1. Get students to repeat chorally and individually, making sure they use the correct intonation patterns.

3 **T 4.11** **[CD 1: Track 57]** Tell students they are going to hear six short conversations. Give students time to look at the nouns and adjectives and deal with any vocabulary queries.

Play conversation 1 as an example. Then play the rest of the recording and get students to complete the task. Only play the recording a second time if students missed a lot of the answers. If appropriate, elicit any further information that students understood, e.g. the location of the flat, the colour of the shoes, etc.

Refer students to **T 4.11** **[CD 1: Track 57]** on SB p172. Put students into pairs to practise the conversations. Remind them to think about the intonation of the sentences with adjectives. Monitor and check. If students sound 'flat', play key lines of the conversations again and get students to repeat chorally and individually. Students then repeat the closed pairwork.

Answers and tapescript

Alice's new boyfriend – lovely
Ben's new flat – fantastic/fabulous
the weather – horrible/terrible
a meal/the wine – excellent/wonderful
new shoes – great/amazing
the new teacher – nice/awful

T 4.11

1 **A** Do you know Alice has a new boyfriend?
B Really? Is he OK?
A Mm! He's lovely!
B Ooh! What's his name?
A James.
B Good for Alice!

2 **C** Ben has a new flat.
D Wow! Where is it?
C In the centre of town.
D Is it nice?
C Oh, yes. It's fantastic! The living room is fabulous!

3 **E** What a horrible day!
F Yes, it is! Rain, rain, rain. It's terrible weather at the moment.
E Oh, well! Tomorrow's another day!

4 **G** Mmm! This is an excellent meal!
H Thank you! I'm pleased you like it.
G And the wine is wonderful! Where's it from?
H I think it's French. Yes, it is. French.

5 **I** I love your shoes! They're great!
J They're nice, aren't they? They're Italian.
I The colour's amazing! Red! Wow!

6 **K** We have a new teacher. Her name's Nancy.
L Is she nice?
K No, she's awful! I hate her.
L Why?
K I don't understand her. She talks, and talks, and talks all the time!

4 Focus attention on the conversation starters. With weaker classes, elicit possible adjectives for each question. You could also elicit whole lines for some of the conversations.

If possible, put students in new pairs to do this activity. Give them time to think about ways of continuing the conversations. Monitor and help as necessary. Check for correct pronunciation of the adjectives and for lively intonation. Drill key lines if necessary and let students practise again.

Adverb + adjective

This section practises common modifiers of adjectives. This is a regular feature of language, particularly in speaking, and will help students at this level further improve their range of expression.

5 Focus attention on the pictures and the explanations. Elicit sentences using each of the words/phrases. Check the sentence stress, e.g.

My caravan isn't very big.

My mother's house is big.
My boss's house is very big.
Our new office block is really big.

Point out that in a sentence *not very* … is usually contracted, e.g. *She isn't very old*, but students will also hear *She's not very old*.

6 **T 4.12** **[CD 1: Track 58]** Tell students they are going to hear five short conversations. They need to listen to the key information to complete the chart but they don't need to understand every word. Pre-teach/check *enormous*, *jeans*, *make* (noun), *clever*, and *intelligent*. Write the proper nouns on the board to help students with spelling: *Angela*, *Tom*, *Maria*, *Peter*.

Play conversation 1 as an example. Then play the rest of the recording and get students to complete the task. Remind them to record the phrases *not very/very/really* + adjective where relevant. Only play the recording a second time if students missed a lot of the answers. If appropriate, elicit any further information that students understood, e.g. the type of car, the make of jeans, etc.

Refer students to **T 4.12** on SB p172. Put students into pairs to practise the conversations. Remind them to think about the intonation of the sentences with adjectives. Monitor and check. If students sound 'flat', play key lines of the conversations again and get students to repeat chorally and individually. Students then repeat the closed pairwork.

Answers and tapescript

What/Who are they talking about?	How do they describe it?
1 Angela's car	really expensive, very fast
2 Tom's house/money	really beautiful, very big, very rich
3 jeans	really nice, not very expensive
4 Peter's new girlfriend	pretty, not very old
5 Maria	very clever, really intelligent, not very nice

T 4.12

1 **A** Look at Angela's car! It's a Mercedes!
B Wow! They're really expensive! Is it fast?
A Very fast.
2 **A** Does Tom have a lot of money?
B Well, he has a really beautiful house with a very big garden, and a swimming pool.
A Mm. He's very rich, isn't he?
3 **C** Do you like my new jeans?
D Yeah! They're really nice! What make are they?
C They're Prada.
D How much were they?
C They weren't expensive. Well, not *very* expensive.
4 **E** Look! That's Peter's new girlfriend!
F Mmm! She's pretty. How old is she?
E 28.
F Wow! That's old!
E 28? That isn't very old!
5 **G** Maria's very clever, isn't she?
H Oh, yes. She's really intelligent. She knows everything.
G Do you like her?
H No, not really. She isn't very nice to talk to.
G No, I don't like her either.

7 Focus attention on the questions in the Student's Book and the example conversation. Get students to read it aloud across the class. With weaker students, elicit possible adjectives for the other conversations:

school: small/not very big/dark/untidy/old/new

flat: small/not very big/dark/old/new

Then get students to continue the conversations in pairs.

EVERYDAY ENGLISH (SB p51)

Numbers

The functional syllabus continues with a focus on numbers up to 1,000,000, ways of reading different numbers, and understanding and talking about prices.

> **⚠ POSSIBLE PROBLEMS**
>
> Most students will need regular practice to be able to produce numbers spontaneously. They often have problems distinguishing *-teen* and *-ty* numbers because of the different stress:
>
> *fifteen* *fifty*
>
> There is also a set of 'rules' for saying different categories of number:
>
> **Fractions:** When a fraction follows a whole number, we use *and*, e.g. 1½ = *one and a half*, 2¼ = *two and a quarter*.
>
> **Decimals:** We use a point (.), not a comma, in decimals. The stress falls on the last figure, e.g. 1.75 = *one point seven five*.
>
> **Phone numbers:** We usually give phone numbers using single figures 0–9, and 0 is pronounced 'oh'. Repeated numbers can be expressed with *double*. Longer numbers are grouped into series with a pause in between. The intonation is rise, rise, fall, e.g.
>
> ↗ ↗ ↘
> 020 7225 8133 = *oh two oh, seven double two five, eight one double three*
>
> **Prices:** We express prices in pounds and/or *p* /piː/, e.g. £17 = *seventeen pounds*, 99p = *ninety-nine p*. We don't say *pounds* and *p* in the same price, i.e. we do not say **one pound sixty p* but *one pound sixty*. In dollar/euro prices, both words can be plural, e.g. $17.25 = *seventeen dollars and twenty-five cents*.

1 Briefly review numbers 1–20 by getting students to count round the class. Repeat until they can say the numbers accurately without hesitation. Then get students to count to 100 round the class in tens, to review *twenty*, *thirty*, etc. Drill the words to deal with any pronunciation problems as necessary.

Focus attention on the photos and elicit the correct numbers. Point out that in numbers such as *215* we say *two hundred and fifteen*, NOT **two hundreds and fifteen*. Point to the pictures in random order and elicit the numbers again. Repeat, getting faster and faster until students can say all the numbers with confidence.

Answers
one nineteen twenty-one thirty-six forty-five
ninety-one ninety-four a hundred and seventy-one
two hundred and fifteen a million

2 **T 4.13** **[CD 1: Track 59]** Elicit the first line of numbers with the whole class. Then put students in pairs to continue saying the numbers. Monitor and check.

Play the recording and let students check their answers. Students practise the numbers again. If students have problems, play the recording or model the numbers yourself and get students to repeat chorally and individually.

Answers and tapescript
eight ten twelve fifteen
twenty thirty-two forty-five sixty
seventy-six ninety-nine a hundred and eighty-seven
two hundred and fifty
three hundred a thousand a million

3 **T 4.14** **[CD 1: Track 60]** Check students understand the different categories of number (fractions, decimals, and phone numbers). Students work in pairs and try to read the numbers. Monitor and check.

Play the recording and let students check their answers. Students practise the numbers again. If students have problems, play the recording or model the numbers yourself and get students to repeat chorally and individually. If necessary, highlight the 'rules' for saying numbers in *Possible problems* on TB p48.

Answers and tapescript
one and a half
two and a quarter
six point eight
seventeen point five
oh two oh, seven four eight one, six four nine oh
oh seven eight six one, five double six seven eight

4 **T 4.15** **[CD 1: Track 61]** This is a number dictation activity. Tell students they are going to hear eight numbers of different types, including a decimal, a fraction, and a phone number.

Focus attention on the example and tell students they should write the numbers as numerals, not words. Play the recording. If necessary, pause after each number to give students time to write their answers. Check the answers with the class.

Answers and tapescript
1 30, 17, 13 2 62, 07629 34480 3 460, 16 4 280,000

Tapescript
1 There are thirty students in my class – seventeen boys and thirteen girls.
2 I live at number 62, Station Road. My mobile number is 07629 34480.
3 My father works in a big hotel. There are 460 rooms on sixteen floors.
4 The population of my town is 280,000.

EXTRA ACTIVITY
Get students to do number dictations in pairs to consolidate the range of numbers covered in this section. Students prepare a list of random figures to dictate to their partner. They take it in turns to dictate their list. The student who is taking down the dictated numbers writes the figures, not the words, and then reads the list back to their partner to check the answers.

Prices

5 Pre-teach/check *pound*, *dollar*, *cent*, and *euro* /ˈjʊərəʊ/. Focus attention on the use of *p* /piː/ for prices under a pound. Elicit the first price and then get students to continue, working in pairs. Monitor and check.

If necessary, highlight the 'rules' for saying prices in *Possible problems* on TB p48.

Answers
1 seventy-five pounds
2 one pound fifty
3 forty-five p
4 nineteen dollars ninety-nine cents
5 two hundred and seventy pounds
6 twelve euros

6 **T 4.16** **[CD 1: Track 62]** This is another dictation activity. Tell students they are going to hear eight prices of different currencies, including pounds, dollars, and euros.

Play the recording. If necessary, pause after each price to give students time to write their answers. Check the answers with the class.

You can get students to do price dictations in pairs following the technique for numbers (see *Extra activity*).

Answers and tapescript
1 £6.50 2 £24 3 £18,000 4 £9,500 5 60p 6 $49
7 €150 8 $1.4

Tapescript
1 'How much is this book?' 'Six pounds fifty.'
2 'How much are these pictures?' 'Twenty-four pounds each.'
3 I only earn £18,000 a year.
4 'How much is this car?' '£9,500.'
5 'Just this postcard, please.' 'That's 60p, please.'
6 'Can I have these jeans, please?' 'Sure, that's $49.'
7 'How much is a return ticket from Paris to Madrid?' '€150.'
8 There are about 1.4 dollars to the euro.

7 This activity practises prices in a free activity. Briefly review the questions *How much is this (bag)?* for items in the singular and *How much are these (glasses)?* for items in the plural.

Ask two students to read the example conversation aloud. If students sound flat, focus on the stress and voice range on the lines. Remind students to start high and fall on the exclamations:

A *Excuse me! How much are these …?*

B *Oh, they're very special! They're two hundred pounds.*

A *What! That's crazy! That's much too expensive! No, thanks. Not today.*

With weaker students, elicit ways of continuing the conversation, e.g. *Well, what about this (bag)?/Well, we've also got these (glasses); It's only (£35)./It's in the sale./There's a 20% discount today*, etc.

Divide the students into A/B pairs. Students practise the conversations, adapting the model in the Student's Book. Monitor and help as necessary. If you have time, you could get students to act out their conversations to the class.

8 Demonstrate the activity by talking about one or two numbers or prices that are significant to you, e.g. *£1,000 – My rent is £1,000 a month*. If necessary, feed in useful vocabulary, e.g. *to cost, to pay (price) for something, bill, mortgage, ticket, bus/train pass*, etc.

Focus attention on the examples in the Student's Book. Then get students to continue in pairs or small groups. Elicit a few examples from the class in a short feedback section.

SUGGESTION

You can give students extra practice with numbers and prices by bringing in adverts, leaflets, and menus that show prices and getting students to practise *How much is/are ... ?*

Photocopiable Activity

UNIT 4 Numbers and prices TB p151/TRD

Note: For the discussion stage in exercise 2, it is useful to get students to check the exchange rate with the currency in their country before you do this activity in class. UK prices have been provided which are accurate at the time of publication but you may need to adapt these depending on when you use the quiz.

Materials: One copy of the worksheet for each student.

Procedure: Explain that students are going to do a quiz to find out how much they know about numbers. This is followed by a group task to compare prices of everyday items/services in different countries. Pre-teach/check *piano keys, vote, coin*, and *speed limit*.

If appropriate, you could set up exercise 1 as a competition by keeping a record of students' answers on the board and then making the student/pair with the most correct answers the winner.

- Hand out a copy of the worksheet to each student. Ask question 1 as an example and elicit a range of answers. Don't confirm the correct answer at this stage.
- Give students time to answer the questions in the quiz, working individually. Students then check their answers in pairs.
- Check the answers with the class by eliciting a range of answers and encouraging discussion across the class. Then confirm the correct answers.

Answers
1c 2b 3a 4c 5b 6c 7a 8b

- Check students know the exchange rate between pound sterling and their currency (see *Note* above). Ask students to read through the chart. Deal with any vocabulary queries. Give them time to complete the chart for their country and for the UK. Tell them it doesn't matter if they are unsure. The activity is for general discussion of prices, not a test of their knowledge.
- Feed in useful language, e.g. *I think (a coffee) is about (price). Yes, I think so, too./No, I think it's more/less, maybe (price)*. Put the students in small groups to compare their ideas. Monitor and help as necessary.

  Check for accurate use of prices, noting any common errors. Don't interrupt or over-correct at this stage, as this is a fluency activity.
- Go over the possible answers for the UK (accurate at the time of publication). If you have access to the most recent figures, then use those. Elicit students' reactions to the figures. Establish which countries in the world they think are expensive.

Possible answers

	price in the UK
a day travel-card in the capital city	£8.80 (to cover central zones)
a coffee and a daily newspaper	£3 (a large coffee); £1 (e.g. *The Times*)
a cinema ticket for an adult	£10 (after 5 p.m.); £7 (before 5 p.m.)
a week's food shopping for two adults	£60–£80
dinner in a 3-star restaurant	£90–£120
a top-20 CD	£8.99–£12.99
a litre of petrol	£1.35
a month's rent in a small flat in the capital city	£600–£750 (1 bedroom, depending on the area)

ADDITIONAL MATERIAL

Teacher's Resource Disc
Communicative activity Unit 4 Houses board game

Don't forget!

Grammar Reference (SB p186 and Teacher's Resource Disc)
Unit 4

Word list (SB p209 and Teacher's Resource Disc)
Unit 4

Tests (Teacher's Resource Disc)
Unit test 4A
Unit test 4B
Stop and check 1 (Units 1–4)
Skills test 1 (Units 1–4)

Video (DVD)
Unit 4 A new home

5 Super me!

***can/can't* • *was/were/could* • Words that go together • Polite requests**

Skills and ability are the themes of this unit. These are particularly suitable topics to introduce and practise *can/can't* (ability). However, the unit has two main aims in that we also introduce some past tenses for the first time: the past of *can* (ability) – *could*, and the Past Simple of the verb *to be* – *was/were*. The skills work includes a listening about the artist Picasso and a jigsaw reading about two talented members of the same family. These provide contexts for and practice of the grammar. **Note** The recordings for Units 5–8 are on CD2.

LANGUAGE INPUT

GRAMMAR	
can/can't (SB p56)	• Practising *can/can't* to talk about ability.
Past – *was/were/could* (SB p58)	• Practising *was/were/could* to talk about the past.
VOCABULARY	
Words that go together (SB p62)	• Understanding and practising collocations: noun + noun, verb + noun, prepositions.
Adjectives (SB p60)	• Understanding adjectives in context.
EVERYDAY ENGLISH	
Polite requests (SB p63)	• Understanding and practising *can/could* to make polite requests.

SKILLS DEVELOPMENT

READING	
A talented family (SB p60)	• A jigsaw reading about the life and success of two members of the same family.
LISTENING	
Child prodigies (SB p59)	• Listening for key words in a short monologue. **T 5.11** (SB p173/TRD)
Pablo Picasso (SB p59)	• Listening for key words in a short conversation. **T 5.13** (SB p173/TRD)
Three conversations (SB p62)	• Listening for noun + noun combinations in three short conversations. **T 5.14** (SB p173/TRD)
SPEAKING	
Talking about you (SB p58/p59)	• Talking about the past and things you could do in the past.
What do you think? (SB 60)	• Talking about relationships.
WRITING	
A formal email – Applying for a job (SB p158)	• Understanding key content points and more formal style, then writing an email to apply for a job.

MORE MATERIALS

Photocopiable worksheets – Words that go together (TB p152/TRD), The job fair (TRD) **Test** (TRD) **Video** (DVD)

Students have already practised *can* in the *Everyday English* sections of Units 1, 2, and 3. In those units, it is used as a polite request in a range of useful expressions *Can I have … ?/ Can you tell me the time?/Can I open the window?/Can you help me?* and an offer *Can I help you?*

In Unit 5, the use of *can* is extended to cover ability, and all aspects of the form (statements, questions, negatives) are presented and practised.

> **⚠ POSSIBLE PROBLEMS**
>
> - Sometimes after sustained practice of the Present Simple, students want to use *do/don't* and *does/doesn't* to form the question and negative of *can*.
>
>   **Do you can swim?*
>   **I don't can swim.*
> - The pronunciation of *can* and *can't* can also create problems for students. They often find the different vowel sounds (/ə/ or /æ/ in *can* and /ɑː/ in *can't*) confusing. Because the final *t* in *can't* tends to get lost, it's difficult to recognize whether the sentence is positive or negative. Students also often have difficulty producing the correct sounds themselves.
>
> | | |
> |---|---|
> | *I can swim.* | /aɪ kən swɪm/ |
> | *Can you swim?* | /kən ju swɪm/ |
> | *Yes, I can.* | /jes aɪ kæn/ |
> | *I can't come.* | /aɪ kɑːnt kʌm/ |
>
>   For these reasons, we give special attention to the pronunciation in the unit by including exercises for recognition and production.

STARTER (SB p56)

This is intended to be a fun introduction to *can* for ability. Students talk about the comic hero Superman and what he can do.

T 5.1 [**CD 2: Track 2**] Focus attention on the photo of Superman and elicit any information that students know. Ask *What can he do?* and elicit a range of answers but do not go into a full presentation of *can* at this stage.

Play the recording and let students compare the ideas in the recording with their ideas.

> **Tapescript**
> Superman comes from the planet Krypton. He can fly at the speed of light; he can see through walls; he can jump 250 metres; he can speak every language; he can turn back time. There's nothing Superman can't do!

SUPERMAN IS FANTASTIC! (SB p56)

can/can't

This presentation continues the theme of Superman and his skills. The speakers are two children, Alfie /ˈælfi/ and Ivy /ˈaɪvi/. They are cousins and the tone of the script is teasing but lighthearted, typical of the way children and teenagers often communicate. The recording is divided across three exercises, a first section presented as a gap-fill and then the whole conversation as an unseen script with key information questions. Students then listen to the whole conversation again and complete gapped sentences with the target language.

1 **T 5.2** [**CD 2: Track 3**] Focus attention on the photos and ask students to point to Alfie and Ivy. *Ask How old are they?* and get students to estimate their ages. Ask *What does Alfie like doing?* (skateboarding).

Give students time to read the gapped conversation. Play the recording and get students to complete the missing words.

Check the answers with the class.

> **Answers and tapescript**
> **A = Alfie I = Ivy**
> **A** Superman's fantastic!
> **I** Hmm! What can he do?
> **A** He can do everything!
> **I** No, he can't!
> **A** Yes, he can. He **can fly** at the speed of light, he **can see** through buildings, *and* he **can speak** every language in the world!

2 **T 5.3** [**CD 2: Track 4**] Tell students they are going to hear the rest of the conversation between Alfie and Ivy. Read the questions as a class, then play the recording through once without stopping.

Check the answers.

> **Answers and tapescript**
> They talk about French and Spanish.
> They talk about skateboarding and skiing.
>
> **T 5.3**
> **A = Alfie I = Ivy**
> **A** He can speak every language in the world!
> **I** Really? I don't believe that.
> **A** Well, he can! Can you speak any languages?
> **I** Yes, I can. I can speak French and Spanish a little bit. We learn them at school.
> **A** Well, I can speak French too.
> **I** Oh, yes?!
> **A** I can say 'Bonjour' and 'Merci'.
> **I** That's nothing! You can't speak French at all!
> **A** Well, I can skateboard. You can't!
> **I** I don't want to skateboard. I like other things. What about skiing? Can you ski?
> **A** Yeah, I can ski a bit, but my mum and dad can ski brilliantly!
> **I** I love skiing. I can ski really well.
> **A** OK, OK, we can do some things, but Superman can do everything. There's nothing Superman can't do.
> **I** Oh, you and Superman! Remember he's not real, he's only a …

3 **T 5.4** [**CD 2: Track 5**] The sentences in this exercise present the key forms of *can* and also provide exposure to adverbs that describe how well you can do something. These are further practised and personalized in *Practice* exercises 4 and 5.

Check comprehension of *ski*. Focus attention on the example. Then give students time to complete the sentences. Remind them to use the information from the conversation in exercise 2. With weaker students, go through the sentences orally with the class and then get them to write their answers.

Allow students to check in pairs before playing the recording as a final check.

If you think students will need help with pronunciation at this stage, focus on the *Grammar Spot* before students practise the conversation.

Answers and tapescript

1 'Can you **speak** any languages?'
'Yes, I can. I **can speak** French and Spanish.'
2 'You **can't speak** French at all!'
3 'I **can** skateboard! You **can't**!'
4 '**Can** you **ski**?'
'I **can ski** a bit, but my mum and dad **can ski** brilliantly.'
5 'Superman **can do** *everything*. There's nothing Superman **can't do**!'

GRAMMAR AND PRONUNCIATION (SB p57)

1 Focus attention on the *Grammar and Pronunciation* box. Students work in pairs and say all the persons of *can/can't*. Ask them what they notice about the verb form for each person. Check students are clear about the answer.

Answer
Can/can't are the same for all persons, so there is no *-s* added in the *he/she/it* forms. We do not use the auxiliary *don't/doesn't* to form the negative.

2 **T 5.5** **[CD 2: Track 6]** This activity focuses on the pronunciation of *can/can't* in the positive, questions, and short answers.

Play the recording and get your students to read and listen very carefully to the pronunciation of *can* and *can't*. First, ask generally *Can you hear differences?* If necessary, repeat the sentences yourself, exaggerating the vowel sounds in *can* and *can't* and isolating them /ə/, /æ/, /ɑː/, so that your students can fully appreciate the differences. Elicit the main stresses in each sentence. Ask *When is 'can' pronounced* /kən/*?* (When it is unstressed.) Play the recording again and get students to repeat chorally and individually.

3 Focus attention again on the sentence stress in the positive and negative sentences. Drill the sentences and then get students to practise in pairs.

▶▶ Read Grammar Reference 5.1 on SB p187 together in class, and/or ask students to read it at home. Encourage them to ask you questions about it.

SUGGESTION

If your students need more practice with the pronunciation of *can/can't*, write out simple sentences in phonetic script and then get students to practise saying the sentences in pairs, e.g.

1 /ʃiː kən skiː/
2 /wiː kən drɔː bət wiː kɑːnt raɪt/
3 /aɪ kən sɪŋ kwaɪt wel/
4 /kən juː pleɪ tenɪs/ /nəʊ aɪ kɑːnt/
5 /kən ðeɪ dɑːns/ /jes ðeɪ kæn/

PRACTICE (SB p57)

Ivy can't cook. Can you?

1 **T 5.6** **[CD 2: Track 7]** This is a recognition exercise that moves into production stages in exercises 2 and 4. This time the recording is a monologue with Ivy talking about her abilities.

Ask students what they can remember about Ivy and elicit a range of answers. Pre-teach/check *foreign*, including the pronunication /ˈfɒrən/. Check students understand the convention of ticks and crosses – they need to put a tick (✓) next to things Ivy can do or a cross (✗) next to the things she can't do in the first column of the chart.

Play the recording as far as *I can't cook at all* and focus attention on the examples. Then play the rest of the recording and get students to complete the task.

Put students into pairs to compare their answers. Then conduct a full class feedback to establish the correct answers. Let students listen again if necessary.

Answers and tapescript

Can ...?	Ivy
speak a foreign language	✓
cook	✗
skateboard	✗
swim	✓
play tennis	✓
ski	✓
play any musical instruments	✗

T 5.6
Ivy: So what can I do? Speak a foreign language ... Hmm. Well, yes, I can speak French and Spanish a little bit, but just holiday Spanish! Cooking? No, I can't cook at all. My mum can, she's a fantastic cook. Hmm. Sports – well, I think I'm quite good at sports – my cousin Alfie says I'm not because I can't skateboard, but skateboarding's not a sport. I can swim of course. Everyone can swim, can't they? I can swim very well. I like swimming, and I like tennis. I can play tennis quite well. But skiing is my best sport, I love it, and I can ski really well, really fast. Musical instruments? Er ... well, no, I can't play any musical instruments. My dad can play the guitar brilliantly, and my mum can play the piano a bit, but I can't play anything at all.

2 This stage consolidates the question and answer forms. Practise the questions in the Student's Book in open and closed pairs. Encourage students to distinguish between the strong and weak forms of *can*, and to use the correct intonation. Also make sure that they pronounce the *t* on the end of the negatives. The two consonants *nt* together are difficult for many speakers.

Students work in pairs and ask and answer questions about Ivy and each of the activities in the chart. Monitor and help as necessary, checking for accurate question formation and pronunciation.

3 **T 5.7** **[CD 2: Track 8]** This exercise highlights adverbs for saying how well you can do things. Students may make mistakes with the word order due to interference from their own language. Be prepared to highlight and correct any problems in this area.

Focus attention on the photo of Ivy and elicit a few examples of things she can and can't do. Then focus attention on words and phrases in the box. Explain that they are in order of meaning from 'no talent' (*not at all*) to 'enormous talent' (*brilliantly*). Give a couple of true examples to reinforce these two extremes, e.g. *I can't play tennis at all. Tommy Haas can play tennis brilliantly.*

Focus attention on the example. Then give students time to complete the sentences, working in pairs. With weaker students, go through the sentences orally with the class and then get them to write their answers.

Play the recording and get students to compare their answers.

Students practise saying the sentences across the class. If they have problems with the sentence stress or any individual words, play the recording again and get students to repeat chorally and individually.

Answers and tapescript

1 She can speak Spanish a little bit.
2 She can't cook **at all**.
3 She can swim **very well**.
4 She can play tennis **quite well**.
5 She can ski **really well**.
6 Her dad can play the guitar **brilliantly**.
7 Her mum can play the piano **a bit**.
8 She can't play anything **at all**.

4 The exercise is another personalized phase. Students complete column 3 of the chart in exercise 1 about their partner.

Practise the questions in the Student's Book in open and closed pairs. Encourage students to distinguish between the strong and weak forms of *can*, and to use the correct sentence stress. Drill the questions and answers as necessary.

Students work in pairs and ask and answer questions about each of the activities in the chart. Go round and monitor and help as they do this. Check for accurate question formation, pronunciation, and use of the adverbs.

Feed back on any common errors. If necessary, highlight the position of the adverbs in exercise 3 to reinforce that they come at end of the sentence,

5 Focus attention on the examples and highlight the contrastive stress:

José can speak Spanish really well, but I can't.

Ask a few students to tell the others about their and their partner's abilities. In larger groups, students can do this stage in small groups and then feed back to the class.

6 **T 5.8** **[CD 2: Track 9]** This is a discrimination activity to check that your students can recognize what they hear. Play the first sentence and elicit the answer as an example (*can*). Play the rest of the recording and get students to underline the correct words.

Check the answers with the class, playing the recording again as consolidation if necessary.

Answers and tapescript

1 She can cook.
2 I can't hear you.
3 They can't come to the party.
4 Can you see my glasses anywhere?
5 You can't always get what you want.
6 Can you do the homework?

7 Demonstrate the activity by reading one of the sentences, changing the use of *can/can't* from the wording in exercise 6. Students choose the correct words.

Students continue in closed pairs. Encourage them to do the activity briskly to make it fun and to ensure that the pronunciation doesn't become too laboured.

EXTRA ACTIVITY

Set up a short discussion activity with the class by asking *What can/can't computers do?* Elicit a few examples from the class, then ask students to continue in pairs/small groups. This in an opportunity to generate some freer speaking in English, so don't focus too closely on accuracy and don't worry if the activity is quite short.

Sample answers

Computers can …

do fast calculations, translate, check spellings, speak English (in a limited way), play music/DVDs, play chess, store a lot of information/images

Computers can't …

write poetry, feel ill, laugh, think (because they work completely in numbers), fall in love

ADDITIONAL MATERIAL

Teacher's Resource Disc

Communicative activity Unit 5 The job fair

TODAY AND YESTERDAY (SB p58)

Past – *was/were/could*

These forms are the first introduction of a past tense in *Headway English A2*. They are presented by building on the present forms that students already know. The use of a set of parallel present and past sentences helps to make the form and meaning as clear as possible.

⚠ POSSIBLE PROBLEMS

- Students may have pronunciation problems with the past of *to be*. The vowel sounds in *was* and *were* can be both weak and strong: *was* /ə/ and /ɒ/; and *were* /ə/ and /ɜː/.

He was at home. /hiː wəz ət həʊm/

Was he at home? /wəz hiː ət həʊm/

Yes, he was./No, he wasn't.
/jes hiː wɒz/ /nəʊ hiː wɒznt/

Were they at home? /wə ðeɪ ət həʊm/

Yes, they were./No, they weren't.
/jes ðeɪ wɜː/ /nəʊ ðeɪ wɜːnt/

- The groups of consonants in the negatives *wasn't* /wɒznt/, *weren't* /wɜːnt/ and *couldn't* /kʊdnt/ may be difficult for some students and may need extra choral and individual repetition.

1 **T 5.9** **[CD 2: Track 10]** This is a very direct presentation of the past of the verbs *to be* and *can*. It revises the present forms of the verbs and then moves straight to the past tense equivalents.

Focus attention on the photos to reinforce the concepts of present and past. Pre-teach/check *yesterday* and *last month/last year*. Play number 1 and elicit true answers to each question. Play the rest of the recording. Students listen and write in the answers.

When they have finished, go through the exercise with them, modelling the questions and answers for them to repeat, and focusing on the weak vowel sounds of *was* and *were* (/wəz/ and /wə/) in statements and questions, and the strong vowel sounds (/wɒz/, /wɒznt/, /wɜː/, /wɜːnt/) in short answers and negatives.

GRAMMAR AND PRONUNCIATION (SB p58)

1 Focus attention on the examples. Then put your students into pairs to complete the chart with the past of *to be*. Quickly check through the answers with the whole class.

Answers

	Positive	**Negative**
I	was	wasn't
you	were	weren't
he/she/it	**was**	**wasn't**
we	were	**weren't**
they	**were**	**weren't**

2 Students complete the positive and negative forms of the past of *can*.

Answers
Positive could (all persons)
Negative couldn't (all persons)

3 **T 5.10** **[CD 2: Track 11]** This is a repetition exercise to help consolidate the pronunciation. Play the recording through once and let students just listen. Play the recording again and get students to repeat. Insist on accurate pronunciation of the strong and weak forms. Ask students *When are 'was/were' pronounced* /wəz/, /wə/? (When they are unstressed.)

Tapescript
1 It was Monday.
2 We were at school.
3 'Was it sunny?' 'Yes, it was.'
4 'Was it cold?' 'No, it wasn't.'
5 'Were you at school?' 'Yes, we were.'
6 'Were they at school?' 'No, they weren't.'

▸▸ Read Grammar Reference 5.2 and 5.3 on SB p187 together in class, and/or ask students to read it at home. Encourage them to ask you questions about it.

2 Get students to ask and answer the questions in open pairs across the class. Use the opportunity to check and correct them carefully. Students then ask and answer the questions again in closed pairs.

3 This exercise consolidates the positive, negative, and, question forms. There is an example of a regular Past Simple form in number 3 (*phoned*). If students query this, just explain that it is a past form but don't go into a detailed explanation of the Past Simple at this stage.

Pre-teach/check *ill* and *on holiday*. Focus attention on the example and elicit the second verb (*was*). Give students time to complete the sentences, working individually. Then check with the class.

Answers
1 I wasn't at school yesterday because I **was** ill.
2 My parents **weren't** at work last week. They **were** on holiday in Spain.
3 Where **were** you last night? I phoned, but you **weren't** at home.
4 I **could** read and write when I **was** just five.
5 My sister **couldn't** read until she **was** seven.

Talking about you

4 Drill the first question and possible answers in open pairs. Students continue asking and answering the questions in closed pairs. Monitor and help as necessary. Encourage students to ask about times other than those listed in the Student's Book. Round the activity off by asking one or two students to tell the class about their partner.

EXTRA ACTIVITY

Extend the pairwork activity in exercise 4 by getting students to build a conversation about places/events they have been to recently. Put some skeleton dialogue prompts on the board and ask pairs of students to create conversations, e.g.

... the football match last weekend?

... good?

... many people?

... the score?

Students can act out their conversation for the rest of the class.

PRACTICE (SB p59)

Child prodigies

This section brings together the past of *can* and *to be*, and it also introduces *to be born*. It continues the theme of skills and talents, but this time focuses on some very talented children. Students are also given the opportunity to personalize the language.

⚠ POSSIBLE PROBLEMS

- *Was/Were born* is taught here as an expression, not as an example of the passive. Don't be tempted to go into the grammar of the passive at this stage. Some students translate directly from their own language and say **I am born*, so be prepared to highlight and correct this.
- There are Past Simple forms (*played*, *made*) and also a past participle (*sold*) included in this section for recognition. There's no need to give a full grammar explanation of these forms at this stage. If students query them, just explain that they are a past form of the relevant verb. Student will cover the Past Simple in Units 6 and 7, and the Present Perfect in Unit 12.

1 Focus attention on the photos and ask students to guess how old they think the children are. Elicit information about what the children can do, and why they are 'child prodigies'.

Answers
Marc Yu can play the piano.
Cleopatra Stratan can sing.
They are 'child prodigies' because they are young but they have special talents.

2 **T 5.11** **[CD 2: Track 12]** Pre-teach/check *prodigy* /ˈprɒdədʒi/, *cello* /ˈtʃeləʊ/, and *to be a success*. Give students time to read the gapped information so they know what to listen for. If they query the use of *played*, just explain that it is a past form of *play*.

Play the first two lines of the recording and elicit the missing information in sentence 1. Play the rest of the recording and let students complete their answers.

Students take it in turns to read the sentences aloud. Monitor and check for correct pronunciation. If students have problems, play the recording again as a model and drill key lines chorally and individually. Students then repeat the pairwork.

Answers and tapescript
Marc Yu, pianist.
1 He was born on January **5, 1999**, in California, USA.
2 He **can play** the piano and the cello.
3 He **could play** the piano when he **was three**.
4 He **could play** the cello when he **was four**.
Last year, he played with Lang Lang, the famous Chinese pianist, in New York. They **were** a big success.

3 **T 5.12** **[CD 2: Track 13]** Pre-teach/check *make an album*. Give students time to read the gapped information about Cleopatra (the title of her album means 'At the age of three'). If students query the use of *made* and *sold*, just explain that they are past forms of *make* and *sell*.

Elicit the information about when/where Cleopatra was born. Put students in pairs to continue the task. With weaker classes, elicit the information with the whole class first and then get students to repeat the task in closed pairs. Monitor and check for correct use of *was born*, *could*, *was/were*, and accurate pronunciation. Note any common errors.

Play the recording and let students check their answers. Correct any major errors from the pairwork stage with the class.

Answers and tapescript
Cleopatra Stratan, singer.
She was born on October 7th, 2002 in Moldova, near Romania. She could sing beautifully when she was just two years old. When she was three, she made an album, *La vârsta de trei ani*. Her album was a big success. 150,000 were sold round the world.

4 Elicit example questions and answers about Marc (*When was he born? In 1999. Where was he born? In California. How old was he when he could play the piano? He was three.*) Drill the questions if necessary. Students continue working in pairs, asking and answering questions about the children. Monitor and check for correct use of *was born*, *could*, *was/were*, and accurate pronunciation. Note any common errors for correction during the feedback stage.

Listening

ABOUT THE LISTENING

The theme of talented youngsters is continued with a listening on one of the most influential artists of the 20th century. Born in Málaga in the south of Spain, Picasso was an accomplished and prolific artist from an early age. He trained as an artist in Madrid and Barcelona before moving to Paris, where he lived for many years. He helped to develop cubism and other forms of abstract art and his work is characterised by different periods such as the 'Blue Period' and the 'Rose Period'. His works are held in prestigious museums all over the world, one of the largest collections being in the 'Museu Picasso' in Barcelona.

In the listening script, there are three Spanish words: *Don* (= a title of respect used before a man's first name), *Doña* (= a title of respect used before a woman's first name), and *lápiz* (= pencil).

5 **T 5.13** **[CD 2: Track 14]** Focus attention on the photos. Elicit students' reactions to them and then ask students what they know about Picasso's life and work. Give students time to read and complete the conversation individually. Then play the recording as a check.

Put students in pairs to practise the conversation. If students have problems with pronunciation, play key lines of the conversation again, getting students to repeat chorally and individually. Students then do the pairwork again.

Answers and tapescript
Pablo Picasso, October 25th, 1881 to April 8th, 1973
A Hey, look at that painting! It's a Picasso!
B Oh yes! Fantastic!
A Where was Picasso born?
B In Málaga.
A Ah! So he **was** Spanish?
B Yes, he **was**.
A **Were** his parents rich?
B Well, they **weren't** rich and they **weren't** poor. His father, Don José, **was** a painter and a professor of art. His mother, Doña Maria, was a housewife.
A So, **was** Picasso good at drawing when he **was** young?
B Oh, yes. He **was** a child prodigy. He **could** draw before he **could** speak. His first word **was** *lápiz*, which is Spanish for pencil.
A Wow! What a story!

Talking about you

6 Drill the questions in the *you* form, getting students to repeat chorally and individually. Make sure students can hear the difference between *where* and *were*, and again insist on accurate intonation.

Students work in pairs and ask and answer the questions. At the end of the activity, ask a few students to tell you what they can remember, e.g. *Laura was born in Madrid in 1988. She could read when she was five.*

SUGGESTION

Students could think of some famous talented people, both children and adults, that they know and make similar sentences about where/when they were born and what skills they had at different ages.

If appropriate, you could extend this into a mini-project, getting students to research their chosen person and then give a short presentation to the class, using visuals if possible.

WRITING (SB p158)

A formal email

Applying for a job

Unit 5 introduces a change of tone in the writing syllabus with a focus on more formal writing. Some of the key conventions of writing more formal emails, including greetings and endings, are shown in a model text. Students complete the model and then do a guided writing task, based on an advertisement for a job. This is the type of email students may well need to write at some stage in their learning.

1 Focus attention in the photo of Carl. Ask *What does he do?* (He's a student.) *What does he want?* (a holiday job). Briefly review the ways we read phone numbers and email addresses. Focus on the prompt *Last job* and check the verb form *Is or was?* (*was*).

Divide the class into pairs to ask and answer the questions. With weaker classes, go through the questions as a class first and then get students to repeat the questions and answers in closed pairs. Monitor and help as necessary.

2 Give students time to read the advertisement. Deal with any vocabulary queries. Elicit the answers to the question.

Answers

Carl is interested in the job because:
he is over 18 (22)
he lives in Bath and so probably knows it well
he can speak French and German
he's interested in travel.

3 Focus attention on the email headings. Ask *Who is the email from?* (Carl), *Who it is to?* (Linda Yates), *What is it for?* (to apply for the job of tourist guide). Elicit the answer to the first gap as an example. Then give students time to complete the email, using the information about Carl. Check the answers with the class.

Answers

1 tourist guide
2 22
3 live
4 student
5 free
6 ski instructor
7 can
8 languages
9 like
10 was

Focus attention on the model email again and ask check questions, e.g. *How many email addresses are there?* (two), *How do you begin the email? (Dear…), Does the email use full or short forms, 'I am' or 'I'm'* (full forms), *What is a more formal way of saying 'Please reply'? (I look forward to hearing from you.), How do you end the email? (Yours sincerely).* Also ask *Why do you use 'Ms' and not 'Miss' or 'Mrs'?* (because we don't know if Linda Yates is married or not). If necessary, establish the difference between *Miss* (for a single woman) and *Mrs* (for a married woman).

4 Focus attention on the advertisement and elicit the job (*receptionist*). Check comprehension of the details, e.g. *Who do you email?* (Anne Watson), *Where?* (awatson@international.school.com), *What are the 'qualifications'?* (like working with people, speak two languages and English, have experience working in an office, use a computer, know your town well). Get students to answer the questions in the advertisement about themselves.

Remind students to use Carl's email in exercise 3 as a model and to use the information provided in each paragraph as a guide. Give students time to write their email in class or set it for homework.

5 Allow students to compare each other's emails, both for interest and to help each other with mistakes. When you collect in the emails, check for the correct use of greeting, ending, and full forms. Point out errors but allow students to correct them themselves. Try to limit correction to major problems to avoid demoralizing the students.

READING AND SPEAKING (SB p60)

A talented family

ABOUT THE TEXT

This activity is another jigsaw reading task. This means it should result in not only reading practice, but also some freer speaking. The class divides into two groups and each group reads a different, but similar text about a talented member of the same family. It's important to remind students to read only their text and to get information about the other text via speaking. If necessary and possible, give the instructions for the jigsaw reading in L1.

The texts are based on real people and have been written to consolidate the grammar taught in this and previous units. There are also examples of Past Simple forms (*came, saw, started, wanted*) included in this section for recognition. There's no need to give a full grammar explanation of these forms at this stage. If students query them, just explain that they are a past form of the relevant verb.

Gio Benedetti /ˈdʒiːəʊ benəˈdeti/ is a successful businessman, originally from near Lucca /ˈluːkə/ in Tuscany, central Italy. Despite humble beginnings, he has gone on to become a self-made millionaire and chairman of several companies.

Nicola Benedetti /ˈnɪkələ benəˈdeti/ is his daughter and a world-famous violinist. Born in Scotland, she started playing at the age of four and went on to attend the prestigious Yehudi Menhuin School for young musicians. She lives in Chiswick /ˈtʃɪsɪk/ near her sister Stephanie /ˈstefəni/, also a violinist.

Encourage students to use the context to help them with new vocabulary and to pool knowledge with other students. With weaker classes or if you are short of time, ask students to check some of the following vocabulary before the lesson:

Homework prior to the lesson

Introduction: *passion, businessman* /ˈbɪznəsmən/

Nicola: *to be like someone, close* (adjective = connected by shared feelings and interests), *family occasions, Christmas*.

Gio: *to afford something, dry-cleaning, independent, concert, proud, country and western music, classical music, to cry, I can't help it* (= I can't stop myself), *sentimental*.

SUGGESTION

If possible, play a short section of music by Nicola Benedetti at some stage during the lesson. This will help to put the information in the text into a broader context.

1 Discuss the questions in exercise 1 with the whole class. Elicit a range of examples of talented people and what they can do.

2 Focus attention on the photos of Nicola and Gio. Elicit any information students know about them. Give students a short time to read the introduction to the article and answer the questions in pairs. Check the answers with the class.

Answers
1 She's a violinist.
2 She was BBC Young Musician of the Year.
3 She lives in Chiswick, west London, near her sister.
4 She's a violinist too.
5 He's a businessman.

3 Put students into two groups, A and B. (With larger classes, you may need to have multiple sets of the two groups.) Assign a text to each group and remind students to read only their text:

Group A – Nicola

Group B – Gio

Get students to read their text quite quickly, asking others in their group for help with vocabulary if you didn't pre-teach the items listed in *About the text*. Monitor and help with any queries.

Give students time to read the questions and deal with any queries. Get them to work in their groups and answer the questions about their text, noting down the answers to each one. Monitor and help as necessary. The answers for each group are provided below for reference but don't check the answers with the whole class at this stage.

Answers
Nicola
1 No, it wasn't.
2 She was four.
3 Yes, he did.
4 They were poor.
5 Money is important to Gio but for Nicola success isn't about money.
6 No, he doesn't.
7 She teaches him about music, he teaches her about business.
8 At family occasions, like weddings and at Christmas.

Gio
1 He was born near Lucca in Italy.
2 He couldn't afford it.
3 It was a dry-cleaning business.
4 She was four.
5 No, he can't.
6 He likes country and western music. He doesn't like classical music.
7 Yes, she does.
8 He often cries when he sees Nicola play. He's very sentimental.

4 Re-group the students, making sure there is an A and a B student in each pair. Demonstrate the activity by getting a pair of students to talk about the person in their text. Students continue talking about the answers to the questions in exercise 3 and exchanging the information about their person. Monitor and help. Also check for correct use of the present and past of *can* and *to be*. Note down any common errors but feed back on them at a later stage. Bring the whole class together to conduct the feedback. Encourage students to expand on their answers where applicable.

Language work

5 This section focuses on the use of adjectives in the text. Focus attention on the example. Then give students time to complete the task, working in pairs.

Check the answers with the class, getting students to give full sentences to show the use of each adjective. Also check for correct use of the present and past of *to be*.

Answers

hard-working	Gio/Nicola's father was very hard-working.
poor	Gio's parents were poor.
important	Money is important to Gio/Nicola's father.
classical	Gio doesn't like classical music very much.
close	Nicola and her sister are very close.
difficult	It was difficult for Gio when he first came to Scotland.
expensive	The Jaguar was too expensive.
independent	Nicola was always independent.
proud	Gio is proud of Nicola and Scotland is proud of her.
passionate	Nicola is passionate when she plays the violin.
sentimental	Gio often cries because he's very sentimental.

EXTRA ACTIVITY

Students personalize the adjectives in exercise 5 by writing true sentences about themselves/someone they know. They can write present or past tense examples and then compare with a partner.

What do you think?

> ⚠ **POSSIBLE PROBLEMS**
>
> If students become involved in discussion activities, they often start to talk in L1 in their frustration to get their point across. Don't worry too much if this happens, at least it shows that they are interested! Just give them a gentle reminder to try in English as much as they can.

This is an attempt to generate some personalized discussion and give further freer practice of the Present Simple. Don't worry if at this level it turns out to be quite a short activity – even a little freer speaking is still worthwhile. Don't correct students too much. The aim of this activity is fluency, not accuracy.

It can be helpful to ask students to discuss the topic in small groups, before you conduct feedback with the whole class. It would also be a nice idea to encourage students to ask you questions about your family and who you are close to.

> **SUGGESTION**
>
> You could get students to roleplay an interview between a journalist and Gio or Nicola. Assign roles of the journalist and Gio or Nicola, or allow students to choose the role they want. Get students to prepare their interview, using the questions in exercise 3 to help them. Allow sufficient time for students to make notes, but discourage them from writing out the interview word for word. Get students to practise the interview in pairs and then act it out in class.

VOCABULARY AND LISTENING (SB p62)

Words that go together

Collocation and word groupings are a key feature of English and it's important that students start to become familiar with them as early in their learning as possible. This vocabulary section focuses on compound nouns (noun + noun combinations), verb + noun collocation, and the use of prepositions in a range of high-frequency phrases/structures.

Noun + noun

1 Explain that this task focuses on noun + noun combinations. Focus attention on the examples. Point out that the first is written as two words and the second as one. Highlight the main stress on the words:

post office *businessmann*

Ask *Where is the stress, on the first or second word?* (the first word). Drill the words as necessary.

Get students to write their answers to the task, so that they can focus on whether to write them as one or two words.

Check the answers, making sure students have written them correctly and that they stress the words accurately.

Answers
bookshop/store
motorway
motorbike
sunglasses
living room
bus stop
handbag
railway station
car park
traffic lights
petrol station

2 Focus attention on the examples in the book and get students to say the exchanges in open pairs. Elicit one or two more example definitions and then get students to test each other in pairs.

3 **T 5.14** **[CD 2: Track 15]** Tell the students they will hear three short conversations and that they should listen for noun + noun combinations from exercise 1. Focus attention on the example and play conversation 1. Elicit the other nouns from exercise 1 (*bus stop*, *traffic lights*).

Play the rest of the recording and let students complete their answers. Check with the class.

If you have time, ask students to turn to **T 5.14** on SB p173 and practise the conversations with a partner.

Answers and tapescript
1 post office, bus stop, traffic lights
2 sunglasses, handbag, living room
3 petrol station, railway station, car park, motorway

T 5.14
1 A Excuse me! Is there a post office near here?
B Yes. Can you see the bus stop over there?
A Yes, I can.
B Well, it's next to the bus stop. Near the traffic lights.
A Thanks.
2 A I can't find my sunglasses.
B Not again! Look in your handbag!
A Where's my handbag?
B It's in the living room.
A Oh yes! There it is, and there they are!
3 A Excuse me! Is there a petrol station near here?
B A petrol station? Yeah. Go past the railway station and the car park. It's just before the motorway.
A That's very kind. Thank you.

4 With weaker classes, ask students what they can remember from the conversations in exercise 3, and elicit ideas for a new conversation with the whole class. Students then continue writing their own conversation in closed pairs. Monitor and help, and feed in vocabulary as necessary.

Ask some students to perform their conversations for the class.

Verb + noun

5 Students have met most of these phrases as lexical items in earlier units. Point out that this task has verbs in list A and nouns in B. Focus attention on the example and then get students to complete the task. Let students check in pairs before checking with the whole class.

Answers
send a lot of text messages
drive a car
ride a motorbike
speak three languages
earn a lot of money
live on the third floor
play the guitar
wear a suit and tie
look after children
watch TV a lot

SUGGESTION

Ask students to brainstorm other nouns that go with the verbs, e.g. *play the piano/violin, drive a bus/taxi, ride a horse/bike*, etc. This can be done in class if you have time, or for homework. Remind students to record the verbs + nouns in their vocabulary notebook.

6 Focus attention on the example questions and answers in the Student's Book. If necessary, drill the pronunciation, paying attention to the sentence stress. With weaker classes, elicit other possible questions before the pairwork stage, e.g. *Can you speak three languages? Do you watch television a lot?*

Students ask and answer questions in closed pairs. Monitor and help as necessary.

7 **T 5.15** **[CD 2: Track 16]** Tell the students they are going to hear ten short conversations and that they should listen for the verb + noun combinations from exercise 5.

Play number 1 as an example and elicit the verb + noun. Play the rest of the recording without stopping. Give students time to check their answers in pairs before checking with the class.

Answers and tapescript
1 send a lot of text messages
2 earn a lot of money
3 live on the third floor
4 wear a suit and tie
5 play the guitar
6 ride a motorbike
7 drive a car
8 look after children
9 watch TV a lot
10 speak foreign languages/German/Spanish

T 5.15

1 **A** You send a lot of text messages!
B I know. My mobile phone is my best friend!
2 **A** Do you earn a lot of money?
B What a question! Mind your own business!
3 **A** Do you live on the third floor?
B Yes, I have a great view. I can see right over the town.
4 **A** Do you wear a suit and tie when you go to work?
B No, no. Where I work is very casual. I wear jeans and a T-shirt.
5 **A** Can you play the guitar?
B Yes, I can. And the piano. And the violin.
6 **A** Can you ride a motorbike?
B I can. Do you want to come for a ride? You can sit on the back.
7 **A** Can you drive a car?
B Of course not! I'm only 16!
8 **A** You have a full-time job. Who looks after your children?
B They go to playschool.
9 **A** Do you watch TV a lot?
B No, not really, just in the morning, and in the evening, and sometimes in the afternoon.
10 **A** I can't speak any foreign languages.
B I can. German and Spanish.

8 Refer students to **T 5.15** on SB p173. Get students to learn two conversations by heart and practise them in closed pairs. Monitor and help as necessary. Ask some pairs to perform their conversations for the class.

Prepositions

9 **T 5.16** **[CD 2: Track 17]** Pre-teach/check *What sort?* (= What type?), *iPod/iPhone, be on the Internet* (= using the Internet). Focus attention on the example. Give students time to complete the task, working individually. Tell students that the lines are each part of a longer conversation. Play the recording and let students check their answers. Elicit as many replies as students can remember, then play the recording again.

Refer students to **T 5.16** on SB p174 and get them to practise the conversations with a partner.

Answers and tapescript
1 **A** Do you like listening **to** music?
B Yes, of course. I have it all on my iPod.
2 **A** What sort **of** music do you like?
B All sorts but especially jazz.
3 **A** Where's your girlfriend **from**? Is she Mexican?
B No, she isn't. She's from Brazil. She speaks Portuguese.
4 **A** Is Paula married **to** Mike?
B That's right. Do you know her?
5 **A** Do you want to come shopping **with** me?
B Oh, yes. Can you wait a minute? I'll get my coat.
6 **A** Were there any good programmes **on** television last night?
B I don't know. I was on the Internet all evening.
7 **A** What do you want **for** your birthday?
B Can I have an iPhone? Or is that too expensive?
8 **A** Can I speak to Dave? Is he **at** work today?
B Sorry, he's on holiday all this week. He's back next week.

SUGGESTION

Ask students to personalize the language in the conversations in exercise 9. They can change the wording of the sentences but keep the language around the preposition the same, e.g. *I like listening to pop music.*

EVERYDAY ENGLISH (SB p63)

Polite requests

⚠ POSSIBLE PROBLEMS

Students have already met *can* for ability and its past form *could* earlier in this unit. This section focuses on *Can I … ?/Could I … ?* and *Can you … ?/Could you … ?* in polite requests. Students should recognize *Can I … ?* from earlier *Everyday English* sections, but may be confused at the use of *could* with present meaning. Although *Could you (do me a favour)?* has the same form as the past of *can*, the concept is in fact present. The *Caution box* covers the request and ability uses of *can/could*, but be prepared to check the time reference of key sentences with the class, e.g.

Can/Could I use your phone? (= present)
Can/Could you give me a lift? (= present)
I can drive. (= present)
I could drive when I was 17. (= past)

1 **T 5.17** **[CD 2: Track 18]** Start this section by making a couple of natural requests to students in the class, e.g. *Can you close the door, please? Could you switch on the lights, please?* etc. Focus attention on the photos. Give students time to read the conversations and guess the missing words. Play the recording and check the answers. Elicit where each conversation takes place (*1 in a café, 2 coming out of a building, 3 in a restaurant, 4 at a railway station*).

Answers and tapescript
1 A Can I have a **coffee**, please?
B Yes, of course.
2 A Can you open the **door** for me, please?
C Sure. No problem.
A Thanks.
3 A Could I have the **menu**, please?
D Certainly, madam.
4 A Could you **tell** me the **time**, please?
E It's 10.30.
A Thanks a lot.

2 Read the questions as a class. Give students time to discuss the answers in pairs before checking with the class.

Answers
In conversations 1 and 2, the speaker uses *Can I/you …?*, in 3 and 4, he/she uses *Could I/you …?*
Could …? is a little more polite than *Can …?*

Read the information on *can* and *could* as a class. Check students understand the difference between *Can/Could I … ?* (to ask for things) and *Can/Could you … ?* (to ask other people to do things).

Review the ability use as a class.

If necessary, also check the time references in the sentences (see *Possible problems* above).

3 **T 5.18** **[CD 2: Track 19]** Focus attention on the intonation in the examples. The recording divides each sentence into three parts to make imitating the intonation easier. Play the recording. Students repeat each section of the sentences, paying special attention to the intonation. Get students to practise the conversations in exercise 1 with a partner.

Tapescript

Can I …?	Can I have a …?	Can I have a coffee, please?
Could you …?	Could you tell me …?	Could you tell me the time, please?

4 **T 5.19** **[CD 2: Track 20]** Focus attention on the example. Check comprehension of *give me a hand* (= help me) and then get students to complete the task.

Play the recording and let students compare their answers. Elicit as many replies as students can remember, then play the recording again.

Refer students to **T 5.19** on SB p174 and get them to practise the conversations with a partner. If students have problems with the request intonation, play key lines of the recording again and get them to repeat.

Answers and tapescript
1 A Can I have a cheese sandwich, please?
B In white or brown bread?
2 A **Could you** post this letter for me, please?
B Yes, of course. No problem.
3 A **Can you** give me your email address?
B I think you have it already.
4 A **Can I** speak to you for a moment?
B Can it wait? I'm a bit busy.
5 A **Could you** lend me £20 till tomorrow?
B I can lend you ten but not 20.
6 A **Can you** give me a hand with this box?
B Of course. Do you want it upstairs?

5 Ask two students to read the example conversation across the class. Give students time to read through the list of prompts and deal with any vocabulary queries.

Put students in pairs to practise the conversations. Monitor and help as necessary.

SUGGESTION

Integrate the language of requests into your lessons in a natural way and encourage students to use the language themselves, e.g. asking students to open/close the window, hand out books/materials, sit in a particular place/work with a particular student, asking to borrow an object, asking for help with a word/exercise, asking someone to pass something over.

Photocopiable Activity

UNIT 5 Words that go together TB p152/TRD

Materials: One copy of the worksheet for each group of three/four students, cut up into dominoes. An uncut version of the game for you to use as a check.

Procedure: Explain that students are going to play a game to help them remember some of the language from the *Vocabulary* and *Everyday English* sections of the SB.

- Divide students into groups of three or four and give each group a set of dominoes placed face down on the table.

- Pre-teach/check useful language for playing the game: *Whose turn is it? It's my/your turn. I can't go. Take another card. Do these cards match? I don't think that's right. Can you check with the teacher?*
- Students take three dominoes each and leave the rest in the pile face down.
- Explain the rules: the first student places a card on the desk face up. The second student looks at his/her dominoes and tries to find a card that will match with the words on one of the sides. If he/she can't go, they have to take another card. He/She can put this card down if it matches, otherwise play passes to the next person. The game continues in the same way around the group. The first player to get rid of all their dominoes is the winner.
- Students play the game in their groups. Remind students to think about the context of the words and to go for the most logical matches that might occur in everyday situations. Go around listening, helping and correcting any wrongly matched cards as necessary. (The answers appear on the uncut worksheet, reading from the bottom right up to top left and then across.)
- After playing the game, students take turns to choose a card and then try to complete each sentence half orally. They can either try to remember what was on the dominoes, or they could come up with their own version.

Don't forget!

Grammar Reference (SB p187 and Teacher's Resource Disc)
Unit 5

Word list (SB p210 and Teacher's Resource Disc)
Unit 5

Test (Teacher's Resource Disc)
Unit test 5A
Unit test 5B

Video (DVD)
Unit 5 A music school

6 Life's ups and downs

Past Simple (1) – regular and irregular • Describing feelings • What's the date?

The theme of 'Life's ups and downs' provides the context for the presentation of both regular and irregular forms of the Past Simple. The formation of the question and negative is also introduced briefly as a lead-in to Unit 7, where it is one of the main grammatical aims. The skills work includes a *Reading and listening* section with a story on what matters in life and a *Writing* section which focuses on linking words. These also provide further practice of the Past Simple.

LANGUAGE INPUT

GRAMMAR

Past Simple – regular verbs (SB p68) Past Simple – irregular verbs (SB p70)	• Understanding and practising the addition of *-ed* in Past Simple forms. • Understanding and practising irregular verb forms to talk about the past.

VOCABULARY

Describing feelings (SB p74)	• Understanding and practising adjectives ending in *-ed* and *-ing* in the context of talking about feelings.

EVERYDAY ENGLISH

What's the date? (SB p75)	• Understanding and practising ordinal numbers in the context of talking about dates (months and years).

SKILLS DEVELOPMENT

READING

The meaning of life (SB p72)	• A short fable about a fisherman and a businessman, and what is important in life.

LISTENING

A dotcom millionaire (SB p70) The meaning of life (SB p72) Four conversations (SB p74)	• Listening for key information in an interview. **T 6.8** (SB p174/TRD) • Listening for key words in a short story. **T 6.11** (SB p175/TRD) • Listening for adjectives ending in *-ed* and *-ing* in four short conversations. **T 6.13** (SB p175/TRD)

SPEAKING

Talking about you (SB p71) What do you think? (SB p72)	• Talking about what you did yesterday and last week/month/year, etc. • Discussing the moral of a story and what you think happened next.

WRITING

A biography – Combining sentences (SB p159)	• Reviewing and understanding linking words, then writing a biography of someone successful.

MORE MATERIALS

Photocopiable worksheets – Focus on feelings (TB p153/TRD), The Everyday English game (TRD) **Tests** (TRD) **Video** (DVD)

STARTER (SB p68)

SUGGESTION

It is helpful to bring a set of family photos of your grandparents and, if possible, great-grandparents to provide context for the *Starter* section. Encourage students to bring a set of photos of their family to the lesson, too.

Check comprehension of *great-grandparents*. Demonstrate the activity by telling the class about your own grandparents and great-grandparents, dealing with each question in turn and giving as much information as you can. Use photos you have brought to class if appropriate.

Focus attention on the examples. Then elicit information from the students about their grandparents and great-grandparents. In larger classes, students can work in pairs/small groups and then feed back to the class.

AMERICA'S RICHEST WOMAN (SB p68)

Past Simple (1) – regular verbs

This presentation takes the form of a profile of the American TV star and chat show presenter Oprah Winfrey. When learning the Past Simple, students build on their knowledge of the Present Simple, in that both tenses use a form of *do* as an auxiliary in the question and negative. It is not such a big leap to learn that the same auxiliary is used in its past tense form, *did*, to make the Past Simple tense, especially as this form remains the same in all persons.

Many of the exercises in this unit provide opportunities to contrast the Present Simple and Past Simple tenses. There are examples of the superlative adjective *richest* just for recognition.

⚠ POSSIBLE PROBLEMS

- Although students should be helped by their knowledge of the Present Simple (see above), the use of *did* can still cause problems. Students often mis-use the form or forget to use the auxiliary altogether:

  **Where you lived when you were young?*

  **When she start school?*

  **She no liked her job.*

- The different ways of pronouncing the *-ed* at the end of regular verbs is a problem. Students often want to pronounce the *-ed* in its entirety – /ed/ – and not the /t/, /d/, /ɪd/ endings:

  cleaned * /kliːned/ instead of /kliːnd/

  worked * /wɜːked/ instead of /wɜːkt/

  visited * /vɪzɪted/ instead of /vɪzɪtɪd/

There is an exercise on SB p70 to help students perceive the different endings, but we suggest you avoid spending too much time getting students to produce the endings at this stage so as not to overload them.

1 Focus attention on the photos of Oprah /ˈəʊprə/ Winfrey and ask students if they recognize her. Elicit any information/guesses about her as a child and now as an adult.

Pre-teach/check *billionaire, to give money to charity, childhood, coal mine, to clean houses, clever, receive a scholarship, drama, to read the news.*

2 **T 6.1** **[CD 2: Track 21]** Text **A** is about Oprah Winfrey's life now and so revises the Present Simple before moving to the introduction of the Past Simple in texts **B** and **C**. Ask students to read and listen to text **A** and complete the missing verbs. Play the recording and then check the answers. Make sure students have spelt their answers correctly.

Answers and tapescript

Oprah Winfrey is a famous American TV star. She **lives** in California but she also **has** an apartment in Chicago, where she **works**. Oprah is one of the richest women in America. She **earns** millions of dollars every year. She **gives** a lot of money to charity.

Elicit the answers to the questions in exercise 2.

Answers

Yes, she is.
She lives in California. She works in Chicago.
She earns millions of dollars every year.

Ask a few additional questions about Oprah's life now, e.g. *What does she do?* (She's a TV star.) *Where is her apartment?* (In Chicago.) *What does she do with her money?* (She gives a lot of it to charity.)

3 **T 6.2** **[CD 2: Track 22]** Tell your students that they are going to listen to and read about Oprah's past in text **B**. Play the recording through once. Then check the answers to the questions in exercise 3.

Answers

She was born in Kosciusko /ˈkɒzɪʌskəʊ/, Mississippi on January 29, 1954.
No, they weren't.
Yes, she was. She could read before she was three.

GRAMMAR SPOT (SB p68)

Go through the exercises one by one, establishing the answers after each exercise.

1 Students complete the sentences with the correct form of *live*. Check the answers.

Answers

Now she **lives** in California.
When she was a child she **lived** with her grandmother.

2 Refer students to text **B**. Get them to find examples of the verbs. Check the answers.

Answers

Her father **worked** in a coal mine.
Her mother **cleaned** houses.
She **received** a scholarship.
She **studied** drama.
She **started** reading the news.

Then get students to work out the rule for forming the Past Simple of regular verbs.

Answer
To form the Past Simple of regular verbs, add *-ed* or *-d* to the infinitive.

▶▶ Read Grammar Reference 6.1 on SB p188 together in class, and/or ask students to read it at home. Encourage them to ask you questions about it.

4 **T 6.3** **[CD 2: Track 23]** Check comprehension of *interview* and *move*. Students work in pairs to decide on the Past Simple form of the verbs in the box. Let them try and practise the pronunciation.

Play the recording and let students check their answers. Play the recording again and get students to repeat. Students spell the Past Simple forms. Pay particular attention to the change of *-y* to *-ied* in *study–studied*.

You can point out that the endings can be grouped according to pronunciation, but do not spend too long on this, as students will focus on pronunciation on SB p70.

Answers and tapescript
watched interviewed studied talked moved started
earned opened

5 **T 6.4** **[CD 2: Track 24]** Explain that text **C** gives more information about Oprah's work and her more recent life. Explain that students need to use the verbs in exercise 4 in the Past Simple form and that they need to use one verb twice (*watch*).

Focus attention on the example and play the first sentence on the recording. Play the rest of the recording straight through without pausing and get students to complete the text. Alternatively, students try to fill in the gaps with the verbs before they listen, and then listen and check against the recording.

Go through the answers as a class, getting students to take turns at reading aloud part of the text. Correct their pronunciation of past tense verbs in preparation for the exercise on pronunciation in the Practice section on SB p70.

Answers and tapescript
C Her success
In 1984, Oprah moved to Chicago to work on a TV talk show called *A.M. Chicago*. She **talked** to lots of interesting people about their problems. Oprah says, 'People's problems are my problems.' The show was very successful, so in 1985, it was renamed *The Oprah Winfrey Show*. 49 million people in 134 countries **watched** it every week. In 1993, she **interviewed** Michael Jackson and 100 million people **watched** the programme. Last year she **earned** $260,000,000.

Her charity work
In 1998, Oprah **started** the charity *Oprah's Angel Network* to help poor children all over the world. In 2007, she **opened** a special school in Johannesburg, the *Oprah Winfrey Academy for Girls*. She says, 'When I was a kid, we were poor and we didn't have much money. So what did I do? I **studied** hard.' There are 152 girls at the school, Oprah calls them her daughters – the children she didn't have in real life.

GRAMMAR SPOT (SB p69)

1 Refer students back to text **C** about Oprah and get them to find a question and two negatives. With weaker classes, review how to form Present Simple questions and negatives with *do*/*does* and *don't*/*doesn't*.

Answers
So what did I do?
We didn't have much money.
The children she didn't have in real life.

2 Go through the notes on the formation of questions with the whole class. Point out the use of the past auxiliary *did* in the *Wh*-question, *Yes*/*No* question, and short answer. Point out that *did* is followed by the infinitive without *to*: *did … work* (NOT **did … worked*).

3 Go through the notes on the formation of the negative with the whole class. Point out that *didn't* is followed by the infinitive without *to*: *didn't go* (NOT **didn't went*). Having the main verb in the Past Simple form, although incorrect, may seem more logical to students.

▶▶ Read Grammar Reference 6.2 on SB p188 together in class, and/or ask students to read it at home. Encourage them to ask you questions about it.

6 **T 6.5** **[CD 2: Track 25]** This exercise focuses on question formation in the Past Simple. Focus attention on the example and then get students to work in pairs to complete the questions.

Play the recording so that students can check their answers. Play the recording again, pausing after each question (or say them yourself) and get students to repeat them both chorally and individually. Ask other students to provide the answers. Encourage natural falling intonation on each one.

What did she study?

Students continue practising the questions and answers in pairs. Monitor and check for accurate formation of Past Simple questions and negatives. Be prepared to drill the forms again if students have problems.

Answers and tapescript
1 Where did her father work?
In a coal mine.
2 What **did** her mother do?
She cleaned houses.
3 Who **did** Oprah **live** with?
Her grandmother.
4 What **did** she **study**?
Drama.
5 When **did** she **interview** Michael Jackson?
In 1993.
6 How much **did** she **earn** last year?
$260 million.
7 When **did** she **open** the girls' school?
In 2007.
8 **Did** her parents **earn** much money?
No, they didn't.

PRACTICE (SB p70)

Talking about you

1 This activity brings together the past of *to be*, *to be born*, and *did* in Past Simple questions, so that students become aware of the difference between the past of the verb *to be* and full verbs. Focus attention on the example and elicit the missing verb forms in number 2.

Get students to complete the questions on their own first and then check in pairs. Check the answers with the whole class, asking individuals to read out their answers. Drill the questions, encouraging natural falling intonation.

Answers
1 Where were your parents born?
2 Where **did** you live when you **were** a child?
3 **Did** you live in a house or a flat?
4 When **did** you start school?
5 Who **was** your first teacher?
6 Who **was** your best friend?
7 When **did** you learn to read and write?
8 When **did** you get your first mobile phone?

2 Put students in pairs or groups of three to ask and answer the questions. Monitor and check for correct Past Simple question formation and intonation. (Alternatively, you could do this activity as a class mingle. Ask students to get up and walk round the class asking each question to a different student.)

3 After a few minutes, bring the class back together to feed back what information they can remember. Focus attention on the examples in the Student's Book and remind them of the third person singular form *was born*.

Sample answer
Wolfgang's father was born in Mannheim and his mother was born in Frankfurt. He lived in a flat in Mannheim when he was a child. He started school in 1987. His first teacher was Herr Becker. His best friend was Martin Schiller. He learned to read and write when he was five. He got his first mobile phone in 2002.

EXTRA ACTIVITY
As consolidation of exercise 1, ask students to write a short paragraph about themselves for homework.

Pronunciation

4 **T 6.6** **[CD 2: Track 26]** Play the recording. Students listen to and repeat the three different pronunciations of the *-ed* ending.

5 **T 6.7** **[CD 2: Track 27]** Play the recording. Students write the verbs in the correct column. Get them to check their answers with a partner before checking with the class.

Play the recording again. Students practise saying the verbs.

Answers and tapescript
/t/ talked watched
/d/ cleaned received studied moved interviewed opened
/ɪd/ wanted decided

T 6.7
cleaned received studied wanted moved talked watched interviewed opened decided

BEN'S UPS AND DOWNS (SB p70)

Irregular verbs

⚠ POSSIBLE PROBLEMS
- See the notes on TB p65 on the use of *did*.
- There are a large number of irregular verbs to learn. From now on students should be encouraged to consult the irregular verb list on SB p202 and learn the irregular verbs as and when needed. You could start setting some to learn for homework and giving short tests on them at the beginning of some lessons!

The context for the introduction of irregular verbs is a profile of another real-life millionaire – Ben Way, who made his fortune in the computer boom of the 1990s. The term *dotcom* refers to a company or person that uses the Internet to sell products/services. Ben Way's company 'Rainmakers' was created to exploit existing technologies on the Internet and develop new ones.

SUGGESTION
All of the irregular verbs in exercise 1 appear at some point later in this unit, so your students need to become familiar with them as quickly as possible. You could set exercise 1 for homework prior to the lesson and then go through it quickly in class.

1 Refer students to the irregular verb list on SB p202. Make sure they understand that it is an important resource that they should refer to regularly.

Elicit one or two examples of the Past Simple forms. Ask students to work with a partner and check the other irregular forms. If appropriate, let students use dictionaries to look up new words.

Students read out the correct answers around the class. Model pronunciation of the verbs and get students to repeat chorally and individually. Check pronunciation of the more difficult forms, e.g. *caught* /cɔːt/.

Read Grammar Reference 6.3 on SB p188 together in class, and/or ask students to read it at home. Encourage them to ask you questions about it.

Answers

be, was, were	leave, left
begin, began	lose, lost
can, could	make, made
catch, caught	meet, met
come, came	send, sent
get, got	take, took
give, gave	win, won
go, went	write, wrote
have, had	

2 Check comprehension of the expression *ups and downs* (good and bad periods of life). Elicit a few examples of ups and downs that students have experienced.

Focus attention on the photos of Ben Way and check comprehension of *dotcom millionaire* (a person who made a lot of money through selling products/services on the Internet). Give students time to read the introduction about Ben. Ask *What were Ben's ups and downs in life?* (He made his first million at 17. He was one of the first dotcom millionaires. Then he lost all his money, but now he's a millionaire again.)

3 Pre-teach/check *dyslexic*, *software program*, *company*, and *entrepreneur*. Read the first sentence of the profile on SB p71 with the class and then elicit the missing verb for number 2 (*went*).

Give students time to complete the profile, working individually. Students check their answers in pairs before listening to the recording in exercise 4.

Listening

4 **T 6.8** **[CD 2: Track 28]** Tell students that the recording is in the form of a conversation between Ben and an interviewer and that the profile in exercise 3 is a summary of what the speakers talk about. Students are required only to select key points to check the verbs in the profile.

Play the recording. Students listen and check their answers to exercise 3. Play the recording again if students have missed any of the key verbs. Check the answers with the class.

Play the recording again. Give students time to discuss any further information they understood in pairs. Elicit examples in a brief feedback session.

Answers and tapescript

1 was	7 began
2 went	8 left
3 couldn't	9 made
4 gave	10 had
5 took	11 won
6 wrote	12 lost

T 6.8

I = Interviewer B = Ben Way

I Hi Ben. Nice to meet you. Can you tell us a bit about your life?
B Well, I was born on September 28th 1980 in Devon in the south-west of England.
I And what did your parents do?
B My dad was an accountant and my mum was an artist.
I Did you go to school in Devon?
B Yes, I did. I went to a small village school.
I Did you enjoy school?
B No, I didn't enjoy it at all. I had problems because I was dyslexic and couldn't read and write ...
I Ah, that's difficult ...
B Yes, but when I was nine, my dad gave me a computer and it changed my life. I loved it, I took it everywhere with me. I helped my friends and my parents' friends with their computers.
I Very good – and then ...?
B Then, I wrote my first software program when I was just 11, and when I was 15, I began my own computer company.
I That's fantastic! Was it successful?
B Yes, very successful – so successful that I left school at 16 and ...
I Yes, I know ... you were a millionaire at 17!
B Yes, I made my first million at 17 and at 19, I had £18.5 million.
I And at 20 you won 'Young Entrepreneur of the Year'.
B Yes, I did. I often went on TV and radio and talked about it. It was amazing!
I And then one year later ...?
B Yes, and then just a year later, when I was 21, I lost everything. Disaster! Dotcom businesses everywhere went down.
I Yeah, but now you're up again! Another company, another million!
B I know. I work hard but I'm also very lucky!

Note This interview with Ben Way is fictitious and is based on factual information from a number of sources.

5 Briefly review how to say 19– dates and if you think your students need to practise dates, ask the class to chant the years from 1990 to 2000.

Focus attention on the example question. Give students time to write the other questions in the exercise. Monitor and help as necessary. With weaker classes, go through the question formation as a class activity before students do the pairwork.

Focus attention on the example again and elicit the complete answer. Students work in pairs to ask and answer the rest of the questions. Insist on full answers so that they get practice with the irregular past forms. Check for accurate question formation and falling intonation. If students have problems, drill the questions and answers in open pairs and then get students to repeat the pairwork.

Check the answers with the whole class. Correct any mistakes in the question formation and use of irregular pasts carefully.

Answers

1 What did Ben's parents do? His father was an accountant and his mother was an artist.
2 Where did he do to school? He went to a small village school in Devon.
3 Why did he have problems at school? He was dyslexic.
4 What did his dad give him in 1989? He gave him a computer.
5 Who did he help with their computers? He helped his friends and his parents' friends with their computers.
6 Why did he leave school at 16? He left school at 16 because his first computer company was very successful.
7 When did he win 'Young Entrepreneur of the Year'? He won 'Young Entrepreneur of the Year' in 2000.
8 Why did he lose his money? He lost his money because dotcom businesses everywhere went down.

PRACTICE (SB p71)

Regular and irregular verbs

1 **T 6.9** **[CD 2: Track 29]** This exercise gives controlled practice with both regular and irregular past forms. Focus attention on the example. Give students time to complete the rest of the sentences. Remind them to look at the list of irregular verbs on SB p202 if they need help with any of the forms.

Play the recording and let students check their answers. With weaker students, go over each verb form and ask *Regular or irregular?* Also drill the pronunciation if students have problems.

Answers and tapescript

1 My granddad was born in 1932. He **died** in 2009.
2 My parents **met** in London in 1983. They **got** married in 1985.
3 I **arrived** late for the lesson. It **began** at two o'clock.
4 I **caught** the bus to school today. It **took** just 40 minutes.
5 I **had** a very busy morning. I **sent** 30 emails before 10 o'clock.
6 Our football team **won** the match 3–0. Your team **lost** again.
7 My brother **earned** a lot of money in his last job but he **left** because he **didn't like** it.
8 I **studied** Chinese for four years, but when I **went** to Shanghai, I **couldn't** understand a word.

Talking about you

2 Focus attention on the example. Give some true sentences about yourself, using a range of different prompts from the exercise. Give students time to make their own sentences. If you want students to get written consolidation, they can write the sentences out in their notebook. Monitor and help as necessary.

Demonstrate exchanges starting with both positive and negative forms. Highlight the use of extra information and follow-up questions to make the exchange more interesting, e.g.

A *I watched TV yesterday.*
B *Oh, what did you watch?*
A *A film about a poor man who became a millionaire. What about you?*
B *I watched a football match but my team lost.*
C *I didn't watch TV yesterday. I was out with friends. What about you?*
D *I watched the news and then I listened to music. Where did you go with your friends?*
C *We went to the cinema. We saw the new Johnny Depp film.*
D *Was it good?*
C *Yes, not bad.*

Put the students in pairs to continue the pairwork. Alternatively, students can do the task as a whole-class mingle. Monitor and check for accurate use of Past Simple forms and question formation. Highlight and correct any common errors carefully.

3 Focus attention on the time expressions, pointing out that we can't use *last* with parts of a day, except *night*. Check pronunciation and then get students to give a few examples of the time expressions in context, e.g. *I went to the cinema last night.*

Check pronunciation of the question form, highlighting the main stresses, e.g.

When did you last have a holiday?

Drill the question form chorally and individually. Then put students in pairs to ask and answer the questions. You could suggest that they take notes about each other. Monitor and help as necessary.

4 With weaker classes, briefly check the past form of the verbs in the list in exercise 3. Bring the class together and elicit examples of what students learned about their partner.

SUGGESTION

You could provide further practice of the Past Simple by asking students to write a short description of the year they were born. Tell students where and when you were born and give examples of key people/events/trends in that year, e.g. world leaders, sports events, science, popular songs/artists/films, trends in cars/fashion/design, famous people, etc. Write the above categories on the board and get students to find out information about the year they were born for homework. If you have access to computers, students could do this during class time.

With weaker classes, build a skeleton on the board with the students to help them with the writing task, e.g.

I was born on … in … . In that year … was the leader of my country. Other important leaders were… . In sport … won … and … became world champion in … . In science … made … . Millions of people bought a … . In music, … sang … and … had hit records.

When students have written about the year they were born, put them into pairs or small groups to exchange information. Elicit any interesting examples during class feedback.

WRITING (SB p159)

A biography

Combining sentences

The writing syllabus continues with the second focus on linking words. Students practised *and*, *so*, *but*, and *because* in Unit 4. This section reviews those linking words and also includes *however*, *when*, and *until*. The theme of the biography is a successful person and the subject of exercise 1 is Ben Way, the dotcom millionaire students learned about on SB pp70–1. Students do a matching and then a gap-fill exercise to practise the use of the linkers, before writing a short text about a successful person that they know. The writing task also consolidates the use of the Present Simple and the Past Simple.

1 Focus attention on the photo of Ben Way and ask students what they can remember about him. Elicit a range of information.

Pre-teach/check *to continue*, *to run a company*, *to win a business award*, *to do well*. Check comprehension of *however* and *until* via translation or by getting students to check in dictionaries.

Focus attention on the sentence halves in columns **A** and **C**. Explain that they are in the correct order and students have to choose the correct word in column **B** to join them. They also need to pay attention to the punctuation at the end of column **A** to help them choose the correct answer. With weaker students, highlight the use of the capital letter in *However* to indicate the start of a new sentence.

Focus on the example and elicit the correct word to join the first sentence (*and*). Then give students time to complete the task, working in pairs.

T 6.10 **[CD 2: Track 30]** Play the recording and let students compare their answers. Students then take it in turns to read the sentences aloud. Correct any pronunciation, drilling key lines as necessary.

Answers and tapescript

Ben Way is 35 years old **and** he runs a company called 'Rainmakers'.
Ben's a computer millionaire. **However**, he wasn't always so successful.
As a child, he was dyslexic **so** he didn't do well at school.
He didn't learn to read and write **until** he was nine and his father gave him a computer.
He wrote his first software program **when** he was 11.
He didn't go to university **because** at 15 he started his own company.
He first became a millionaire **when** he was just 17.
He continued to be very successful **until** he was 21.
He won a business award in 2000, **but** then in 2001 he lost it all.
One year later he started 'Rainmakers', **and** now he's a millionaire again.

2 Give an example by answering the questions in exercise 2 about someone you know who is successful. Then give students time to write notes about their chosen person, using the questions as prompts.

Divide the class into pairs and get students to exchange information about their person, using the questions in the exercise and their notes. Check for correct use of the Present Simple and Past Simple and, if necessary, briefly review the use of the tenses for present habits and past events.

3 Focus attention on the photo and pre-teach/check *dress designer*, *artistic*, *fashion school*, and *stay in touch*. Give students time to read through the text quickly to get a general idea of what it is about. Elicit the first two missing linking words as examples and then get students to complete the text. With weaker students, remind them to look carefully at the punctuation to help them choose their answers.

Give students time to check in pairs before checking with the class.

Answers

1 and 2 when 3 because 4 until 5 However 6 so
7 because 8 but 9 when 10 so 11 However 12 because

4 Draw up a paragraph plan from the questions in exercise 2 for students to follow when they write their own text:

Paragraph 1: What is his/her name? How old is he/she? What does he/she do?

Paragraph 2: How do you know him/her?
Was he/she clever at school?
How did he/she become successful?
Did he/she have any ups and downs?

Paragraph 3: When and where do you see him/her?

With weaker students, elicit the key structures needed to write the biography, e.g. *My* [person and name] *is* [age] … . *He is a* [job] … . *We met in* … [place] *when we were* … [age], etc.

Give students time to write their text in class or set it for homework. If possible, display the texts on the classroom wall/noticeboard to allow students to read each other's work. You could ask them to vote for the most interesting biography. When you check the students' work, point out errors but allow students to correct them themselves. Try to limit correction to major problems to avoid demoralizing students.

LISTENING AND READING (SB p72)

The meaning of life

ABOUT THE TEXT

The reading section in this unit is in the form of a fable (a traditional story which teaches a moral lesson). It gives students the opportunity to enjoy a change of genre from the more factual texts of the earlier units.

The story has narrative and dialogue sections and so provides recycling of Present Simple and Past Simple forms (regular and irregular). The conversation in **T 6.11** is a summary of the wording of the main story. Even though the wording in the recording isn't exactly the same as the main story, the key sections are close enough for students to be able to pick out the key words. There are examples of comparatives in the story but these are for recognition only.

Harvard /'hɑːvəd/ is a prestigious university in Cambridge, Massachusetts. It is the oldest institution of higher education in the USA. LA is short for *Los Angeles* /lɒs 'ændʒəliːz/, the second largest city in the US, in California on the Pacific Coast. *Señor* is the Spanish for *sir* and *papa* is the Spanish for *daddy*. The yellowfin tuna is one of the biggest species of tuna, found near the Hawaiian Islands, in the Indian Ocean, Caribbean and Western Pacific.

Encourage students to use the pictures in the SB and the context to help them with new vocabulary, and to pool knowledge with other students. With weaker classes or if you are short of time, ask students to check some of following vocabulary before the lesson:

Homework prior to the lesson

fishing village, *boat*, *tuna fish*, *to take* (= need a particular amount of time), *to smile*, *to take a siesta* (= have a short sleep in the afternoon), *fleet of boats*, *to export*, *to sell*, *gentleman*, *advice*.

1 Lead in to the theme of the story by asking students *What does a businessman do? And a fisherman? How are their lives different?* Elicit a range of answers from the class.

Focus attention on the picture and ask students to point to the fisherman and the businessman. Elicit any other basic information about the situation.

Read the questions as a class and then give students time to read the introduction to the story. Deal with any vocabulary queries if you didn't pre-teach the items listed in *About the text*. Check the answers.

Answers
He was on holiday in a fishing village in the south of Mexico.
He met a young fisherman.
Yes, he did.
He said, 'What beautiful tuna!'
The businessman was American and the fisherman was Mexican.

2 **T 6.11** **[CD 2: Track 31]** With weaker students, pre-teach/check some of the key vocabulary from the conversation (see *About the text*). Tell students they are going to hear a conversation between the two men. They don't need to understand every word, but should listen for key information about the fisherman's life and the suggestions that the businessman makes.

Play the recording through once. Elicit who the students think has a better life. Encourage them to give reasons for their answers.

Tapescript
B = Businessman F = Fisherman FC = Fisherman's children

B Good morning. What beautiful tuna! How long did it take to catch them?
F Oh, about two hours.
B Only two hours! Amazing! Why didn't you fish for longer and catch more?
F I didn't want to fish for longer. With this I have enough fish for my family.
B But what do you do with the rest of your day? Aren't you bored?
F I'm never bored. I get up late, play with my children, watch football, and take a siesta with my wife. Sometimes in the evenings, I walk to the village to see my friends, play the guitar, and sing some songs.
B Really? That's all you do? Look, I am a very successful businessman. I went to Harvard University and I studied business. I can help you. Fish for four hours every day and sell the extra fish you catch …
F But …
B … Then, you can buy a bigger boat, catch more, and earn more money.
F But …
B … Then buy a second boat, a third, and so on, until you have a big fleet of fishing boats.
F But …
B … and you can export the fish, and leave this village, and move to Mexico City, or LA or New York, and open a fishing business.
F OK, OK, but how long will all this take?
B Er- let me think -er, probably about 15 to 20 years.
F 15 to 20 years! And then what, Señor?
B Why, that's the exciting part. You can sell your business and become very rich, a millionaire.
F A millionaire? Really? But what do I do with all the money?
B Well, let me think. Erm- I know, you can stop work and -er, move to a lovely, old fishing village where you can sleep late, play with your grandchildren, watch football, take a siesta with your wife, and walk to the village in the evenings where you can play the guitar, and sing with your friends all you want.
F Mmmm – well …
FC Papa, Papa, did you catch many fish?
F I caught enough for us today and tomorrow, and also some for this gentleman. Please, Señor, have some of my beautiful fish. Goodbye Señor. Come on children, let's go home.

3 Put students in pairs to do the true/false task. Encourage them to do as many sentences as they can from memory. If students have problems, play the recording again and let them check/complete their answers.

Answers
1 True
2 False. He took two hours to catch the tuna.
3 True
4 False. He is never bored.
5 True
6 True
7 True
8 False. He went home with his family.

4 **T 6.11** **[CD 2: Track 31]** Give students time to read and complete the story. Monitor and help as necessary.

Allow students to check their answers in pairs. Point out that the recording doesn't have exactly the same wording as the story in the SB, but the dialogue sections are the same and so students should be able to pick out the key words to check their answers.

Play **T 6.11** again. Check the answers with the class. Ask students to spell the Past Simple forms or to write their answers on the board.

Answers

1 two	5 some	9 about
2 didn't	6 went	10 stop
3 have	7 studied	11 did
4 late	8 earn	12 caught

T 6.11
See exercise 2 above.

5 This stage gives students the opportunity to retell the story, using their own words where possible. If you have a large class, students can work in groups of about six to give everyone the opportunity to tell a part of the story. Read out the opening of the story: *An American businessman was on holiday in a fishing village in the south of Mexico. One morning …* . Then get the class to continue the story, each telling a small section before moving on to the next student. Encourage the class to help and prompt each other if they get any of the main events wrong or if they can't remember what happened next. With weaker students, write key words for each section on the board as prompts.

What do you think?

Check comprehension of *moral* (the main lesson of the story) and *what matters* (what is really important).

Put students into groups of three or four to discuss their answers. Monitor and help as necessary but don't interrupt or over-correct as this is primarily a fluency task.

Allow the discussion to continue for as long as students' interest is held, and exchanges are taking place mainly in English! Elicit a range of opinions from the class and establish the moral of the story ('*Understand what really matters in life*.')

EXTRA ACTIVITIES

- Ask students to imagine that the fisherman and the businessman meet again five years later. Students roleplay the conversation between the two men in pairs. They can then act out their conversations for the class and compare their ideas.
- If your students are interested in story-telling, get them to research a fable or traditional short story from their own country for homework. They should make notes about the main characters and events but not simply print out the complete story. Students then work in pairs/small groups to tell each other their story. This works particularly well in multilingual groups as students can exchange stories from a range of cultures.

VOCABULARY AND LISTENING (SB p74)

Describing feelings

1 Demonstrate the activity by getting students to find the correct picture for *bored* (picture a). Students match the rest of the feelings to the pictures.

Check the answers with the whole class. Drill the pronunciation of the adjectives.

Answers

a bored	d interested
b excited	e worried
c tired	f annoyed

2 **T 6.12** **[CD 2: Track 32]** Elicit the answer to number 1 as an example. Students continue the activity in pairs. Then play the recording and let students check their answers.

Answers and tapescript

1 I went to bed late last night, so I'm very **tired** today.
2 My football team lost again. I'm really **annoyed**!
3 I won £20,000 in the lottery. I'm so **excited**!
4 I can't find my house keys. I'm really **worried**.
5 I have nothing to do and nowhere to go. I am so **bored**!
6 The professor gave a great lecture. I was really **interested**.

-ed and *-ing* adjectives

Read the notes on *-ed* and *-ing* adjectives with the whole class. Using L1 if appropriate, explain that adjectives ending in *-ed* often describe a person's feeling or reactions, and that adjectives ending in *-ing* often describe the person or thing that provokes those feelings or reactions.

3 Focus on the pair of sentences in number 1 as an example and elicit the missing adjectives (*exciting*, *excited*.) Students complete the rest of the exercise.

Check the answers with the whole class. Drill the pronunciation of the pairs of adjectives, making sure students can clearly distinguish the *-ing* and *-ed* forms. If students need further practice, drill the complete sentences in exercise 3 chorally and individually.

Answers

1 Life in New York is very **exciting**.
It's my birthday tomorrow. I'm really **excited**.
2 The marathon runners were very **tired**.
That game of tennis was very **tiring**.
3 The child's behaviour was really **annoying**.
The teacher was **annoyed** because nobody did the homework.
4 We were very **worried** when they heard the news.
The news is very **worrying**.

SUGGESTION

You can give students further practice by asking a range of questions and getting students to respond with a suitable adjective in the correct form (sample questions and answers are given below). Elicit a range of answers by asking several students the same question.

Did you enjoy the last film you saw? (Yes, it was interesting.)
Why don't you run six kilometres every morning? (Because it's tiring.)
How do you feel after the lesson? (A bit tired.)
How do you feel before an exam? (Very worried.)
How do you feel if your friend is late? (A bit annoyed.)
Do you like football? (No, it's very boring.)
Do you like learning English? (Yes, it's interesting, but a bit tiring.)

4 **T 6.13** **[CD 2: Track 33]** Give students time to read through the gapped conversations. Deal with any vocabulary queries and check the pronunciation of *laugh* /lɑːf/. Students complete the conversations, working in pairs. With weaker students, write the missing adjectives on the board in random order to help them with the gap-fill.

Play the recording and let students check the answers. Students practise the conversations in their pairs. Monitor and check. If students have problems, play selected sections of the recording again and get students to repeat. Students then practise the conversations again.

Answers and tapescript

1 A Did you enjoy the film?
B No, I didn't. It was **boring**.
A Oh, I loved it. It was really **interesting**, and very funny.
B I didn't laugh once!
2 A How was your exam?
B Awful. I'm very **worried**.
A But you worked really hard.
B I know, I studied until two in the morning, but then I was so **tired** today, I couldn't read the questions.
A Don't worry. I'm sure you'll be OK.
3 A That was a great match! Really **exciting**!
B Only because your team won. I was **bored**.
A But it wasn't **boring** at all! It was a fantastic game!
B Well, I didn't enjoy it, and now I'm **annoyed** because I paid £45 for my ticket.
4 A When's Nina's birthday?
B You mean 'When was her birthday?' It was last Friday, March 24th.
A Oh no! Was she **annoyed** that I forgot?
B No, no, she was just **worried** that you didn't like her any more.

5 Refer students back to the text on SB page 73 to find examples of *-ed* and *-ing* adjectives.

Answers
Aren't you bored?
Why, that's the exciting part!
The young fisherman didn't look excited.

Photocopiable Activity

UNIT 6 Focus on feelings TB p153/TRD

Materials: One copy of the worksheet for each student.

Procedure: Explain that students are going to complete a worksheet to practise the language of feelings from the *Vocabulary and listening* section of the SB.

- Pre-teach/check the following *-ed/-ing* adjectives: *frightened/frightening, embarrassed/embarrassing, irritated/irritating, surprised/surprising*. There are examples of superlative adjectives in the sentences but these are for recognition only.
- Hand out a copy of the worksheet to each student. Give the class time to read through the statements in exercise 1. Deal with any vocabulary queries. Students choose the correct adjectives in the statements 1–10. Check the answers with the class, dealing with any pronunciation difficulties.

Answers

1 tiring	6 interesting
2 frightened	7 bored
3 annoyed	8 worried
4 embarrassed	9 exciting
5 irritating	10 surprised

- Focus attention on the underlined sections of the sentences. Elicit different endings for sentence 1 from a range of students. With weaker students, go through all the sentences and check students know which are present and which are past. Give students time to personalize each of the sentences, working individually. Monitor and help as necessary.
- Put students into pairs or small groups to compare their answers. Monitor and help as necessary but do not interrupt or over-correct as this is the fluency stage of the activity. Note down any common errors but feed back on them at a later stage.
- As an extension, get students to write out three of their personalized sentences on strips of paper without writing their name. Students exchange the sentences across the class, read them out, and then try to guess who wrote them.

EVERYDAY ENGLISH (SB p75)

What's the date?

⚠ POSSIBLE PROBLEMS

Students will need regular reviews and practice to be able to say a range of dates fluently.

- One of the main problems with ordinals is pronunciation. The sound /θ/ causes difficulty, and there are a lot of consonant clusters, e.g. *sixth* /sɪksθ/, *twelfth* /twelfθ/. In rapid speech, sounds are often dropped, for example /twelθ/ instead of /twelfθ/ and /fɪθ/ instead of /fɪfθ/.
- Saying dates can also cause problems of form. We can begin with the month (April the third) or the date (the third of April), but in both cases we need to add *the*, which is never written, and in the latter case we need to add *of*, which is also never written. Years beginning 20– can also be read in two ways, e.g. 2012 = *two thousand and twelve* or *twenty twelve*. Students often miss out *and* in dates like 2005 = *two thousand and five*.
- Some languages divide the date differently, e.g. 1999 – **one thousand nine hundred and ninety-nine*, so students need help with dividing the century and years correctly. Note that in American English, 3/8/12 means *the eighth of March 2012*, whereas in British English it means *the third of August 2012*.

1 **T 6.14** **[CD 2: Track 34]** Focus attention on the example. Students work in pairs to match the words to the correct ordinals.

Check the answers by writing the ordinals on the board and eliciting the correct words.

Play the recording, pausing after each number and getting students to repeat chorally and individually. Drill the ordinals, correcting any mistakes carefully.

Answers and tapescript

1st	first	6th	sixth	17th	seventeenth
2nd	second	10th	tenth	20th	twentieth
3rd	third	12th	twelfth	22nd	twenty-second
4th	fourth	13th	thirteenth	30th	thirtieth
5th	fifth	16th	sixteenth	31st	thirty-first

2 Ask *What's the first month?* and elicit *January*. Students continue saying the months in order round the class. If necessary, review the pronunciation and word stress, drilling any difficult words chorally and individually. Check students get the correct word stress in *January* /ˈdʒænjueri/ and *February* /ˈfebrueri/ and that they can distinguish *June* /dʒuːn/ and *July* /dʒuˈlaɪ/. Repeat until students can say all the months quickly and accurately, but don't let this stage go on too long.

3 Focus attention on the example and then get students to ask and answer questions about the other months of the year. You don't need to let this go on for very long.

Focus on the notes about the different ways of writing and say the dates. Highlight on the board how we divide dates beginning 18-, 19-, into two pairs of numbers and give practice of similar dates. Also highlight the use of *and* and get students to practise a range of 20- dates.

4 **T 6.15** **[CD 2: Track 35]** Elicit an example and then get students to practise saying the dates. For the first five dates, they should practise saying them both ways. Students often have a lot of difficulties saying dates, so do the activity as a class and correct mistakes carefully.

Play the recording. Students listen and check.

Answers and tapescript
1 The first of April. April the first.
2 The second of March. March the second.
3 The seventeenth of September. September the seventeenth.
4 The ninth of November. November the ninth.
5 The 29th of February, 1976.
6 December the nineteenth, 1983.
7 The third of October, 1999.
8 May the 31st, 2005.
9 July 15th, 2015.

5 **T 6.16** **[CD 2: Track 36]** Tell students they are going to hear six dates in total and they are given just as dates, not in a sentence or conversation context. Play number one as an example first.

Students listen and write down the dates they hear. Let them check in pairs before checking with the class.

Answers and tapescript
1 October the 31st.
2 The 23rd of June.
3 July the 15th.
4 March the 4th, 2012.
5 The 18th of February, 2020.
6 The 17th of September, 1960.

6 Students work in pairs to ask and answer the questions about dates. Monitor and feed back on any common errors before checking the answers with the whole class.

Answers
(We can only give some of the answers.)
3 The 25th of December.
4 The 14th of February.
7 The 21st century.

7 Give a few examples of dates that are important to you, e.g. your birthday/wedding day, the start of your next holiday, the date of your next dentist's appointment, etc.

Students work in pairs to ask and answer the questions about dates. Monitor and help as necessary. Note any common errors and correct them carefully after a short feedback stage with the whole class.

EXTRA ACTIVITY

You can give more practice on saying years by getting students to talk about key events in their country/around the world and getting the rest of the class to guess the year, e.g. *The Olympics were in Beijing* (2008). *Spain won the World Cup* (2010).

ADDITIONAL MATERIAL

Teacher's Resource Disc
Communicative activity Unit 6 The Everyday English game

Don't forget!

Grammar Reference (SB p188 and Teacher's Resource Disc)
Unit 6

Word list (SB p212 and Teacher's Resource Disc)
Unit 6

Tests (Teacher's Resource Disc)
Unit test 6A
Unit test 6B
Progress test 1 (Units 1–6)
Skills test 2 (Units 1–6)

Video (DVD)
Unit 6 A dancer's life

7 Dates to remember

Past Simple (2) • Questions and negatives • Time expressions • Adverbs • Special occasions

This is the second unit on the Past Simple tense, and it provides further practice and reinforcement of the input in Unit 6, focusing particularly on question and negative forms. The title of this unit is 'Dates to remember' and the topics in the unit lend themselves to practice of the Past Simple and *ago*. The unifying theme of the unit is important moments in the past, with a quiz on important events in the 20th century, a *Speaking* section on talking about my life, and reading texts on progress in aviation.

LANGUAGE INPUT

GRAMMAR

Past Simple – questions and negatives (SB p81)	• Understanding and practising questions and negatives in the Past Simple.
Time expressions (SB p82)	• Understanding and practising *in/at/on* and *ago*.

VOCABULARY

Adverbs (SB p86)	• Understanding and practising regular and irregular adverbs in the context of telling a story.

EVERYDAY ENGLISH

Special occasions (SB p87)	• Understanding and practising the language of talking about special occasions; comparing special occasions in different countries.

SKILLS DEVELOPMENT

READING

Sixty years of flight (SB p84)	• A jigsaw reading about the pioneers of air and space flight.

LISTENING

Alisa's life story (SB p83)	• Listening for key information in a conversation. **T 7.6** (SB p176/TRD)
Noises in the night! (SB p86)	• Listening and ordering adverbs in a short story. **T 7.8** (SB p176/TRD)

SPEAKING

Bill's life (SB p82)	• Information gap about a man's past.
Talking about my life (SB p83)	• Telling your own life story.
Retelling a story (SB p84)	• Retelling the story of the pioneers of air and space flight.

WRITING

Telling a story – Using time expressions (SB pp160–1)	• Reviewing and understanding time expressions, then writing a description of a historical character.

MORE MATERIALS

Photocopiable worksheets – Adverb acting (TB p154/TRD), Celebrations (TRD) **Test** (TRD) **Video** (DVD)

STARTER (SB p80)

⚠ **POSSIBLE PROBLEMS**

The adverb *ago* is introduced in the multiple-choice answers in the *Starter* quiz. *Ago* is used when the point of reference is the present and it means 'before now'. It is used only with past tenses, not present or present perfect tenses. *Ago* can cause problems with word order, as it always comes after an expression of time, which may be different in the students' own language.

Different languages realize this concept in various ways.

two years ago – *vor zwei Jahren* (German)
– *il y a deux ans* (French)
– *hace dos años* (Spanish)
– *due anni fa* (Italian)

Common mistakes

- *I went there ago two weeks.*
- *I went there before two weeks.*
- *My cat died for two years.*

SUGGESTION

You could pre-teach *ago*, especially with weaker classes (see *Possible problems* above). Ask questions such as the following to help show the meaning of *ago*:
When was your last English lesson? (On Tuesday.)
How many days ago was that? (Two days ago.)
When did you last have a holiday? (In June.)
How many months ago was that? (Five months ago.)
When did you last go to the cinema? (Last Friday.)
How many days ago was that? (Five days ago.)

1 Lead in to the theme of the unit by asking *What was the most important event of the 20th century?* Elicit a range of answers from the class.

Briefly review the Past Simple irregular forms in the *Starter* quiz. Say the infinitive and elicit the past (*be – was/were, sell – sold, come – came, have – had*). Also review the way we say dates, e.g. *1903 – nineteen oh three, 1989 – nineteen eighty-nine*, etc.

Focus attention on the photos, ask *Who can you see?* and elicit any people/events that students recognize. Put students in groups of three to do the history quiz. Monitor and help as necessary.

2 **T 7.1** **[CD 2: Track 37]** Play the recording and let students check their answers. Elicit which group won and any reactions to the answers. Ask if students learned anything new.

If you didn't pre-teach *ago*, focus attention on questions 3 and 5 and explain its use now (see *Possible problems* and *Suggestion* above).

Answers and tapescript

1b Henry Ford sold the first Model-T in 1908.
2c The first talking movie, *The Jazz Singer*, was in 1927.
3a Einstein published his theory of relativity about 100 years ago.
4c The Russian Revolution was in 1917.
5b The first non-stop flight around the world was about 60 years ago.
6b About 60 million people died in the Second World War.
7c The Berlin Wall came down in 1989.
8a Man first landed on the moon on July 20, 1969.
9b The Beatles had 17 number one hits in the UK.
10b The twentieth century ended at midnight on 31st December, 2000.

THE GOOD OLD DAYS (SB p81)

Past Simple – questions and negatives

⚠ **POSSIBLE PROBLEMS**

See the introduction to the Past Simple and problems associated with it on TB p64. There are a lot of opportunities to practise positive forms in this unit, but the main focus is on question forms and negatives. These present few problems of concept, but there can inevitably be mistakes of form.

Common mistakes

- *When you went home?*
- *When did you went home?*
- *Where did go Peter?*
- *I no went out last night.*

Write the section heading *The Good Old Days* on the board. Explain that if you talk about *the good old days*, you mean a time in the past when you believe life was better. Ask students *How was life different when your grandparents were young?* Elicit a range of examples about everyday life from the class, e.g. work, school, transport, holidays, etc.

1 **T 7.2** **[CD 2: Track 38]** Focus attention on the photo of the people and ask students to identify Tommy and Bill. Also elicit what is shown in the other photos (*a seaside holiday, an old car, an old black and white TV, an old-fashioned boys' comic*).

Check comprehension of the topics in exercise 1, making sure students don't confuse *housework* and *homework*. Tell students they are going to hear Tommy and Bill talking about the past, but that they don't need to understand every word to be able to do the task. Play the recording through once. Check the answers with the class.

Answers and tapescript

programmes on TV pocket money housework comics holidays

T 7.2

T = Tommy B = Bill

T Granddad, when you were a boy did you have television?
G Of course we had television! But it wasn't a colour TV like now, it was black and white.
T And were there lots and lots of channels? How many TV channels were there?
G Only two. But that was enough! We loved it! And there weren't programmes all day long. Nothing in the morning and nothing in the afternoon!
T Oh, no! What time did programmes begin?
G At 4.30 when children's TV started. There were some great programmes for us children, I can tell you! We had real stories in those days!
T Did your mum and dad give you pocket money?

G Yes, but I worked for it! I cleaned the kitchen and did the washing-up. We didn't have dishwashers in those days!
T That's terrible! How much pocket money did you get?
G My dad gave me sixpence a week. That's two and a half p these days! He didn't give me much, did he? But we bought comics and sweets.
T What sort of comics did you buy?
G Well, I bought a comic called the *Eagle*, and it was full of adventure stories. And *Superman*! That was really exciting!
T Wow! Did you have holidays?
G Yes, but not like nowadays. People didn't go abroad. I never took a plane like people do now! It was too expensive!
T Where did you go on holiday?
G To the seaside, in England.
T How did you get there?
G My father drove. We had a Ford car, a Ford Prefect it was. We went to the same place every year.
T Why did you go to the same place? Why didn't you go somewhere different?
G Because we all liked it there!
T I'm pleased I wasn't alive then! It sounds really boring!
G Oh, no! That's where you're wrong! It was the best fun ever!

2 **T 7.2** **[CD 2: Track 38]** Pre-teach/check *TV channel, sixpence* (a coin worth six old pennies, used in the UK before 1971*), dishwasher, go to the seaside, go abroad*, *what sort?*, *adventure stories* and *drove* (past of *drive*). Focus attention on the example, then play the recording again and get students to complete the questions. Ask them to write down the answer to each question in note form.

T 7.3 **[CD 2: Track 39]** Play **T 7.3** and let students check their answers. Check the answers with the class.

Answers and tapescript
1 How many TV channels were there?
2 **What time** did programmes begin?
3 **How much** pocket money **did** you get?
4 **What sort** of comics **did** you **buy**?
5 **Where did** you **go** on holiday?
6 **How did** you **get** there?
7 **Why did** you go to the same place?

Students ask and answer question 1 in open pairs and then continue the task in closed pairs. With weaker classes, you could write the answers from the script in random order on the board (see *Answers* below). Monitor and help as necessary. If students have problems with the sentence stress and intonation, play the recording again and drill the questions. Check the questions and answers with the class.

Answers
1 How many TV channels were there?
Only two.
2 What time did programmes begin?
At 4.30.
3 How much pocket money did you get?
Sixpence a week.
4 What sort of comics did you buy?
A comic called the *Eagle*, full of adventures stories, and *Superman*.
5 Where did you go on holiday?
To the seaside, in England.
6 How did you get there?
My father drove.
7 Why did you go to the same place?
Because we all liked it there.

3 Focus attention on the example. Point out that the answer is in the negative, and students should focus on the negative things that Bill says. Put students in pairs to try the task. If students can't remember all the information, play **T 7.2** again, or play it again as a check. With weaker students, write the sentences in gapped form on the board, e.g. *There ___ programmes all day long*, etc.

Answers
It wasn't a colour TV like now.
There weren't programmes all day long.
I never took a plane like people do now!
He didn't give me much, did he?
We didn't have dishwashers in those days!
People didn't go abroad.

4 Check comprehension of *theme parks* and *fast food*. Focus attention on the example and then get students to write sentences, using the other prompts. Check the answers, making sure students stress the sentences correctly.

We didn't have computers in those days.

Answers
We didn't have computers in those days.
We didn't have/use mobile phones in those days.
We didn't have/eat fast food in those days.
We didn't have/go to theme parks in those days.

GRAMMAR SPOT (SB p81)

1 Focus attention on the Grammar Spot. Elicit the answers in the *Past Simple* column orally first. Then check the answers with the whole class again, writing the sentences on the board for students to copy.

Answers

Present Simple	Past Simple
I want to go.	I wanted to go.
He loves it.	**He loved it.**
Do you watch TV?	**Did you watch TV?**
Where does she work?	**Where did she work?**
I don't buy sweets.	**I didn't buy sweets.**
They don't go on holiday.	**They didn't go on holiday.**

Remind students that *he/she/it* has a different form in the Present Simple from the other persons, but that all forms in the Past Simple are the same. Highlight the use of *do/does* to form questions in the present and *did* in the past. Then highlight the use of *don't/doesn't* to form negatives in the present and *didn't* in the past.

2 This exercise covers *ago* and the prepositions of time *in/on/at*. Give students time to complete the sentences. Then check the answers. Highlight the position of *ago* after the time expression but don't spend too long on this section, as students will practice time expressions again on SB p82.

Answers
Henry Ford sold the first Model-T **in** 1908.
I was born **on** 17 April 1991.
Our lessons begin **at** nine o'clock.
Tommy saw Bill two days **ago**.

▶▶ Read Grammar Reference 7.1 and 7.2 on SB p189 together in class, and/or ask students to read it at home. Encourage them to ask you questions about it.

EXTRA ACTIVITY

You can give more practice on days, months, and years by getting students to create an 'important year' quiz. Students do the research for world events of the 20th century nationally and internationally for homework. Students then work in small groups and form questions to 'test' the other groups.

Pre-teach expressions like *in the (1950s), in about (1995)* to enable students to give an answer if they can't give an exact year. Get students to ask their questions to another group. Conduct brief feedback with students saying sentences about the most interesting/popular events.

PRACTICE (SB p82)

1 **T 7.4** **[CD 2: Track 40]** This task consolidates the formation of Past Simple questions with question words. Focus attention on the example, then give students time to complete the task.

Play the recording and let students check their answers. Put students in pairs to ask and answer the questions. Monitor and help as necessary. If students have problems with the stress and intonation, play the recording again and drill the questions. Students then repeat the pairwork.

Answers and tapescript
1 Where did you go?
To the shops.
2 When did you go?
Yesterday.
3 Who did you go with?
A friend from work.
4 How did you get there?
By bus.
5 Why did you go?
Because I wanted to.
6 What did you buy?
A shirt.
7 How many did you buy?
Only one.
8 How much did you pay?
£29.

Bill's life

2 Focus attention on the photo and ask students what they can remember about Bill and his life.

Divide the class into pairs, getting students to work with a different partner than in exercise 1. Ask the A students to turn to SB p194 and the B students to SB p197. Demonstrate the activity by getting students to ask and answer the example questions in the Student's Book in open pairs. Encourage a good, wide voice range. Remember that students may have difficulty in selecting the correct short response (*wasn't, didn't*), so you might want to go through them as a class first, especially with weaker groups.

Students work in closed pairs. Monitor and check for accurate question formation and irregular past forms. Correct any grammar and pronunciation errors carefully after the task. Students can check their answers by looking at their partner's text.

Time expressions

⚠ POSSIBLE PROBLEMS

Exercise 3 focuses on preposition + noun collocations, e.g. *on Saturday* and *in summer*. These prepositions can cause a lot of confusion and so will need a lot of practice and regular reviewing.

3 Elicit the first answer as an example (*at*). Monitor and check. If students have problems, give them these rules to help:

on + day/day of the week plus part of the day, e.g. *on Saturday morning*

in + part of the day (except *night*)/month/season/year/century

at + time

This leaves only *at night* and *at the weekend* that do not fit any of the categories.

Check the answers with the class.

Answers

at seven o'clock	**in** the morning
on Saturday	**on** Sunday morning
at night	**in** July
in 2009	**at** the weekend
in summer	**in** the twentieth century

4 Demonstrate the activity by getting students to practise the examples in the Student's Book in open pairs. Students continue in closed pairs asking questions with *When …?*, and answering the questions in the two different ways. Monitor and check that the questions are well formed, and that the voice starts high. Feed back on any common errors in grammar or pronunciation after the pairwork.

5 Give an example by telling students about your day so far and then get students to tell the class about their day. If you have a small group and sufficient time, you could ask each student to give their example. If you have a lot of students, you could get students to work simultaneously in small groups, making sure the students who worked together in exercise 4 talk to different students.

Listening and pronunciation

6 **T 7.5** **[CD 2: Track 41]** This is another discrimination activity. Play sentence 1 as an example. Then play the rest of the recording and ask students to tick the sentences they hear.

Answers and tapescript
1 **a** Where do you want to go?
2 **b** I didn't go to college.
3 **b** Where was he?
4 **a** Do you like it?
5 **a** Why did he come?
6 **a** She doesn't work there.

You can make this receptive exercise productive by modelling each pair of sentences and getting students to repeat chorally and individually. Check for accurate pronunciation and differentiation between the sentences.

SPEAKING (SB p83)

Talking about my life

1 **T 7.6** **[CD 2: Track 42]** Focus attention on the photo of Freddy and Alisa and ask students to identify the two characters. Focus on the top photo and ask students where they think it is. Explain that it shows Alisa when she was a young child.

Explain that Freddy and Alisa are meeting for the first time and Freddy is keen to find out more about Alisa. Give students time to read Freddy's questions. Check comprehension of *grew up*. Give students time to read Alisa's answers through and deal with any vocabulary queries. Check the pronunciation of *St Petersburg* /sənt ˈpiːtəzbɜːg/, *psychology* /saɪˈkɒlədʒi/, *Moscow* /ˈmɒskəʊ/, and *junior* /ˈdʒuːnɪə/. Ask students to read Freddy's first two questions aloud and elicit Alisa's answers from the notes. Students work in pairs to continue working out the wording for Alisa's answers from the notes.

Play the recording and get students to compare their wording. With weaker students, refer them to **T 7.6** on SB p176 to read the script after they have listened.

Tapescript
A = **Alisa** **F** = **Freddy**
F You aren't English, are you, Alisa? Where are you from?
A No, I'm Russian. I was born in St Petersburg.
F Is that where you grew up?
A Yes, I lived with my parents and two sisters in a house near the university. My father worked at the university.
F Oh, how interesting! What was his job? Was he a teacher?
A Yes, he was a professor of psychology.
F Really? And what did your mother do?
A She was a doctor. She worked in a hospital.
F So, where did you go to school?
A I went to a Catholic High School. I was there for ten years, then, when I was 18, I went to university.
F What did you study?
A I studied philosophy and education at university in Moscow. I was there for four years.
F Wow! And did you start work after that?
A No, I travelled in the States for six months. I worked in a summer camp near Yellowstone National Park. It was amazing!
F It sounds great! And what's your job now?
A I work in a junior high school in Paris. I teach Russian and English.
F Your English is really good! Well, it was very nice to meet you, Alisa!
A Nice to meet you too. Bye!

2 Demonstrate the activity with two students. Student A covers the questions and tries to ask them from memory, then Student B covers the answers and tries to answer from memory. Put students in pairs to practise the conversation. Monitor and help as necessary. Check for accurate question formation and use of Past Simple forms. Highlight and correct any Past Simple errors carefully.

3 Write a few notes about your own life on the board, making sure students understand they don't need to give complete sentences, e.g. *born in York, lived with mum – a brother – house in suburbs; mother – worked in office.*

Give students time to write their notes. Monitor and help as necessary. With weaker students, you could write key words on the board as prompts, e.g. *born, family, school, university, first job,* etc.

4 Focus attention on the prompts and elicit possible questions, e.g. *Did you enjoy university? What did you study? How long did you stay there? Who did you meet?* Put students in small groups to compare their life stories. Monitor and help as necessary. Check for accurate question formation and use of Past Simple forms and note any common errors but don't interrupt the groupwork. You can highlight and correct any errors at a later stage.

EXTRA ACTIVITY

Students give a short presentation of the life story of someone they admire. They can do the research for homework and make brief notes about the person's early life, family, education, career, and achievements. Make sure they don't just print out pages of information from Wikipedia or a similar source! Students then take turns to give their presentation to the class (or they can work in groups if you have a large class). The other students should be encouraged to ask questions about the speaker's chosen person. If you have access to video equipment, the talks could be recorded as an added incentive. They can be played in class and commented on and can also be referred back to at a later date to show students how much progress they have made.

READING AND SPEAKING (SB p84)

Sixty years of flight

ABOUT THE TEXT

This is another jigsaw reading task, which gives students an opportunity for not only reading practice, but also some freer speaking. The class divides into two groups and each group reads a different, but similar text about a pioneer of aviation. It's important to remind students to read only their text and to get information about the other text via speaking. If necessary and possible, give the instructions for the jigsaw reading in L1.
The texts continue the theme of keys dates in history with a focus on groundbreaking developments in aviation. They have been chosen to consolidate Past Simple forms and time expressions. The use of a range of numbers in the texts provides for a number referencing task as part of the *Speaking* section.

Louis Blériot /ˈluːi ˈblerɪəʊ/ (1872–1936) was a French aviator, engineer, and inventor. He is best known for his flight over the English Channel, the first crossing of a large body of water in an aircraft, in 1909. The first text in this section is an account of the flight.

Neil Armstrong /niːl ˈɑːmstrɒŋ/ (1930–2012) was one of the three astronauts who took part in the Apollo 11 moon mission in 1969. He is best known as the first man to walk on the moon and for his words 'That's one small step for man, one giant leap for mankind.'

Encourage students to use the context to help them with new vocabulary and to pool knowledge with other students, or use a dictionary. With weaker classes or if you are short of time, ask students to check some of following vocabulary before the lesson:

Homework prior to the lesson

Introduction: *rocket, aviation, phenomenal.*

Louis Blériot: *flight, injury, compass, to take off* (leave the ground), *field, cliff, altitude, foot* (plural *feet*; 1 foot = approximately 30 cm), *fog, to wave a flag, to cut the engine, to crash, pioneer.*

Neil Armstrong: *to lift off, astronaut, to circle, landing, lunar module, to land, to rest, to take a step, leap, mankind, to collect samples, to set up scientific equipment, to put up a flag, earth, inscription, peace, exploration.*

1 Focus attention on the pictures. Check students recognize the two men and can pronounce their names /ˈluːi ˈblerɪəʊ/ and /niːl ˈɑːmstrɒŋ/. Elicit the answers to the questions in exercise 1 and any additional information students know about the two men.

Answers
Louis Blériot made the first air journey in 1909.
Neil Armstrong was the first man on the moon in 1969.

2 Students read the title and introduction. Check the answer to the question.

Answers
The progress in aviation in the 20th century was phenomenal.

3 Put students into two groups, A and B. (With larger classes, you may need to have multiple sets of the two groups.) Assign a text to each group and remind students to read only their text:

Group A – the first air journey

Group B – the first man on the moon

Get students to read their text quite quickly, asking others in their group for help with vocabulary if you didn't pre-teach the items listed in *About the text* or set them for homework. Monitor and help with any queries.

Give students time to read the questions and deal with any queries. With weaker students, briefly review how to read numbers and years. Get them to work in their groups and answer the questions about their text, noting down the answers to each one. Monitor and help as necessary. The answers for each group are provided below for reference but don't check the answers with the whole class at this stage. Ask students to give full statements where possible in order to practise past forms.

Answers
The first air journey
1 The journey began in Calais in the north of France on July 25, 1909.
2 It took 37 minutes.
3 It was 22 miles.
4 He flew at 40 miles per hour.
5 The journey ended in Dover in the south of England.
6 It was the start of modern aviation.

The first man on the moon
1 The journey began at the Kennedy Space Center in Florida on 16 July, 1969 at 9.30 in the morning.
2 It took three days.
3 It was 250,000 miles.
4 They flew at 21,600 miles an hour.
5 The journey ended on a part of the moon called the Sea of Tranquility.
6 It was the beginning of man's exploration of space.

4 Re-group the students, making sure there is an A and a B student in each pair. Demonstrate the activity by getting a pair of students to talk about the person in their text. Students continue talking about the answers to the questions in exercise 3 and exchanging the information about their person. Monitor and help. Also check for correct use of the present and past of *can* and *be*. Note down any common errors and feed back on them at a later stage. Bring the whole class together to conduct the feedback. Encourage students to expand on their answers where applicable.

5 Students now look at both texts to get further information about each journey. Encourage students to help each other with vocabulary, or use a dictionary. With weaker students, you could pre-teach some of the items listed in *About the text* if you didn't set them for homework.

Students work with the same partner to find the answers to the questions. Monitor and help as necessary.

Check the answers with the whole class, again getting students to give full statements where possible in order to practise past forms.

Answers

Blériot

1 He couldn't swim, he couldn't walk very well because of an injury to his leg, and he didn't have a compass.
2 No, it was foggy/there was fog.
3 He saw a French journalist waving a flag.
4 He won £1,000.

Armstrong

5 They were too excited.
6 'That's one small step for man, one giant leap for mankind.'
7 They spent two and a half hours walking on the moon.
8 They left a US flag and an inscription on the moon.

Speaking

6 **T 7.7** **[CD 2: Track 43]** Elicit the reference for the first two numbers, *37* and *4.30* (see *Answers*.) Then give students time to complete the task, working in pairs. Monitor and help as necessary.

Play the recording and let students check their answers.

Answers and tapescript

In 1909 Blériot made the first air journey from Calais to Dover.

1 Blériot was just 37 years old when he flew across the Channel. It took him just 37 minutes.
2 He took off from France at 4.30 in the morning.
3 He flew his plane at 40 miles per hour.
4 He flew at 250 feet above the sea.
5 He won a prize of £1,000.

In 1969 Neil Armstrong became the first man to walk on the moon.

6 Three astronauts flew in Apollo 11. The rocket took three days to get to the moon.
7 It circled the moon 30 times.
8 It landed at 8.17 a.m. on 20 July, 1969.
9 Six hundred million people watched on TV.
10 Neil Armstrong said, 'That's one small step for man, one giant leap for mankind.'
11 The astronauts spent 22 hours on the moon.

SUGGESTION

Students can play a memory game based on the facts and figures in the story. Students take it in turns to say a number and their partner guesses what it refers to. Encourage them to use different numbers from those in exercise 6, e.g.

A 9.30 a.m.

B The time Apollo 11 lifted off.

A Yes, that's right.

7 Ask students to close their books. Elicit some information about the start of each of the journeys from a few students.

Students continue retelling the stories in pairs. With weaker students, write key words and dates on the board as prompts. Monitor and help as necessary but don't interrupt or over-correct. Note any common errors for correction at a later stage.

VOCABULARY AND LISTENING (SB p86)

Adverbs

⚠ POSSIBLE PROBLEMS

The word order with adverbs can cause difficulties. We do not overtly give the rules for the order of adverbs (front position, mid-position, end position), because the rules are rather complicated. We do not suggest that you try to go into them at this stage. You could perhaps point out that adverbs usually follow the verb and object if there is one, whereas adjectives go before the noun (unlike many other languages). Otherwise, let students see how they get on with exercise 4, and simply correct any mistakes.

1 Focus on the sentences and ask students to read them aloud. Explain that an adverb describes a verb. Elicit the adverb and verb in each example (*went well, flew beautifully, quickly went round, finally put up*).

GRAMMAR SPOT (SB p86)

1 Read the notes as a class. Ask students to identify the adjective that each adverb is formed from (*quick, slow, careful, quiet, bad, real*).
   Highlight the spelling change in adjectives ending in *-y* to *-ily*, e.g. *happy – happily, noisy – noisily*.
2 Read the notes as a class. Explain that irregular adverbs are those that don't add *-ly* to the adjective.

▶▶ Read Grammar Reference 7.3 on SB p189 together in class, and/or ask students to read it at home. Encourage them to ask you questions about it.

2 Focus on the first pair of sentences as an example. Elicit the answers (*bad* – adjective, *badly* – adverb). Students then work in pairs. Check the answers with the whole class.

Answers

1 **a** *bad* – adjective
  b *badly* – adverb
2 **a** *carefully* – adverb
  b *careful* – adjective
3 **a** *hard* – adjective
  b *hard/hard* – adverb (*hard* is irregular)

3 This activity focuses on adverbs that collocate with common verbs and phrases. Elicit adverbs that can go with *work* as an example (*work carefully/fast/hard*).

Students work in pairs and continue the activity. Check the answers with the whole class. Elicit which adverbs in the chart are irregular (*fast, late, hard*).

Answers
work carefully/fast/hard
speak English fluently/carefully/fast
breathe hard/deeply (take a lot of air into your lungs)
do my homework carefully/fast/late
drive carefully/fast
arrive late

4 Elicit the correct answer to number 1 as an example. Students put the word in brackets in the correct place in the sentences. Tell them that sometimes more than one answer is possible. Students can work in pairs, or alone and then check with a partner.

Check the answers with the class and elicit if each word in brackets in an adjective or adverb (see *Answers*).

Answers
1 We had a **terrible** holiday in Italy. (adjective)
2 **Unfortunately**, I lost my passport. (adverb)
3 I contacted the police **immediately**. (or I **immediately** contacted ...) (adverb)
4 It was a **long** journey because the traffic was bad. (adjective)
5 Fortunately, Sally's a **good** driver. (adjective)
6 She speaks Italian **well**. (adverb)

Telling a story

5 Point out that adverbs are often used in storytelling to make the actions sound more vivid. Focus on sentence 1 as an example. Elicit a range of other possible endings that will fit with the adverb *fortunately*, e.g. ... *we were inside/ the rain didn't last long.*

Check comprehension of *fast asleep* (in a deep sleep). Students continue working in pairs. Monitor and check if their answers fit with the adverbs given. Where possible, elicit a range of answers for each sentence that highlight the meaning of the adverb. If you want to double-check that students have understood the adverbs, explain or translate them. You could get students to look up the definitions in dictionaries.

Possible answers
1 ... fortunately, I had an umbrella/we were inside/the rain didn't last long.
2 ... unfortunately, I couldn't go/I was ill/I was on holiday.
3 Fortunately, we had enough food/there was enough for everyone/ they weren't very hungry.
4 Unfortunately, it was closed/I couldn't afford them/they didn't have then in my size.
5 ... suddenly the phone rang/I heard a loud noise/the dog started to bark.
6 Immediately, I called an ambulance/went to help/told a police officer.
7 I really liked her/thought she was beautiful/didn't want to see her again.
8 ... went slowly across the room/to the window/down the stairs.

6 **T 7.8** **[CD 2: Track 44]** Focus attention on the picture. Ask *How do you think the man feels? Why?* (scared/frightened/ nervous. He doesn't know who is downstairs.) Play the recording and elicit the answer to the question.

Answers and tapescript
He heard a noise./He heard two men talking.

T 7.8
It was about two o'clock in the morning, and ... suddenly I woke up. I heard a noise. I got out of bed and went slowly downstairs. There was a light on in the living room. I listened carefully. I could hear two men speaking very quietly. 'Burglars!' I thought. Immediately I ran back upstairs and phoned the police. I was really frightened. Fortunately the police arrived quickly. They opened the front door and went into the living room. Then they came upstairs to see me. 'It's all right now, sir,' they explained. 'We turned the television off for you!'

7 **T 7.8** Play the first sentence of the recording again and elicit the first adverb as an example (*suddenly*). Students listen to the rest of the story again and number the adverbs in the correct order. Check the answers.

Answers
8 quickly
4 quietly
2 slowly
1 suddenly
5 immediately
3 carefully
7 fortunately
6 really

8 Pre-teach/check *to wake up, burglar, to come upstairs, to turn off the TV*. In pairs, students retell the story either one sentence at a time each, or one student first, then the other. Remind them to use the order of adverbs to help them. With weaker classes, you could write up key words on the board as prompts.

Photocopiable Activity

UNIT 7 Adverb acting TB p154/TRD

Materials: One copy of the worksheet cut up for each group of three to six students.

Procedure: Explain that students are going to play a miming game to practise adverbs. Demonstrate the activity by miming a simple activity and eliciting the verb + adverb, e.g. *run fast, breathe deeply.*

- Divide the class into teams of three to six students. Put a set of shuffled cards face down on the desk for each team. Explain how to play the game. Students need to give the exact wording on the card. If students suggest, for example, *drive slowly* and the wording required is *drive carefully*, the person miming needs to indicate that a similar word is needed. This helps students focus on suitable adverbs that collocate with the verbs. Students are not allowed to speak but can make noises/give 'sound effects'. They should also give their answer in the form of verb + adverb rather than with *You ...* . (This would require Present Continuous, which is covered later in the course in Unit 10.)
- Ask the first student in each team to stand up, take the first card from the pile and mime the action and adverb for the other students in his/her team to guess.
- When the team guesses the verb + adverb correctly, play passes to the next player. The team that guesses all the cards first wins the game.

WRITING (SB pp160–1)

Telling a story

Using time expressions

The writing section is in the form of a historical narrative. This gives the opportunity to revise and extend students' use of time expressions and also recycle Past Simple regular and irregular forms.

ABOUT THE TEXT

The theme of the narrative is the life of Christopher Columbus /kə'lʌmbəs/ (1451–1506), an Italian sailor and explorer, traditionally thought of as the first European to discover America. Current belief is that the Icelandic Leif /liːf/ Ericson actually preceded Columbus by 500 years. He is referred to in the text as a *Norseman* (an ancient Scandinavian, especially a Viking). Columbus was given money for his travels by the reigning monarchs of Spain at the time, Queen Isabella and King Ferdinand. His three ships were the *Santa Maria*, the *Pinta*, and the *Niña* /'niːnjə/.

There are a number of places referred to the text, so it would be helpful to bring in a map to help students plot Columbus's travels. The pronunciation of the following places may need checking: *Genoa* /'dʒenəʊə/, *Madeira* /mə'dɪərə/, *Cuba* /'kjuːbə/, and *Haiti* /'heɪti/.

Encourage students to use the context to help them with new vocabulary, to pool knowledge with other students, or to use dictionaries. With weaker classes or if you are short of time, ask students to check some of following vocabulary before the lesson:

Homework prior to the lesson

explorer, to discover, sailor, to agree, voyage /'vɔɪɪdʒ/, *to sail, island* /'aɪlənd/, *to hit rocks, gold* (n), *wool, hero, to beg, pain, arthritis.*

The students' writing task is in the form of a project on a historical character from their own country. This will require students doing some research, so make sure you build in time for them to do this, probably for homework.

1 Write the name *Christopher Columbus* on the board and check the pronunciation. Ask *What do you know about him?* and elicit one or two ideas from the class. Focus attention on the pictures on SB p160 and put students in pairs to share their ideas about Columbus's life.

Elicit a range of ideas from the class, but don't confirm or reject them at this stage.

2 Give students time to read lines a–h and deal with any vocabulary queries. If you didn't set the vocabulary in the text for homework (see *About the text*), you could use the pictures to check some of the key words now.

Elicit the answer for line a (3). Students continue matching the lines and pictures, working in pairs. Check the answers with the class.

Answers
a 3 b 1 c 2 d 7 e 5 f 4 g 8 h 6

3 With weaker students, pre-teach/check the main vocabulary if you didn't set it for homework (see *About the text*). Give students time to read the main story. Set a time limit for this of about three minutes so that students focus just on the main ideas. Elicit the missing line for the first gap (b).

Students continue completing the main story with the missing lines, working in pairs. Remind them to use the linking words and punctuation to help them choose the correct lines. Check the answers with the class.

Answers
1 b 2 c 3 a 4 f 5 e 6 h 7 d 8 g

4 Focus attention on the first two time expressions and elicit what they refer to (*for a long time* – the time that people believed that Columbus discovered America, *1451* – the year Columbus was born).

Students work in pairs to continue the referencing task. Monitor and help as necessary. Check the answers with the class.

Answers
For a long time – people believed that Columbus discovered America
in 1451 – Columbus was born
Between 1477 and 1485 – Columbus visited many countries
Finally – after a long time/number of events
on August 3, 1492 – Columbus left Spain
After three months – the number of months they were at sea
Two days later – after two days
Next – the next thing that happened
Then – the next thing that happened
Between 1492 and 1504 – Columbus travelled across the Atlantic
In the last years – at the end of his life
on May 20, 1506 – Columbus died

5 Put students in new pairs and ask them to cover the text of the story. Elicit some information about the start of Columbus's life from a few students.

Students continue retelling the story in pairs. With weaker students, write key words and dates on the board as prompts. Monitor and help as necessary.

Project

Read the task as a class and elicit a few examples of characters students would like to write about. If you have access to computers or encyclopaedias, students can do their research and make notes during class time. If not, set the research for homework.

Put students in pairs to talk about their chosen character. Encourage students to ask each other questions.

Give students time to write their story in class or set it for homework. Remind them to use the writing plan on SB p161.

If possible, display the texts on the classroom wall/noticeboard to allow students to read each other's work. You could ask them to vote for the most interesting story. When you check the students' work, point out errors but allow students to correct them themselves. Try to limit correction to major problems to avoid demoralizing the students.

EVERYDAY ENGLISH (SB p87)

Special occasions

Common expressions for special occasions, such as *Happy birthday* and *Happy New Year* are introduced and practised. This provides the opportunity for some very interesting discussion on cross-cultural traditions, especially if you have a multilingual class or if some of your students know foreign countries. What occasions different nationalities celebrate, and how they celebrate them, is a source of great interest to most students.

BACKGROUND NOTES

Here are some notes on how some British people celebrate the special days (though not all British people, of course).

Birthday
There is often a birthday cake, with candles to be blown out and everyone sings *Happy birthday*. People send birthday cards, and there is perhaps a birthday party with friends.

Mother's Day
This is on a Sunday towards the end of March (the fourth Sunday in Lent). Children give cards and a present such as some flowers or chocolates.

Wedding day
People get married in a church for a religious ceremony or a registry office (or other local authority approved premises) for a civil ceremony. Rice or confetti is thrown at the bride and groom to wish them luck, and the bride often carries a horseshoe, again to symbolize good luck. There is a party afterwards called a reception, and the bride and groom may go on a holiday called a honeymoon.

Hallowe'en /hæləʊ'iːn/
This is the evening of 31 October, when it was believed that the spirits of dead people appeared. Customs associated with Hallowe'en in Britain and the US are fancy dress parties, where people dress up as ghosts, witches, etc. Children often celebrate by wearing masks or costumes and going 'trick or treating' – going from house to house collecting sweets, fruit, or money.

Easter /'iːstə/ **Day**
Although there are no fixed traditions of ways to celebrate Easter, a lot of people give chocolate Easter eggs, especially to children. Some people have Easter eggs hunts and young children believe that the eggs were hidden by the Easter Bunny.

New Year's Eve
In Scotland this is called *Hogmanay* and it is a more important celebration than in the rest of Britain. People go to parties and wait for midnight to come, when they wish each other *Happy New Year*. In London many thousands of people celebrate New Year in Trafalgar Square where they can hear Big Ben (the clock on the Houses of Parliament) strike midnight.

Valentine's /'væləntainz/ **Day**
People send Valentine cards to the person they love. Cards are usually sent anonymously! Men may give a gift of flowers or chocolates to the woman they love.

Christmas /'krisməs/ **Day**
This is the 25 December, the main day for celebrating Christmas in Britain, when presents are exchanged. There is a large lunch, traditionally with turkey and Christmas pudding, which is made from dried fruit. People decorate the house, and have a Christmas tree. Young children believe that Santa Claus (or Father Christmas) visits during the early hours of Christmas morning and leaves presents by the children's beds or under the tree.

1 Focus attention on the photos and the list of days in the box. Elicit the first special day (*birthday*) and then let the students continue in pairs. Students match the special days to the photos.

Check the answers with the class, dealing with any pronunciation difficulties as you go.

Answers
(in order from left to right)
wedding day
Mother's Day
Valentine's Day
Easter Day
Hallowe'en
birthday
New Year's Eve
Christmas Day

2 Check pronunciation of *special* /'speʃəl/ and *fireworks* /'faɪəwɜːks/. Ask your students which special days they celebrate in their country. Elicit some examples of how they celebrate, using the ideas given and their own ideas. Students work in small groups to describe to each other how they celebrate. Monitor and help as necessary.

Conduct a brief feedback session with the whole class. Write new vocabulary on the board for students to record in their vocabulary notebooks.

3 Students work in pairs to complete the conversations with words from exercise 1. Also give them time to name each of the occasions.

4 **T 7.9** **[CD 2: Track 45]** Students listen and check their answers. Elicit the name of each occasion/day.

Using the recording as a model, drill the sentences in conversation 3, paying particular attention to stress and intonation. If students sound 'flat', exaggerate the voice range and get them to repeat again. Ask three students to take a role each and act out the conversation to the class.

Put students in pairs and ask them to choose a different conversation (avoid 1, as it is a song). With weaker students allocate conversations 2, 3, 4, 6, and 7. Students practise until they know their lines by heart, paying close attention to stress and intonation. Students take it in turns to act out their conversations to the class.

Answers and tapescript

1 **birthday**
Happy **birthday** to you.
Happy **birthday** to you.
Happy **birthday**, dear Grandma.
Happy **birthday** to you.

2 **Valentine's Day**
A Did you get any **Valentine** cards?
B Yes, I did. Listen to this.
Roses are red. Violets are blue.
*You are my **Valentine**.*
And I love you.
A Wow! Do you know who it's from?
B No idea!

3 **Christmas Day**
C Mummy! Daddy! Wake up! It's **Christmas**!
D Mm? What time is it?
C It's morning! Look. Father **Christmas** gave me this present!
D Oh, that's lovely! Merry **Christmas**, darling!

4 **wedding day**
F Congratulations! It's great news!
G Thank you very much. We're both very happy.
F So, when's the big day?
H Pardon?
F Your **wedding** day! When is it?
G December the 12th. You'll get an invitation!

5 **New Year's Eve**
I It's midnight! Happy **New Year**, everyone!
JKL **Happy New Year**!

6 **Mother's Day**
C Wake up, Mummy! Happy **Mother's Day**!
D Thank you, darling. Oh, what beautiful flowers! And a cup of tea! Well, aren't I lucky!
C And we made you a card! Look!
D It's beautiful! What clever children you are!

7 **weekend**
M Thank goodness it's Friday!
N Yeah! Have a good **weekend**!
M Same to you.

ADDITIONAL MATERIAL

Teacher's Resource Disc
Communicative activity Unit 7 Celebrations

Don't forget!

Grammar Reference (SB p189 and Teacher's Resource Disc)
Unit 7

Word list Unit 7 (SB p214 and Teacher's Resource Disc)
Unit 7

Test (Teacher's Resource Disc)
Unit test 7A
Unit test 7B

Video (DVD)
Unit 7 A special occasion

8 Eat in or out?

Count and uncount nouns • *some* and *any* • *I like* and *I'd like* • *How much?* or *How many?* • Food and drink • Shopping in the High Street

The theme of this unit is food and drink, which lends itself to the presentation and practice of the target items – count and uncount nouns with a review of the determiners *some* and *any* (in Unit 4 they were introduced mainly with count nouns only) and a focus on *much/many*. The verb *like* is contrasted with *would like*, and the vocabulary and *Everyday English* focus is on shopping in the High Street. The skills material includes a reading text on the history of the sandwich, and a listening task on *World Sandwich Week*! There is also a project on students' favourite recipes.

LANGUAGE INPUT

GRAMMAR

Count and uncount nouns – *some, any, a lot of* … (SB p93)	• Understanding and practising count and uncount nouns with determiners *some/any/a lot of*.
I like … and *I'd like* … (SB p93)	• Understanding and practising the difference between *I like* … for general references and *I'd like* … in requests.
some/any, much/many (SB p94)	• Understanding and practising *some/any* and *much/many* to talk about number and quantity.

VOCABULARY

Daily needs (SB p98)	• Understanding the vocabulary of, and practising the pronunciation of, everyday objects.

EVERYDAY ENGLISH

Shopping in the High Street (SB p99)	• Understanding and practising the language of shopping and ordering in a café; practising sounding polite.

SKILLS DEVELOPMENT

READING

Everybody likes a sandwich! (SB p96)	• An article on the history of the sandwich.

LISTENING

What's your favourite sandwich? (SB p97)	• Listening for key information to complete a chart. **T 8.9** (SB p177/TRD)

SPEAKING

How is it made? (SB p95)	• Guessing how to make a dish.
Project (SB p95)	• Researching and presenting your favourite recipe.
What do you think? (SB 97)	• Discussing favourite types of sandwich.

WRITING

Two emails – Informal and more formal (SB pp162–3)	• Understanding the content and comparing the register of two emails, then writing a thank-you email.

MORE MATERIALS

Photocopiable worksheets – *How much/many* … ? (TB p155/TRD), Word stress dominoes (TRD) **Tests** (TRD) **Video** (DVD)

STARTER (SB p92)

> ⚠ **POSSIBLE PROBLEMS**
>
> **Count and uncount nouns** Students often need help with the concept of count and uncount nouns, and need regular practice with the articles and determiners that can be used with them. Students also need to understand that a lot of nouns can be both countable and uncountable, depending on the context in which they are used, e.g.
>
> *Two coffees, please.* (countable and meaning 'two cups of coffee')
>
> *Coffee is expensive.* (uncountable and meaning 'coffee in general')
>
> Students can also have problems with interference from their own language, where some nouns which are uncount in English may be countable. This can lead to misuse, e.g.
>
> **They gave me advices.*
>
> **I'd like some informations.*
>
> ***some/any*** *Some* and *any* were first introduced in Unit 4, mainly with count nouns. This unit introduces and practises them with uncount nouns as well. The often-repeated rule that *some* is used in positive sentences and *any* in questions and negatives is not entirely true, but is still useful at this level.
>
> Students may need ongoing help with the weak pronunciation of *some* /səm/.

1 Check comprehension of *to be a fussy eater*. Answer the questions in exercise 1 about yourself, writing examples of food you didn't like on the board. Ask students to write down their own examples. Then elicit a range of answers from the class, checking and drilling pronunciation as necessary. Revise the alphabet by getting students to spell key words. Build up a vocabulary list on the board and get students to copy it into their vocabulary notebooks. With weaker students, you could brainstorm food vocabulary with the class at the start of the activity and write key words on the board before looking at the questions.

2 **T 8.1** **[CD 2: Track 46]** Elicit one or two examples with the class. Students match the food and drink in columns **A** and **B** with the pictures.

Play the recording and get students to listen and follow in their books. Students then say the list aloud. Drill the pronunciation of any words students find difficult, highlighting the word stress as necessary.

Answers and tapescript

A		B	
l tea	**w** ice-cream	**i** bananas	**e** onions
p coffee	**k** apple juice	**a** apples	**c** tomatoes
j wine	**h** bread	**f** strawberries	**q** eggs
v cheese	**u** milk	**t** potatoes	**b** biscuits
n yoghurt	**o** chocolate	**r** carrots	**g** crisps
d pasta	**s** broccoli	**x** peas	**m** chips

3 Ask students to identify which list (**A** or **B**) has plural nouns (list **B**). Put students into pairs to complete the sentences with *is* or *are*. Check the answers and elicit that we can't count *broccoli* or *apple juice*, but we can count *tomatoes* and *apples*.

Read Grammar Reference 8.1 on SB p189 together in class and/or ask students to read it at home. Encourage them to ask you questions about it.

Answers

Broccoli **is** good for you.
Tomatoes **are** good for you.
Apple juice **is** delicious.
Apples **are** delicious.

WHO'S A FUSSY EATER? (SB p93)

Count and uncount nouns – *some, any, a lot of …*

The aim of this section is to revise count and uncount nouns and provide practice of *some*, *any*, and *a lot of*.

1 **T 8.2** **[CD 2: Track 47]** Focus attention on the photos. Explain that Duncan and Nick are flatmates and that they are talking about what they like and don't like to eat and drink, and what they liked and didn't like as children. Pre-teach/check *kid* (informal for *child*), *green vegetables*, and *fruit*. Play the recording as far as *Ah – you were a fussy eater!* Elicit who was a fussy eater (*Duncan*). Play the full recording and ask students to note down the foods that Duncan did and didn't like when he was a child.

Give students time to check in pairs before checking with the class.

Elicit the answer to the question about where Duncan and Nick go to eat.

Answers and tapescript

Duncan is the fussy eater.
He didn't like green vegetables, other vegetables (apart from potatoes), bananas, coffee, or tea.
He liked chips, some fruit, fruit juice, ice-cream, chocolate, crisps, biscuits, and pasta (with tomato sauce).
They go to Romano's to eat.

T 8.2

D = Duncan N = Nick

N Oh, good, we have some tomatoes.
D Sorry Nick. I don't like them.
N Come on Duncan! Tomatoes are good for you. I didn't like them much when I was a child, but I love them now.
D Hmm – I didn't like a lot of things when I was a kid.
N Ah – you were a fussy eater! What didn't you like?
D I didn't like any green vegetables.
N Did you like any vegetables at all?
D Only potatoes. I loved chips.
N What about fruit? Did you like fruit?
D I liked some fruit, but not all. I didn't like bananas. I liked fruit juice. I drank a lot of apple juice.
N And now you drink beer and wine!

D Yeah – and coffee. But I didn't like coffee or tea when I was a kid.
N So what were your favourite foods?
D I liked ice-cream, chocolate, crisps, biscuits, especially chocolate biscuits. Er- you know, I liked all the usual things kids like.
N All the unhealthy things!
D I liked pasta too. Pasta with tomato sauce. I love that!
N Tomato sauce!? But you don't like tomatoes.
D Tomato sauce is different. Hey, let's not eat in tonight. Let's go out to Romano's.
N Romano's – a great idea! It's my favourite Italian restaurant.

2 **T 8.2** **[CD 2: Track 47]** With weaker classes, give students time to read the gapped lines and try to remember some of the answers before they listen. Focus attention on the example. Play the recording and get students to complete the lines. Check the answers with the class.

Answers
1 Oh, good, we have some tomatoes.
2 I didn't like a **lot** of things when I was a kid.
3 I didn't like **any** green vegetables.
4 Did you like **any** vegetables at all?
5 I liked **some** fruit, but not all.
6 I drank a **lot** of apple juice.
7 I liked **all** the usual things kids like.

GRAMMAR SPOT (SB p93)

Look at the examples and question as a class. Allow students time to think about their answers before checking with the class.

Answer
We use *some* in positive sentences with both singular uncount nouns (*wine*) and plural count nouns (*tomatoes*).
We use *any* in negative sentences and questions with both singular uncount nouns (*beer*, *coffee*) and plural count nouns (*bananas*, *apples*).

►► Read Grammar Reference 8.2 on SB p189 together in class and/or ask students to read it at home. Encourage them to ask you questions about it.

EXTRA ACTIVITY

Give some examples of your own likes and dislikes, now and as a child. Students look at the lists of food and drink on SB p92 and decide what they liked and didn't like as a child, and what they like and don't like now. They then work in pairs and talk about their likes and dislikes. Monitor and check. Get students to feed back briefly, e.g. *Ana likes fruit, but I don't.*

I like ... and I'd like ...

⚠ POSSIBLE PROBLEMS

like* and *would like *Would like* is introduced for the first time, and this is the first time that students have seen the modal verb *would*. It is easy for students to confuse *like* and *would like*. Here are some common mistakes.

**Do you like a coffee?*

**I like a cup of tea, please.*

*Are you hungry? *You like a sandwich?*

It is relatively easy for students to perceive the difference between a general expression of liking and a specific request, but be prepared to deal with mistakes on an ongoing basis as students confuse *like* and *would like*, and especially the two auxiliary verbs *do* and *would*.

***some* in requests and offers** It is quite a subtle concept for students to grasp that *some* can be used in questions when there is no doubt about the existence of the thing requested or offered. The use of L1 might help to clarify this.

Students may hear *Would you like a tea or a coffee?* instead of *Would you like some tea or coffee?* The meaning here is *Would you like a (cup of) tea or a (cup of) coffee?* and that is why the article is used with the uncount noun. This form is a feature of spoken English, so encourage students to use *some* with plural and uncount nouns in offers and requests.

As in Unit 4, we do not suggest that you explore the use of *any* to mean 'it doesn't matter which', as in *Take any drink you want.*

3 **T 8.3** **[CD 2: Track 48]** Focus attention on the photo of Duncan and Nick in the Italian restaurant. Pre-teach/check *spaghetti Bolognese* (spaghetti with a thick tomato and minced meat sauce), *sparkling/still/tap water*. Play the recording through once and get students to follow in their books.

4 Give students time to answer the true-false questions, working in pairs.

Answers
1 True
2 False. He really likes spaghetti.
3 False. Duncan would like a glass of red and Nick would like a glass of white wine.
4 True
5 False. They ask for some water.
6 False. He orders some tap water.

5 Students work in their pairs to practise the conversation in exercise 3. Monitor and check. If students have problems with pronunciation, play the recording again and drill difficult lines as a class.

Students work with a new partner and practise the conversation again, changing the things they order.

SUGGESTION

You could record students' conversations on audio/video equipment and then play them back for intensive correction. Pay attention to all aspects of pronunciation, getting students to repeat as often as necessary to improve their performance.

GRAMMAR SPOT (SB p93)

1 Look at the *Grammar Spot* questions as a class. This section is intended to guide students to the difference between *I like* and *I'd like*. Do not attempt to go into a full presentation of the uses of *would* at this stage, just introduce it as a polite way of making requests and offers.

Answer
Would you like some wine? and *I'd like some red wine* mean *Do you want ...* and *I want ...*

Point out that when we talk about things in general, we do not use an article/determiner with plural count nouns or with uncount nouns. You could write these examples on the board:

I like biscuits. (NOT **I like some biscuits.*)

I don't like tea very much. (NOT **I don't like any tea very much.*)

Do you like Chinese food? (NOT **Do you like any Chinese food?*)

2/3 These sections demonstrate the special use of *some* in requests and offers, and *any* in other questions and negatives. Read the notes as a class.

►► Read Grammar Reference 8.3 on SB p189 together in class, and/or ask students to read it at home. Encourage them to ask you questions about it.

PRACTICE (SB p94)

Would/Do you like ...?

1 **T 8.4** **[CD 2: Track 49]** Elicit the answer to question 1 as an example with the whole class. Students work in pairs or small groups to choose the correct form.

Play the recording and let students listen and check. Students practise the conversations in pairs. Monitor and check for accurate pronunciation. Drill any difficult lines with the class as necessary.

Answers and tapescript
1 **A** Excuse me, are you ready to order?
B Yes. **I'd like** a steak, please.
2 **A** **Would** you like a sandwich?
B No, thanks. I'm not hungry.
3 **A** **Do** you like Ella?
B Yes. She's very nice.
4 **A** **Would** you like a cold drink?
B Yes, please. Do you have any apple juice?
5 **A** Can I help you?
B Yes. **I'd like** some stamps, please.
6 **A** What sports do you do?
B Well, **I like** skiing very much.

2 **T 8.5** **[CD 2: Track 50]** Play the first question and elicit the correct reply as an example. Students listen to the rest of the questions and complete the exercise. (See *Answers and tapescript* below for the questions.)

T 8.6 **[CD 2: Track 51]** Play the recording for students to listen and check their answers. Then get them to practise the conversations in pairs.

Answers and tapescript
1 **A** What kind of wine do you like?
B **I like French wine, especially red wine.**
2 **A** Would you like a cheese and ham sandwich?
B **Just cheese, please. I don't like ham.**
3 **A** Who's your favourite author?
B **I like books by Patricia Cornwell.**
4 **A** What do you want for your birthday?
B **I'd like a new computer.**
5 **A** Do you have any pets?
B **No, but I'd like a dog.**
6 **A** Do you want some ice-cream for dessert?
B **No, thanks. I don't like ice-cream.**

a or *some*?

3 The aim of this exercise is to consolidate the concept of count and uncount nouns and practise the use of *a/an* and *some*. Use the section to check how well students have grasped the concept and be prepared to explain further, using L1 if possible.

Focus attention on the examples. Students then work in pairs to write *a*, *an*, or *some* before the nouns.

Answers

1 a banana	7 **an** apple
2 some fruit	8 **some** toast
3 **an** egg	9 **some** sandwiches
4 **some** bread	10 **some** biscuits
5 **some** milk	11 **a** cup of coffee
6 **some** meat	12 **some** apple juice

EATING IN (SB p94)

some/any, much/many

> **NOTE**
> At the end of this section, there is a project activity on favourite recipes. You will need to build in time for students to do some research on their chosen recipe and make notes on the ingredients and method of preparation, probably for homework. Students can also bring in pictures of their chosen dish, if available.

The aim of this section is to practise *some/any* and introduce *(not) much/many* with both count and uncount nouns. The question forms *How much ...?* and *How many ...?* are also practised.

1 Focus attention on the photo and ask students what they can remember about Duncan and Nick (*They are students and flatmates. They both like Italian food*, etc.). Ask *Who do they want to cook for?* (their girlfriends).

Focus attention on the photo of the Cottage Pie. Explain that this is a traditional dish often served as a family meal or as part of a pub menu. Give students time to read the list of ingredients. Deal with any vocabulary queries, using the photos to help. Cheddar cheese is a type of hard yellow cheese, originally from the village of Cheddar in the county of Somerset, south-west England. Check pronunciation of *thyme* /taɪm/ and that students recognize the abbreviations *tbsp* (*tablespoon*), *g* (*gram*), and *ml* (*millilitre*).

Elicit the ingredients needed for the dish, as listed in the recipe.

2 Focus attention on the photo of the ingredients on the worktop. Read the examples with the class. Drill the pronunciation if necessary, highlighting the weak pronunciation of *some* /səm/.

Put students in pairs to continue talking about the ingredients for the recipe. Monitor and check carefully for correct use of *many* with count nouns and *much* with uncount nouns. If students have major problems, go through the *Grammar Spot* with the class, then get them to repeat the pairwork.

Check the answers with the class. Correct any mistakes carefully. With weaker students, drill the sentences again by saying the ingredients in random order and getting students to say the sentences, e.g. *potatoes – there aren't many potatoes.*

Answers
These are given in the same order as the ingredients in the recipe.
There are some onions.
There isn't any minced beef.
There isn't much oil.
There aren't any carrots.
There aren't many tomatoes.
There isn't much thyme.
There isn't any salt and pepper.
There aren't many potatoes.
There isn't much butter.
There isn't much cheese.
There's some milk.

3 **T 8.7** **[CD 2: Track 52]** Explain that Duncan and Nick are talking about the ingredients they have and don't have for the Cottage Pie. Pre-teach/check *herbs, to be left (in the bottle).*

Read the first four lines as a class, including the example. Ask *Who can cook?* (Nick). Give students time to complete the conversation, working individually. Let students check in pairs before playing the recording as a final check. If students query the use of *ones* in lines 9 and 12 of the conversation, elicit the food items that it refers back to each time (*potatoes, tomatoes*).

Put students in pairs to practise the conversation. Monitor and check. If students have problems with pronunciation and intonation, play the recording again and get students to repeat key sentences before practising the conversation again.

Answers and tapescript
N = Nick D = Duncan
N This recipe for Cottage Pie looks easy.
D But I can't cook at all.
N Don't worry. I really like cooking. Now, vegetables – do we have any onions? Are there **any** carrots or potatoes?
D Well, there are **some** onions, but there aren't **any** carrots, and we don't have **many** potatoes. How **many** do we need?
N Four big ones.
D OK, put potatoes on your list.
N And how **many** tomatoes are there?
D Only two small ones. Put them on the list too.
N How **much** milk is there?
D There's a lot, but there isn't **much** cheese or butter.
N OK, cheese and butter. What about herbs? Do we have **any** thyme?
D Yeah, that's fine. But don't forget the minced beef. How **much** do we need?
N 500 grams. Now, is that everything?
D Er – I think so. Do we have oil? Oh, yeah, there's **some** left in the bottle.
N OK, first shopping, then I'll give you a cooking lesson!
D I'd like that. I hope the girls like Cottage Pie.
N Everyone likes Cottage Pie!

GRAMMAR SPOT (SB p95)

1/2 Read the Grammar Spot as a class. Also point out to students the use of *many* with the plural verb *are* and *much* with the singular verb *is*.

3 Explain to students that *a lot of* is used with both count and uncount nouns. It describes a large quantity or amount of something.

►► Read Grammar Reference 8.4 on SB p189 together in class, and/or ask students to read it at home. Encourage them to ask you questions about it.

SUGGESTION

If you think students need further controlled practice in the use of *Is/Are there any* + count/uncount nouns as well as *How much/many*, write some of the following prompts on the board about the Cottage Pie recipe:

eggs?	oil?	how/cheese?	how/carrots?
vegetables?	wine?	how/butter?	how/potatoes?
herbs?	pasta?	how/milk?	how/onions?

Elicit examples in open pairs, e.g. *Are there any eggs in the recipe? No, there aren't. Is there any oil? Yes, there is. How much cheese is there? 100 grams.*

Students then continue in closed pairs. Monitor and check for the accurate use of *some/any* and *much/many* and be prepared to correct any mistakes carefully.

PRACTICE (SB p95)

much or *many*?

1 Pre-teach/check *petrol*. Focus attention on the example. Ask *Why 'much', not 'many'?* (*toast* is an uncount noun). Students work in pairs to complete the questions using *much* or *many*.

Answers
1 How much toast would you like?
2 How **much** yoghurt do we have left?
3 How **many** people were at the wedding?
4 How **much** money do you have in your pocket?
5 How **much** petrol is there in the car?
6 How **many** children does your brother have?
7 How **many** days is it until your birthday?
8 How **much** time do you need for this exercise?

2 **T 8.8** **[CD 2: Track 53]** Pre-teach/check *slice* and *raspberry*. Focus attention on the example. Students choose an answer for each question in exercise 1.

Play the recording and let students check their answers. Put students in pairs to practise the questions and answers. If students have problems with pronunciation, drill some of the exchanges chorally and individually.

Answers and tapescript
a 4 b 7 c 1 d 2 e 8 f 6 g 3 h 5

1 **A** How much toast would you like?
B Just one slice, please.
2 **A** How much yoghurt do we have left?
B Not a lot. Just one strawberry and one raspberry.
3 **A** How many people were at the wedding?
B About 150.
4 **A** How much money do you have in your pocket?
B Just 50p.
5 **A** How much petrol is there in the car?
B It's full.
6 **A** How many children does your brother have?
B Two. A boy and a girl.
7 **A** How many days is it until your birthday?
B It's tomorrow!
8 **A** How much time do you need for this exercise?
B Two more minutes.

Check it

3 Students work in pairs to complete the task.

Elicit a range of answers from the class for each sentence. If there is disagreement, write the relevant sentences on the board and get students to explain the reason for their choice. Encourage students to correct each other where possible.

Answers
1 How many **eggs** do you need?
2 We don't have much **cheese** left.
3 I'm hungry. I'd like a **sandwich**, please.
4 I'd like **some** fruit, please.
5 I don't like **broccoli**.
6 Would you like some **tea**?
7 How many **cousins** do you have?
8 We have **no** homework today.

Speaking

4 Demonstrate the verbs in the box with simple mimes. Focus attention on the example and then elicit possible ways of continuing the recipe.

Put students into groups of three or four. Remind them to refer to the ingredients list to make sure they have included everything. Monitor and help, writing up any additional cooking verbs on the board as necessary.

Refer students to the recipe on SB p201. Deal with any vocabulary queries and establish how well students predicted the recipe. Also ask if they would like to cook the recipe at home and elicit reasons why/why not.

Project

Make sure students have brought along their notes for their recipe. Put students into groups of three. In a multilingual class, ask students from different countries to work together to encourage an exchange of information.

Students take it in turns to talk about their recipe. Make sure they use their notes just as a reference and don't read out the complete text of their recipe. Encourage the other students to ask questions. Monitor and help as necessary. Check for accurate use of *some/any*, *much/many*, food vocabulary, and cooking verbs. Note down any common errors but don't feed back on these until after the groupwork.

Ask students to choose their favourite recipe from their group and give reasons for their choice.

EXTRA ACTIVITY

If appropriate, you could get students to produce written work and illustrations/photos for their project and display them on the classroom wall. If you have access to a computer network, upload the project work and make it available to your students and other classes in your school. It can also be uploaded onto the Internet and made available to everyone.

SUGGESTION

You could ask students to roleplay Duncan and Nick shopping for the Cottage Pie at a local market. You can do this before the *Everyday English* section on SB p99 to help you assess how well students can deal with the language of shopping, or afterwards as consolidation.

Photocopiable Activity

UNIT 8 How much/many ...? TB p155/TRD

Materials: One copy of the worksheet cut up for each pair of students.

Procedure: Explain that students are going to practise talking about food in a recipe activity. Pre-teach/check the new ingredients in the activity, drilling the pronunciation as necessary: *cloves of garlic*, *ginger* /ˈdʒɪndʒə/, *chicken stock*, *dried apricots* /ˈeɪprɪkɒts/, *almonds* /ˈɑːməndz/, *olive oil*, *anchovies* /ˈæntʃəvɪz/, *couscous* /ˈkuːskuːs/, and *crusty bread*. Also check the cooking verbs *heat*, *mash*, *peel*, *cover*, *sprinkle*, and *serve*.

- Write the following gapped question on the board *______ oil and ______ tuna steaks do you need?* Elicit the answers to review *How much* + uncount nouns (*oil*) and *How many* + count nouns (*tuna steaks*). Also review the abbreviations *tbsp (tablespoon)*, *g (gram)*, *tsp (teaspoon)*, and *ml (millilitre)*.
- Divide the class into A/B pairs. Ideally, ask students to sit face to face so that they can't see each other's recipe. Hand out the relevant half of the worksheet to each student. Demonstrate the activity by getting a Student B to ask a Student A the first question in the ingredients list *How much oil do you need? One tablespoon.* Also elicit the first question in numbered steps *What do you fry in the oil? The onion and garlic.* With weaker students, you could put all the A and B students into groups to prepare the questions before they do the information exchange. Students continue asking and answering to complete the *Aromatic chicken* recipe. Remind them not to show each other their recipe but to exchange the information by asking and answering. Monitor and check for accurate question formation use of *How much/many ...?* Note any common errors to feed back on at the end of the activity.
- For exercise 2, students change roles and Student A asks Student B about the recipe for *Fresh tuna with tomatoes.* Continue monitoring and noting common errors but don't feed back on them at this stage.
- Ask students to put their worksheets together to check their answers.
- For exercise 3, bring the class back together to discuss which recipe they would like to try. Elicit why they wouldn't like to try the other recipe. Also elicit example of dishes students cooked at home and if they were successful.
- Highlight any common errors from the pairwork stage and get students to self-correct where possible.

WRITING (SB pp162–3)

Two emails

Informal and more formal

This section of the writing syllabus allows students to look at aspects of tone and register by comparing two thank-you emails, one to a boyfriend and the other to the boyfriend's parents. Students focus on the choice of greeting and sign off in the emails as well the overall tone of the language and use of emoticons (taken from *emotion* and *icon* – a symbol that shows how you feel, e.g. :-) means happy or friendly).

1 Focus attention on the photo of Duncan on SB p162 and ask students what they can remember about him, e.g. *He's a student. He shares a flat with Nick. They prepared Cottage Pie for their girlfriends.* Now focus attention on the photo of Sally and read the instructions for exercise 1 with the class. Ask *Where is Sally?* (Edinburgh) *And Duncan?* (Manchester). Focus attention in the email and ask *Why is Sally writing to Duncan?* (To say thank you for her visit to Manchester.) With weaker students of if you are short of time, pre-teach/check *Just kidding (= (I'm) only joking)*, *starving hungry*, *coach* (n), *disgusting*, *to be a star* (=someone who does something kind and helpful), *to miss someone.* Give students time to read Sally's email to Duncan. Set a time limit of one to two minutes so that students don't spend too long on it.

Put students in pairs to discuss their answers. Monitor and help as necessary. Check the answers with the class.

Answers

1 Yes, she did.
2 She says the meal was fantastic, but we know from p95 that Duncan says he can't cook.
3 She wants to cook Cottage Pie for her friends in Edinburgh.
4 She travelled by coach.
5 She danced all night and went to bed at 4 a.m.
6 He got up early to take Sally to the coach station.
7 She would like to see him soon.
8 It's informal.
9 She visited him before their exams.

2 Focus attention on Sally's second email and read the instructions for exercise 2 with the class. Ask *Who is the email to?* (Duncan's parents), *When did Sally write it?* (21st April), *Was that before or after the email to Duncan* (before).

Give students time to read Sally's email to Duncan's parents. Again, set a time limit of one to two minutes so that students don't spend too long on it.

Put students in pairs to discuss their answers. Monitor and help as necessary. Check the answers with the class. If appropriate, ask students to refer to relevant parts of the email to support their answers (see text in brackets in *Answers*).

Answers

1 She visited them the weekend of 19th and 20th April. (She sent the email on 21st April and talks about 'last weekend' in the message.)
2 Yes, it was. (She says in the message, 'I was so pleased to meet you at last.')
3 She ate good food ('The meal you made was delicious.') and went for a walk. ('I also enjoyed our walk.')
4 No, she didn't. (the exams finish at the end of June but she went to see him the weekend of 1st and 2nd May. We know this because she sent her thank-you email to him on 3rd May.)

3 Elicit the difference in tone in the beginning and endings of each email as an example (to Duncan: *Hi/Lots of love*; to Mr and Mrs Owen: *Dear Mr and Mrs Owen/Best wishes*). Sally also uses a short form of her name (*Sal*) to Duncan and adds some kisses but uses her full name and leaves out the kisses in the more formal email to his parents.

Put students in pairs to compare the main paragraphs of the two emails. With weaker students, you could put prompts on the board to help, e.g. information included/omitted, full sentences, direct language, informal language, adjectives, linking words, expressive language/emoticons, etc. Monitor and help as necessary.

Elicit the main differences, getting students to refer to the two emails to give examples.

Possible answers

Beginnings/endings: The email to Duncan: *Hi/Lots of love. Sal xxxx*
The email to Mr and Mrs Owen: *Dear Mr and Mrs Owen/Best wishes, Sally* (no kisses)
Content: The email to Duncan refers to dancing all night and going to bed late. Sally teases Duncan a bit about his cooking skills.
The email to his parents talks about studying hard. Sally gives Mrs Owen a compliment on her cooking skills.
Style:
The email to Duncan has the following features:
Incomplete sentences (*didn't know you could cook; not surprising really; can't wait to see you*)
Direct language (*Thanks for last weekend; email me the recipe; email me, or send a text*)
Informal language (*just kidding; you're a star*)
A mix of positive and negative adjectives (*fantastic, boring, disgusting, brilliant, awful*)
Not many linking words in place, short phrases linked by dashes (*The meal was fantastic – didn't know you could cook!; I slept for the rest of the journey – not surprising really – we did dance ALL night!*)
Expressive language (the emoticon ;-); *sooooooooooo long and boring; Yuk!*; use of capitals *ALL night*, lots of exclamation marks
The email to Duncan's parents has the following features:
Complete sentences with the subject pronoun in place (*I had a really lovely time; it's good to be back at university*)
Indirect/more formal language (*I'd like to thank you so much for …; It was very kind of you, Thank you again for everything.*)
Mainly positive adjectives (*lovely, pleased, delicious, excellent, beautiful, kind*)
More linking words in place, fewer dashes to link sections of the text (*I had a really lovely time, and I was so pleased to meet you at last. I know Duncan has exams too, so we can't see each other until the end of June.*)
Little expressive language, no emoticons or capital letters and fewer exclamation marks

4 Give students time to write their email in class or set it for homework. Remind students to use a fairly informal style, as they are writing to a friend. Allow students to exchange their email with a partner and recommend ways to make it more formal.

If possible, display the emails on the classroom wall or noticeboard to allow students to read each other's work. If appropriate, you could get students to send the emails to each other over a computer network. When you check the students' emails, point out errors, but allow students to correct them themselves. Try to limit correction to major problems to avoid demoralizing the students.

READING AND SPEAKING (SB p96)

Everybody likes a sandwich!

ABOUT THE TEXT

The theme of food is carried through in this section with an article on the history of the sandwich. The text plots the development of the sandwich from the 1st–21st century. Students get to brainstorm different types of sandwich, listen to people talking about their favourite sandwich, and then exchange ideas in a *What do you think?* section.

The following people/characters mentioned in the text:

Hillel /ˈhɪlel/ **the Elder** was an important Jewish religious leader during the first century BC. Hillel and his descendants established academies of learning and were the leaders of the Jewish community in the Land of Israel for several centuries. The *matzohs* /ˈmætsəz/ referred to in the text are crisp biscuits of unleavened bread, traditionally eaten by Jews during Passover.

John Montague /ˈmɒntəgjuː/ (1718–1792) was a British nobleman of high rank, with the title Fourth Earl of Sandwich. Now the title of 'Sandwich' has become synonymous with the food sandwich.

Eliza Leslie /ˈlezliː/ (1787–1858), frequently referred to as *Miss Leslie*, was an American author of popular cookbooks during the nineteenth century. She also gained popularity for her books on etiquette.

Dagwood Bumstead /ˈdægwʊd ˈbʌmsted/ is a character in the long-running comic strip *Blondie*. He first appeared in 1933 and became famous for inventing tall, multi-layered sandwiches held together with an olive on a toothpick. The term *Dagwood sandwich* has entered American English.

Encourage students to use the context to help them with new vocabulary and to pool knowledge with other students, or use a dictionary. With weaker classes or if you are short of time, ask students to check some of following vocabulary before the lesson:

Homework prior to the lesson

rabbi, recorded, nuts, spices, to gamble, chef, ham, mustard, supper, portable, cartoon character, layer, salad.

Students can also check the food items in the listening task in exercise 5. *Fish fingers* are long fillets of fish, breaded and then fried or grilled.

1 Lead in to the topic by asking *What's good about sandwiches?* Elicit possible answers (e.g. They are quick to make. You can take them to school/work. You can eat them anywhere. You can use different fillings, etc.) Read the questions in exercise 1 as a class and elicit a range of answers. If appropriate, ask where students think they get the best sandwiches – at home or in a café/sandwich shop.

2 Get students to read the text through quickly and find the information about the four people/characters. Encourage students to focus on finding just the key information and tell them not to worry about new vocabulary at this stage. You might want to set a time limit of one or two minutes to encourage students to scan the text for the correct information.

Answers
Hillel the Elder was a rabbi who made the first recorded sandwich.
John Montague, the Fourth Earl of Sandwich, liked gambling. He was hungry but he didn't want to stop gambling so the chefs at his club put some beef between two pieces of bread and he ate while he gambled. This became fashionable with other men in the club and they called it the 'sandwich' after the Earl.
Eliza Leslie introduced sandwiches to America in her 1837 cookbook with a recipe for ham sandwiches.
Dagwood Bumstead, an American cartoon character, gave his name to the 'Dagwood' sandwich. It is very big and is made with many layers of meat, cheese, tomatoes, egg, salad, and vegetables.

3 Elicit the answer to question 1 as an example (… *some wine, and he put it between two matzohs or pieces of flat bread*). Put students in pairs. They read the text again more slowly and find the missing information from the text. Monitor and help as necessary. Check the answers with the class.

Answers
1 some wine, and he put it between two matzohs or pieces of flat bread
2 open sandwiches
3 gamble
4 some beef between
5 ham sandwiches
6 they were easy to make and they were a wonderful, cheap, portable meal for workers and school children.
7 an American cartoon character
8 a great many layers

4 Focus attention on the photos on SB p97 and elicit the types of sandwich/ingredients shown. Students work in pairs and write down as many types of sandwich as they can think of. If appropriate, set this up as a competition with the students working in small teams to a limit of two–three minutes.

Elicit possible answers, checking pronunciation as you go.

Possible answers
Types: toasted sandwich/toastie, white bread/brown bread sandwich, pitta bread, wrap, baguette/French bread, melt, roll, ciabatta, croque monsieur (a hot ham and cheese grilled sandwich, originally from France), open sandwich, club sandwich, submarine (or *sub*, an oblong roll of crusty bread filled with various meats, cheeses, vegetables, and sauces), and possibly hamburger and hotdog.
Typical fillings: BLT (bacon, lettuce, and tomato), peanut butter and jelly (US English for *jam*), cold meats (ham, beef, chicken, turkey, salami, chorizo, pastrami, bacon, sausage), fish/seafood (tuna, prawns, smoked salmon, crab), eggs, cheese, salad/vegetables (lettuce, cucumber, tomatoes), onions, peppers, avocado, asparagus, gherkin, mayonnaise, chutney, dressing.

LISTENING (SB p97)

5 **T 8.9** **[CD 2: Track 54]** Read the instructions as a class. Check comprehension and pronunciation of the items in the box. (If students have done the above homework task in *About the text*, they should not have too many difficulties.) Also pre-teach/check *butty* (informal word for *sandwich*), *rare*, *tomato ketchup*, *ciabatta*, *bread roll*, *raw*.

Play the recording of Angus and focus on the example in the first section of the chart.

Play the rest of the recording without stopping and get students to write their answers. With weaker students, play a paused version of the recording, stopping after each speaker. Play the recording again to let students check/complete their answers.

Check the answers, then elicit any additional information that students understood about each speaker.

Answers and tapescript

	favourite sandwich
Angus	ham and mustard
Ulla	beef and onions
Tom	bacon and tomato ketchup
Marianne	tomatoes, mozzarella cheese, olives, and basil
John	mackerel and onions

T 8.9

Angus
I come from the north of England and we often call sandwiches 'butties'. My favourite butty is made with thick slices of white bread and thick slices of warm ham with hot mustard. Yes, warm ham! Mmmm, delicious. Would you like to try one?

Ulla
I'm from Denmark so for me it's the open sandwich – of course, and my favourite is with beef – thin slices of beef, rare beef, with some crispy fried onions on the top. I love this.

Tom
Oh, the best sandwich in the world is definitely a bacon sandwich. Hot bacon between thin slices of white bread and with lots of tomato ketchup. Simple, and very, very tasty. There's a café near where I work in London, I sometimes buy one for breakfast – mm, I'd like one right now.

Marianne
I live in Italy so my best is Italian – a ciabatta with chopped tomatoes, mozzarella cheese – with black olives, and basil. Mozzarella's my favourite cheese and I like cooking with it, I make my own pizza.

John
I was in Turkey by the sea, and a fisherman called to me 'Come, try a 'Balik Ekmek''. I think this means 'fish in bread'. He gave me a sandwich – it was fresh mackerel grilled and in a bread roll with raw onions. Fabulous!

6 Give an example of your own favourite sandwich including the type of bread/roll, filling(s), sauces, and seasonings. Give students a few moments to think of their own favourite sandwich. Feed in vocabulary as necessary. Then elicit a range of examples from the class and students' reactions to sandwiches described.

What do you think?

Read through the questions as a class. Students work in small groups and discuss the questions. This will obviously be a very productive activity in a multilingual group, but students in a monolingual group can also discuss their own habits and preferences.

Conduct a brief feedback session with the whole class, encouraging students to compare what is popular in different countries.

SUGGESTION

Students can do a survey with their classmates to find out the most popular sandwich from a list. Put students in groups to invent eight different sandwiches. Remind them to use their imagination and include the type of bread/roll, filling(s), sauces, and seasonings for each sandwich. Students write up their lists and then survey other students to find out what they like/dislike, recording the numbers of votes for each 'recipe'. The results from each group are then checked by the whole class and the three most popular sandwiches chosen.

EXTRA ACTIVITY

Students do a mini-project on their favourite national/regional dishes. Give examples of your own favourite national dishes and describe them in a natural way. Elicit examples of famous national or regional dishes, e.g. goulash from Hungary, paella from Spain, etc. Elicit one or two other examples from the class.

Then give students time to research their favourite dishes, probably for homework, making notes about ingredients, cooking methods, and a little of the history of the dish if appropriate.

Students can then give a short presentation about their chosen dish to the class or discuss their national/regional foods in small groups.

VOCABULARY AND PRONUNCIATION (SB p98)

Daily needs

Having practised a large lexical set of food and drinks, students now focus on the vocabulary of everyday items such as *aspirin*, *envelopes*, and *shampoo*. The pronunciation focus is on stress, with students categorizing key words according to word stress patterns.

⚠ POSSIBLE PROBLEMS

Students may need reminding of the use of *'s* in words like *chemist's*, *newsagent's* and *stationer's*. Explain that this means the *chemist's/newsagent's/stationer's shop* but we don't need to say the word *shop*.

There might not be the direct equivalent of a newsagent's in your students' countries. A newsagent sells newspapers, magazines, cigarettes, sweets, and small items such as birthday cards and soft drinks.

1 Ask students *Apart from food and drink, what everyday items do you regularly buy? Where do you buy them?* Focus attention on the shopping list and the pictures. Focus on the example and the correct picture for *aspirin*. Then get students to complete the task, working in pairs.

Check the answers with the class.

Answers

n	aspirin	e	sellotape
b	chocolate	m	toothpaste
c	notebook	i	shampoo
k	scissors	d	batteries
l	adaptor	a	screwdriver
f	envelopes	g	magazine
j	plasters	h	newspaper

2 **T 8.10** [**CD 2: Track 55**] Focus attention on the example and remind students of the convention of stress patterns in the Student's Book – the circles indicate the number of syllables and the larger circle indicates the main stress.

Say *aspirin* and ask *How many syllables?* (two). With weaker students, go through the list of words in the same way, establishing the number of syllables.

Play the recording, pausing after each word if necessary to give students time to write their answers. Allow students to check in pairs before checking with the class.

Play the recording again and get students to repeat chorally and individually. Make sure they can reproduce *aspirin* and *chocolate* correctly, both of which are pronounced with only two syllables.

Answers and tapescript

●•	•●	●••	•●•	••●
aspirin chocolate notebook scissors plasters toothpaste batteries	shampoo	envelopes sellotape screwdriver newspaper	adaptor	magazine

T 8.10

aspirin	sellotape
chocolate	toothpaste
notebook	shampoo
scissors	batteries
adaptor	screwdriver
envelopes	magazine
plasters	newspaper

3 Focus attention on the picture of the High Street and check pronunciation of the names of the shops in the box. Make sure students understand that a stationer's sells paper and writing materials. Focus attention on the example. Students then work in pairs and continue categorizing the items in exercise 1.

Check the answers with the class. You can extend the activity by getting students to brainstorm other items that can be bought at the shops in exercise 3. Get them to check the spelling and pronunciation, recording both in their vocabulary notebooks.

Answers
newsagent's: chocolate, magazine, newspaper (batteries, notebook, envelopes, sellotape might be sold here too)
hardware shop: adaptor, scissors, batteries, screwdriver
chemist's: aspirin, plasters, toothpaste, shampoo
stationer's: notebook, envelopes, sellotape (scissors might be sold here too)

EXTRA ACTIVITY

Students do a discussion activity on the pros and cons of shopping in a supermarket and in the High Street. Draw a simple table on the board and elicit some examples, e.g.

	Pros	Cons
Supermarket	do all your shopping in one place	no local/individual products
High Street	personal service	can be expensive

Give students time to think about further arguments for and against each way of shopping. Put students in small groups to discuss their ideas. Elicit the main arguments in a feedback session and establish which way of shopping the class prefers and why.

ADDITIONAL MATERIAL

Teacher's Resource Disc

Communicative activity Unit 8 Word stress dominoes

EVERYDAY ENGLISH (SB p99)

Shopping in the High Street

This section focuses on the language of asking for things in shops and cafés, and how to sound polite. It recycles the language of polite requests from Unit 5 *Can/Could I ...?* and also consolidates *would like* from this unit. The conversations in exercise 1 include examples of *too* and *enough*.

NOTE

This is not intended to be a full presentation of the uses of *too* and *enough*, more the opportunity to use the items in context. *Much* and *many* are recycled with *too*, and students also meet *too* + adjective. *Enough* is used in the context of *Four is enough*, so there is no need to go into the adjectival use, e.g. *not big enough*, at this stage.

An example of the Present Continuous *I'm looking for ...* is also provided in context. There's no need to go into a full presentation of Present Continuous at this stage. This is covered in Unit 10.

SUGGESTION

You could help to add authenticity to the roleplays in this section by bringing in some props for exercises 2, 3, and 6. If it is difficult to supply real objects, you could bring in empty packets of aspirin, toothpaste, etc. for exercise 2, and empty (paper or plastic) plates, cups, etc. for exercise 6. Having objects to handle can help students remember their lines, encourage them to interact with their partner more fully, and also build confidence, especially in weaker students.

1 **T 8.11** **[CD 2: Track 56]** Tell students they are going to hear three conversations in high street shops. Give students time to read the gapped conversations quickly. Ask *Where are the people in each conversation?* (1 a hardware shop, 2 a chemist's, 3 a stationer's).

Focus attention on the example and play conversation 1. Give students time to complete the missing words. Play the rest of the recording and get students to complete the task.

Check the answers with the class. If students query *AA* in conversation 1, get them to refer back to the questions *What sort ...?* and elicit that *AA* refers to a type of battery.

Answers and tapescript

1 **A** I'd like some batteries, please.
B What sort do you want?
A AA, please.
B Would you like a packet of four or six?
A Six is **too many**. Four is **enough**.
B Anything else?
A That's **all**, thanks.

2 **C** Can I have some toothpaste, please?
D Small or **large**?
C The large is **too big**. The small is fine.
D Anything **else**?
C No, thanks. How much is that?

3 **E** I'm looking for a nice pen.
F What about this one? It's £25.
E No, that's **too much**. I don't want to spend that much.
F Well, this one is £12.
E That's **better**. And I need some pencils as well.
F There are ten pencils in this packet.
E But I **only** want two!
F I'm afraid I only have packets of ten. Sorry.

2 Check pronunciation of *enough* /ɪ'nʌf/. Then put students into pairs to learn two of the conversations. If possible, pair weaker students with a stronger classmate. Ask students to change roles after the first conversation so that they both play the shopper and the assistant. Monitor and check pronunciation. If students have problems, play the recording again and drill key lines chorally and individually.

Hand out appropriate props if you are using them (see *Note* above). Students act out their conversations for the class. Encourage the class to prompt if students forget their lines.

3 Refer students back to the shopping list in exercise 1 on SB p98. Give students time to choose which shops (newsagent's, hardware shop, chemist's, stationer's) they want to set their conversations in, and which objects they are going to ask for. With larger classes, you may need to allocate shops and objects to ensure there is a spread of content.

Hand out appropriate props if you are using them (see *Suggestion* above). Students roleplay their conversations in closed pairs. Monitor and help, feeding in vocabulary as necessary. Remind students to change roles after each conversation. Note down any common errors but don't feed back on these until after the activity.

If you have time and your students enjoy roleplay, you could get them to act out some of their conversations for the class.

Sounding polite

This section gives students the opportunity to analyse structures they know in terms of politeness and also focus on their pronunciation in order to sound polite.

4 **T 8.12** **[CD 2: Track 57]** Pre-teach/check *smoothie* (a thick, smooth drink of fresh fruit puréed with milk, yogurt, or ice cream) and *latte* (a shot of espresso coffee with frothy steamed milk). Give students time to read the sentences. Then play the recording and ask students to tick (✓) the sentences that sound more polite.

Check with the class. Ask students *What is the problem with the other sentences?* (they are too direct to use with someone you don't know).

Answers
I'd like a coffee, please.
Can I have a sandwich?
Could you bring me a smoothie?

5 **T 8.13** **[CD 2: Track 58]** Pre-teach/check *croissant* /'krwæsã/and *honey*. Give students time to read through the gapped conversation. Check students understand that *Have in*? means the same as *Eat in*?

Give students time to complete the conversation. Remind them of the need to sound polite.

Play the recording and let students compare their answers. Put students in pairs to practise the conversation. Monitor and check for accurate pronunciation and intonation. If students sound flat, focus on the main stress and voice range on the lines. Exaggerate the voice range if necessary, drilling key lines chorally and individually.

Answers and tapescript
A Hi! What can I get you?
B I'd like a latte, please.
A Sure. Have in or take away?
B Have in.
A And what size do you want? Small, medium, or large?
B **Large**, please.
A Would you like anything to eat? A croissant? Some toast?
B **I'd like** some toast, please.
A No problem.
B **Can I have** some honey with the toast?
A Sure. Take a seat, and I'll bring it over.

6 Briefly review food and drinks that you can buy in a café. Put students in new pairs to practise the conversations. With weaker students, elicit an example conversation first with the whole class, getting students to say a line each.

Hand out appropriate props if you are using them (see *Suggestion* above). Students roleplay their conversations in closed pairs. Monitor and help, feeding in vocabulary as necessary. Remind students to change roles after each conversation so that they both play the customer and the assistant. Note down any common errors but don't feed back on these until after the activity.

If you have time and your students enjoy roleplay, you could get them to act out some of their conversations for the class.

Don't forget!

Grammar Reference (SB p189 and Teacher's Resource Disc)
Unit 8

Word list (SB p215 and Teacher's Resource Disc)
Unit 8

Tests (Teacher's Resource Disc)
Unit test 8A
Unit test 8B
Stop and check 2 (Units 5–8)
Skills test 3 (Units 5–8)

Video (DVD)
Unit 8 A world of food

9 City living

Comparative and superlative adjectives • *have got* • Town and country • Directions

This unit has three presentation sections. The theme is describing places: towns and cities, London's biggest market, and megacities. These are useful contexts to practise comparatives and superlatives. We also introduce *have got* in comparison with *have* (for possession). The skills section includes a jigsaw reading and listening about three megacities.
Note The recordings for Units 9–12 are on CD3.

LANGUAGE INPUT

GRAMMAR

Comparative adjectives (SB p104)	• Understanding and practising comparative adjectives.
have got (SB p106)	• Understanding and practising *have got* to talk about possessions.
Superlative adjectives (SB p106)	• Understanding and practising superlative adjectives.

VOCABULARY

Town and country (SB p110)	• Understanding and practising adjectives, nouns and compound nouns related to life in the town and country.

EVERYDAY ENGLISH

Directions (SB p111)	• Understanding and practising prepositions of movement and the language of asking for and giving directions.

SKILLS DEVELOPMENT

READING

Megacities (SB p108)	• A jigsaw reading about the cities of Tokyo, Mumbai, and Mexico City.

LISTENING

People talking about where they live (SB p105/p108)	• Listening for comparative adjectives in a description of life in Paris. **T 9.4** (SB p178/TRD) • Listening for key information in a description of life in Tokyo, Mumbai, and Mexico City. **T 9.11** (SB p179/TRD)

SPEAKING

Comparing cities (SB p105)	• Making comparisons about two capital cities.
I've got a bigger house than you! (SB p106)	• Roleplaying a millionaire.
Project (SB p108)	• Giving a presentation on a megacity.
Your town (SB p110)	• Talking about where you go in your town for different activities.

WRITING

Describing a place – Relative pronouns *which, who, where* (SB p164)	• Understanding relative pronouns for things, people, and places, then writing a description of your capital city.

MORE MATERIALS

Photocopiable worksheets – The best place to live (TB p156/TRD), Town and country crossword (TRD) **Test** (TRD) **Video** (DVD)

STARTER (SB p104)

The *Starter* introduces the topic of city life and gets students thinking about cities they know. Students are not asked to generate comparative forms at this stage – there will be plenty of opportunities to practise these in the activities that follow.

1 **T 9.1** **[CD 3: Track 2]** Focus attention on the prompts. Briefly review *north* /nɔːθ/, *south* /saʊθ/, *east* /iːst/, and *west* /west/ by drawing a simple compass on the board. Elicit more precise locations, e.g. south-east by asking about towns and cities where your students are studying. Check the pronunciation of *mountains* /ˈmaʊntɪnz/. Give students time to think of a town or city in their country and describe its location. If appropriate, you can ask the rest of the class to guess the name of each place.

2 Play the recording and elicit the name of each city.

Answers and tapescript

1 This city is in the south-east of the country. It's very big, and very old. It's about 50 kilometres from the sea and it's on a famous river, the River Thames. (London)
2 This city is in the north and centre of the country. It's about 200 kilometres from the sea and it's on the River Seine. It's one of the most popular tourist destinations in the world. (Paris)

LONDON AND PARIS (SB p104)

Comparative adjectives

⚠ POSSIBLE PROBLEMS

Students usually experience little difficulty with the concept of comparing two things, but experience more difficulty in producing and pronouncing the forms because of all the different parts involved and sometimes because of interference from their own language. Some languages use the equivalent of *more* + adjective for all comparatives and so students forget to apply the *-er* ending for short adjectives. Students may also include *more* and the *-er* ending in the same sentence.

Common mistakes

- *She's more tall than me.*
- *She's more taller than me.*
- *She's taller that me.*

Pronunciation can also present problems if equal stress is given to each word and syllable. In natural speech, the *-er* ending and *than* is usually pronounced with /ə/, e.g.

/ə/ /ə/ /ə/
London's bigger than Paris.

Be prepared to highlight and drill natural-sounding connected speech if students have problems with pronunciation in the early stages.

1 **T 9.2** **[CD 3: Track 3]** Focus attention on the photos and check the pronunciation of *Gherkin* /ˈgɜːkɪn/ and *Eiffel Tower* /ˈaɪfəl ˈtaʊə/. Ask students what they know about London and Paris. Elicit their opinions of the cities if they have been to them.

Pre-teach/check *romantic*. Then play the recording and get students to follow in their book. Focus attention on the example comparison between London and Paris. Then ask students to underline the other differences given in the conversation.

Elicit the key sentences, checking the pronunciation carefully. Drill the sentences chorally and individually, focusing particularly on the /ə/ sounds (see *Answers* below). Ask students whether /ə/ is used on stressed or unstressed words/parts of words (*unstressed*). Tell students that the /ə/ sound is always present at the end of the *-er* comparative and in the pronunciation of *than* /ðən/. Isolate *bigger* and *than* and then drill them together as connected speech: *bigger than* /ˈbɪgəðən/.

Answers

/ə/ /ə/ /ə/
London's bigger than Paris.
/ə/ /ə/
Paris is much smaller, but it's more romantic.
/ə/ /ə/
The food is better.

GRAMMAR SPOT (SB p104)

1 Read the notes as a class. Students work individually to write the comparative forms and try to formulate any rules they can. They may have got a clear idea from doing exercise 1 or they may need prompting and guiding, but try not to just give them the rules. You could write the rules up on the board as you go along. Make sure students understand the doubling of consonants in examples like *big – bigger*.

Answers
big **bigger**
romantic **more romantic**
small **smaller**

-er is used with short adjectives such as *small – smaller*.
Short adjectives ending in one vowel and one consonant double the consonant such as *big – bigger*.
more … is used with longer adjectives such as *romantic – more romantic*.

2 Check students understand that some comparatives are irregular and so don't follow the *-er* rule – we don't say **gooder* or **badder*. Focus attention on the example *good – better* and elicit/teach *bad – worse*, checking the pronunciation /wɜːs/ carefully.

Answers
good better bad **worse**

►► Read Grammar Reference 9.1 on SB p190 together in class, and/or ask students to read it at home. Encourage them to ask you questions about it.

2 This exercise gives students the opportunity to practise the formation of comparative adjectives without having to worry about forming a whole sentence.

Pre-teach/check *tall*, *wet*, and *polite*. Focus attention on the examples *taller* and *more expensive. Ask why '-er' and why 'more'? (-er* with short adjectives, *more* with longer adjectives). Students work individually to write the comparative forms, using their dictionaries if appropriate. Some of the comparative forms were given in exercise 1 and the *Grammar Spot*. Monitor and help as necessary. Then check the answers with the whole class. Point out that adjectives ending in *-e* add just *-r*, e.g. *nice – nicer*. With weaker classes, you could put the examples into groups according to their pattern: + *-er*, doubling of consonant, *more* + adjective, and irregular.

Briefly review the alphabet, reminding students of the word *double* when the same letter appears twice, e.g. *T - A - double L - E - R*. Demonstrate the pairwork with two students:

A *hot*

B *hotter – H - O - double T - E - R*

Then put students in pairs to test each other. Remind them to spell the comparative forms. Monitor and check. Feed back on any form, spelling, or pronunciation errors with the whole class.

Answers

tall – taller	warm – **warmer**
expensive – more expensive	cold – **colder**
hot – **hotter**	polite – **more polite**
cheap – **cheaper**	beautiful – **more beautiful**
nice – **nicer**	bad – **worse**
wet – **wetter**	good – **better**

3 Focus attention on the photos and ask students to identify which show Paris and which London. Focus attention on the example. Check which other adjective in exercise 2 could be used to describe the Eiffel Tower and the Gherkin (*beautiful*) and elicit a comparison, e.g. *I think the Eiffel Tower is more beautiful than the Gherkin*. With weaker students, elicit the adjectives they can use in the rest of the sentences (*Métro/Underground – expensive, weather – hot/wet/warm, buildings – beautiful, people – nice/polite*).

Put students in pairs to compare their ideas. Monitor and help as necessary. Check for accurate formation of comparatives and a natural delivery in the pronunciation. Correct any errors with the class, highlighting the use of /ə/ on the unstressed syllables if necessary.

T 9.3 **[CD 3: Track 4]** Tell students they are going to hear six sentences, using the same prompts as in exercise 3. Play the recording and let students compare the sentences with their own versions. (If students query the height of the Eiffel Tower and the Gherkin, confirm that the Eiffel Tower is 300m and the Gherkin is just 180m!)

Refer students to **T 9.3** on SB p178. Get them to practise the sentences. Monitor and check pronunciation. Focus particularly on the /ə/ sounds. If students have problems, drill the sentences from the recording or model them yourself. If necessary, break up the sentences into sections, isolating the comparative forms + *than*. Try to get a natural 'flow' in the repetition of the sentences.

Tapescript

1 The Eiffel Tower is taller than the Gherkin.
2 The Underground is more expensive than the Métro.
3 Paris is warmer than London.
4 Paris is wetter than London.
5 I think the buildings in Paris are more beautiful.
6 I think the people in London are nicer.

4 **T 9.4** **[CD 3: Track 5]** Focus attention on the photo of Rob. Ask *What nationality is he?* (English) *Where does he live?* (Paris). Pre-teach/check *transport, architecture, Londoner, Parisian,* and *have a good time.* Focus attention on the examples. If students query the spelling of *easier*, point out that adjectives ending in *-y* form the comparative with *-ier*, e.g. *noisy – noisier.*

Give students time to read the gapped sentences. Explain that the recording is in the form of a short monologue but students should be able to pick out the key words to complete the sentences. Play the recording and get students to complete Rob's opinions. Give them time to check their answers in pairs. Play the recording again if necessary and let students check/complete their answers. Check the answers with the class.

Answers and tapescript

1 The Métro is **cheaper** and **easier** to use than the Underground.
2 Paris is certainly **hotter** than London.
3 Paris, in fact, is **wetter** than London; but in London there are **more** wet days.
4 The architecture in Paris is **more beautiful**, but the buildings in London are **more interesting**.
5 Life is **faster** in London.
6 Londoners are generally **more polite** than Parisians.
7 People in London work **harder** and they earn **more**.
8 In Paris, having a good time is **more important**.

T 9.4

Well, I like both London and Paris. But they are very different cities. Take transport for example. The Métro is cheaper and easier to use than the Underground. And the weather ... well, Paris is certainly hotter than London. And Paris, in fact, is wetter than London; but in London there are more wet days. What about the buildings? Well, ... people say that the architecture in Paris is more beautiful, but the buildings in London are more interesting. And living in the two cities? Well ... life is faster in London. And the people? ... Mmm, Londoners are generally more polite than Parisians. People in London work harder, and they earn more. In Paris, having a good time is more important.

5 Ask students to close their books and elicit one or two examples of what Rob said about London and Paris. With weaker classes, you could write key words on the board as prompts, e.g. *transport, weather, buildings,* etc.

Students work in pairs to continue the task. Monitor and check. Feed back on any form or pronunciation errors with the whole class.

Round off the activity by asking if students agree with Rob's opinions and eliciting their reasons.

PRACTICE (SB p105)

Comparing cities

1 **T 9.5** **[CD 3: Track 6]** In this exercise we bring in the use of *much* to emphasize comparatives. Students are only asked to recognize it at first, and not produce it until the following exercise.

Put the conversations in a context and tell your students that two people are discussing different cities they know.

Focus attention on the example. Point out that the students have to fill in the opposite adjectives in B's comments to those that A uses. Then ask students to work in pairs to complete the conversations.

Play the recording and get students to check their answers.

Answers and tapescript
1 **A** New York is older than London.
B No, it isn't! New York is much more modern!
2 **A** Tokyo is **cheaper than** Bangkok.
B No, it isn't! Tokyo's much **more expensive**!
3 **A** Seoul is **bigger than** Beijing.
B No, it isn't! Seoul is much **smaller**!
4 **A** Johannesburg is **safer than** Cape Town.
B No, it isn't! It's much **more dangerous**!
5 **A** Taxi drivers in New York are **better than** taxi drivers in London.
B No, they aren't! They're much **worse**!

2 Focus attention on the example and highlight the main stress and intonation arrow. Drill the pronunciation chorally and individually. Also check the pronunciation of these cities: *Tokyo* /ˈtəʊkiəʊ/, *Seoul* /səʊl/, *Beijing* /beɪˈdʒɪŋ/, and *Johannesburg* /dʒəʊˈhænɪsbɜːg/.

Get individual students to practise the conversations across the class in open pairs. Encourage the Bs to sound really indignant when they disagree with A. If students have problems, give them exaggerated models yourself or play the recording again to make clear that you want them to produce good stress and intonation and connected speech. You could give further support by writing these models on the board:

A *New York is older than London.*

B *No, it isn't. New York is much more modern.*

A *Seoul is bigger than Beijing.*

B *No, it isn't. Seoul is much smaller.*

Students practise the conversations in closed pairs. Remind them to focus on pronunciation, particularly stress and intonation.

3 This is the personalization stage. Decide on two capital cities that you and all, or most, of the students know and demonstrate the activity.

Students continue in pairs. Monitor and check for accurate use of comparative forms and pronunciation.

Get a few students to feed back to the rest of the class. Discuss any common mistakes in grammar or pronunciation after the pair and classwork stages.

SUGGESTION

You can give further practice of comparatives by asking students to write a series of true/false statements comparing town/cities/countries. Students exchange their statements with a partner and 'test' their knowledge.

A PARISIAN IN LONDON (SB p106)

have got

⚠ POSSIBLE PROBLEMS

The verb *have* for possession was introduced and practised in Units 1 and 2. We have purposely delayed the introduction of *have got* for possession until now because of the complications it causes if introduced alongside the Present Simple of *have*, particularly in the question and negative forms. (See the *Note* at the start of Unit 2, TB p18.) In this unit there are exercises to help students contrast *have* and *have got*.

Although both *have* and *have got* can be used for possession, students may need help getting used to the differences in form. You will need to point out that the *have* in *have got* contracts, but that it doesn't in *have* for possession. Students may have trouble saying the contracted and negative forms, especially next to the following consonant, so be prepared to drill the key forms chorally and individually.

I've got a dog.	/aɪv gɒt ə dɒg/
He's got a car.	/hiːz gɒt ə kɑː/
Have you got a dog?	/həv juː gɒt ə dɒg/
Has she got a car?	/həs ʃiː gɒt ə kɑː/
They haven't got a flat.	/ðeɪ hævnt gɒt ə flæt/
It hasn't got a garden.	/ɪt hæznt gɒt ə gɑːdn/

This context for the main presentation of *have got* continues the focus on Paris and London, this time with an interview with a Parisian girl in London.

1 **T 9.6** **[CD 3: Track 7]** Focus attention on the photo of Chantal. Ask *What nationality is she?* and elicit *She's French.*

Tell students to close their books and listen to the interview with Chantal. Play the recording through once. Elicit the answers to the gist questions. Allow students to share any other information about Chantal that they understood.

Answers and tapescript
Chantal lives in London.
She works in a bank.
Yes, she is.

T 9.6
I = Interviewer C = Chantal
I Hello, Chantal!
C Hi!
I Now, you're French, but you live in London. Is that right?
C Yes, that's right.
I And are you … on your own here in London?
C No, no! I'm here with my husband, André.
I Ah, OK. Do you work in London?
C Yes, I do. I've got a good job. I work in a bank.
I And … Where do you live in London? Have you got a flat?
C Yes. We've got a nice flat in Camden.
I Oh, great! Has André got a job?
C Yes, he has. He's got a shop in Camden. He sells French cheese!

I Wow, that's good! And tell me, have you got a car here?
C No, I haven't got a car. I go everywhere on public transport. It's much easier.
I OK! Thank you very much! I hope you enjoy your stay here!

2 Give students time to read through the questions and answers. Ask *Who's André?* (Chantal's husband.) *What's Camden?* (An area of London.)

Play the recording through without stopping. With weaker classes, play the recording again for students to add in any answers they missed. Check the answers with the whole class.

Get students to practise the questions and answers in pairs. If necessary, play the recording again, drilling the questions and answers students have problems with.

Answers and tapescript
We**'ve got** a nice flat in Camden.
Has André **got** a job?
He**'s got** a shop in Camden.
Have you **got** a car?
No, I **haven't got** a car.

T 9.6 See exercise 1.

GRAMMAR SPOT (SB p106)

This *Grammar Spot* contrasts the form and use of *have* with *have got*.

1 Read through the notes with the whole class. Focus especially on the negative forms (*have – doesn't have, have got – hasn't got*). Get students to read the examples aloud. If necessary drill the key forms chorally and individually (see *Possible problems* above).

2 Introduce the past of *have* and *have got*. Elicit a few examples from the class of things they had when they were younger, e.g. *I had a dog. I had a bike.*

▶▶ Read Grammar Reference 9.2 on SB p190 together in class, and/or ask students to read it at home. Encourage them to ask you questions about it.

3 **T 9.7** **[CD 3: Track 8]** This is a very straightforward transformation exercise designed to focus students' attention solely on the difference in form between *have* for possession and *have got*. Focusing on the form of *have got* at this stage should help students when they meet the Present Perfect in Unit 12.

Refer students back to Grammar Reference 9.2 on SB p190 as they do this exercise. Elicit the answer to number 1 as an example and then get students to do the exercise on their own, writing the contracted forms where possible.

Play the recording to check. Then get students to practise the sentences across the class. If necessary, drill the pronunciation chorally and individually, using the recording as a model. Students take it in turns to read the sentences aloud, working in closed pairs.

Answers and tapescript
1 We've got a nice flat.
2 I've got a French husband.
3 He's got a business in Camden.
4 Have you got a lot of friends?
5 How many brothers and sisters have you got?
6 I haven't got any brothers. I've got a sister called Natalie.
7 Natalie's got a big house.
8 You've got a good English accent.

I've got a bigger house than you!

4 This roleplay should be a fun (and not very realistic!) activity. Ask students *What sort of house have millionaires usually got?* and elicit a few suggestions from the whole class (big houses/mansions with a lot of rooms, an indoor/outdoor swimming pool, tennis courts, a helipad, stables and horses, servants, a private plane).

Focus attention on the example in the Student's Book. Say the first line yourself and then in open pairs. Drill the sentences and encourage exaggerated stress and intonation as students boast about their houses! If necessary, highlight the rise, rise, rise, rise, fall of 'list' intonation:

I've got a garden with a swimming pool, stables, tennis courts, and a helipad.

Divide students into A/B pairs and refer them to the appropriate texts. Elicit an example exchange from two confident students and then get the rest of the students to exchange information about their houses. Go round the class checking grammar and pronunciation. Note down any common errors but don't feed back on them until after the task in order to keep the focus on fluency. Then get feedback as to who has the bigger house!

SUGGESTION

You can give further practice of *have got* by playing a describe and guess game. Students describe another student or a famous person, e.g. hair, eyes, family, possessions, etc. and the others have to guess who it is.

LONDON'S BIGGEST MARKET (SB p106)

Superlative adjectives

⚠ POSSIBLE PROBLEMS

As with comparatives, students usually experience little difficulty with the concept of comparing three or more things but experience more difficulty in producing and pronouncing the forms because of all the different parts involved and sometimes because of interference from their own language. Some languages use the equivalent of *(the) most* + adjective for all comparatives and so students forget to apply the *-est* ending to short adjectives. Students may also include *most* and the *-est* ending in the same sentence. One further problem is the tendency to omit *the* in superlative forms.

Common mistakes

- *He's the most tall student in the class.*
- *He's the most tallest student in the class.*
- *He's tallest student in the class.*

Pronunciation can also present problems if equal stress is given to each word and syllable. Be prepared to highlight and drill natural-sounding connected speech if students have problems with pronunciation in the early stages.

1 Focus attention on the photo of Camden and elicit any information students know about the area. Ask any students who have visited Camden to give a brief description of their experience.

Read the introduction to the text with the class. Focus attention on the example and then give students time to complete the chart. Check the answers.

Answers

Adjective	Superlative
1 big	biggest
2 popular	**most popular**
3 busy	**busiest**
4 good	**best**

2 Pre-teach/check *jewellery*, *tattoo shop*, and *cool* (= fashionable/attractive). Give students time to read through the text to get a general idea of the content. Check comprehension of *Camden Market rocks!* (an informal way of saying that the market is very good or impressive).

Check the answers with the class, getting students to spell the superlative forms. Students should be able to identify the *-est* endings in the short adjectives and the *most* form with longer adjectives, but be prepared to prompt them if necessary. (Do not go into a full explanation of the rules, as this is the focus of the *Grammar Spot*.)

Answers

1 most famous
2 largest
3 cheapest
4 most amazing
5 oldest
6 latest
7 coolest

3 **T 9.8** **[CD 3: Track 9]** Focus attention on the example. Put students in pairs to make the other sentences, using the prompts and referring back to the text as necessary. Monitor and check. If students have a lot of problems, do the activity on the board with the whole class.

Play the recording as a check. Get students to read the sentences aloud. If necessary, drill the pronunciation chorally and individually, using the recording as a model.

Answers and tapescript

It's got the largest street market in the UK.
The market's busiest at the weekend.
The food is the cheapest in north London.
It's got the most amazing clothes.
The Electric Ballroom is the oldest nightclub in Camden.
Proud is one of the coolest clubs in Camden.

GRAMMAR SPOT (SB p106)

1 Students look back at the superlatives in exercise 1 and try to work out the rules. Prompt and guide them if necessary. Write the rules up on the board as students work them out, taking the opportunity to remind them of the comparative forms. Make sure students understand the doubling of consonants in examples like *big – biggest*.

Answers

– *(the) … -est* is used with short adjectives. Short adjectives ending in one vowel and one consonant double the consonant such as *big – biggest*. Short adjectives ending in *-y* drop the *-y* and add *-iest* such as *busy – busiest*.
– *(the) most* is used with longer adjectives such as *popular*, *(more popular)*, *the most popular*.
– some superlatives are irregular such as *good – best*.

2 Elicit the forms for *small* as an example. Students write the other comparative and superlative forms, using their dictionaries if appropriate.

Answers

small, smaller, (the) smallest
expensive, more expensive, (the) most expensive
hot, hotter, (the) hottest
easy, easier, (the) easiest
beautiful, more beautiful, (the) most beautiful

►► Read Grammar Reference 9.1 on SB p190 together in class, and/or ask students to read it at home. Encourage them to ask you questions about it.

PRACTICE (SB p107)

It's the biggest!

1 **T 9.9** **[CD 3: Track 10]** This activity consolidates superlative forms in a set of sentences about places in London. Pre-teach/check *spotting celebrities*. Focus attention on the example and explain that students should look at the second sentence in each pair to help them decide on which adjective to choose. With weaker classes, elicit the base form of the missing adjectives before students complete the sentences.

Give students time to complete the task. Play the recording and get students to check their answers.

If you think your students need more pronunciation practice, play the recording again and get them to repeat. Encourage them to imitate the stress and rhythm of the sentences, with the main stress falling on the superlative adjective.

Elicit a few examples about the town/city where your students are studying. Then put students in pairs/groups of three to continue the task. If possible, try to put students from different places together to encourage an exchange of information. Monitor and check for accurate formation of superlative adjectives. Feed back on any common errors and get students to correct them.

Answers and tapescript

1 The tallest building in London is Canary Wharf. It's 235 metres.
2 The **most expensive** hotel is the Lanesborough. It costs £7,000 per night!
3 The **biggest** park in central London is Hyde Park. It's 142 hectares.
4 The **most popular** tourist attraction is the London Eye. It has 10,000 visitors a day.
5 The **most famous** building is Buckingham Palace. Everyone knows who lives there.
6 The **best** restaurant for spotting celebrities is *The Ivy*. They all go there.

Making comparisons

2 This activity consolidates comparative forms and pairs of opposite adjectives. Focus attention on the example and explain that students need the opposite of the adjective in bold to complete the sentences. With weaker classes, elicit the base form of the missing adjectives before students complete the sentences.

Give students time to complete the task. Let students check in pairs before checking with the class.

Answers

1 The music here is too loud. Can we go somewhere quieter?
2 The 10.00 train is too slow. Is the 11.30 train a **faster** one?
3 You're late. Why weren't you here **earlier**?
4 This flat is too far from the town centre. I need somewhere **nearer**.
5 Five minutes is too short for a break. We need a **longer** one.
6 This exercise is too easy. Can I do something **harder/more difficult**?

Check it

3 Elicit the correct sentence in the first pair. Ask students to work in pairs to choose the correct sentence in each pair. Ask them to work quite quickly, then check the answers with the class.

Answers

1 Yesterday was hotter than today.
2 She's taller than her brother.
3 I am the youngest in the class.
4 This exercise is the most difficult in the book.
5 I've got three sisters.
6 Have you got any money?
7 She hasn't got a good job.

SUGGESTIONS

- You can give freer speaking practice in a personalized activity by asking the class to compare different students. This should be good fun, provided you warn students to be careful not to offend other people! Briefly check/review the irregular comparatives *good/better/best, bad/worst/worst, far/further/furthest.* Write a few short and long adjectives on the board as prompts, e.g. *tall, good at English, talkative, funny,* etc. Elicit a few examples from the class, then let students continue in small groups. Give them enough time to describe a few other people, but do not let the activity go on too long.
- Students write the name of their favourite film or sports star and then compare their favourites in pairs/small groups, e.g. *(Johnny Depp) is more popular than (Ben Stiller).* With weaker students you could write possible adjectives on the board, e.g. *talented, successful, good, interesting, rich, famous, old,* etc.

Photocopiable Activity

UNIT 9 The best place to live TB p156/TRD

Materials: One copy of the worksheet for each student.

Procedure: Explain that students are going to complete and discuss a questionnaire to practise superlatives and talking about cities/regions.

- Give out a worksheet to each student. Focus attention on the example. Check comprehension of *reputation*. Give students enough time to complete the gapped questions. Check the answers.

Answers

1 the biggest	6 the busiest
2 the worst	7 the most expensive
3 the most beautiful	8 the friendliest
4 the best	9 the most dangerous
5 the most interesting	10 the most modern

- Students write their answers to the questions. Remind them when they are giving an opinion, they should not always choose their own city/region.
- For exercise 2, divide the class into groups of three. Pre-teach/check useful language for the discussion stage, e.g. *What did you put for question (1)?, I think …, I agree/don't agree with …, I prefer …,* etc. Get students to discuss their answers. Monitor and check for accurate use of superlatives.
- For exercise 3, bring the class back together. Elicit a number of examples promoting different cities/regions. Encourage students to persuade their classmates to accept their choice. This should lead to natural use of comparatives and superlatives, and to some lively debate! Don't interrupt or over-correct students, as this is the fluency stage of the activity.

  With monolingual classes, you could extend the activity by getting students to decide on the best/worst place to live in their country.

READING AND LISTENING (SB p108)

Megacities

NOTE

At the end of this section, there is a project activity on megacities. You will need to build in time for students to do some research and make notes on a megacity, probably for homework. Students then give a short presentation about their chosen city to the class. In larger groups, you may need to stage the presentations across a series of lessons or get students to give their presentations in groups.

ABOUT THE TEXT

This is another jigsaw reading task, which gives students an opportunity for not only reading practice, but also some freer speaking. The class divides into three groups and each group reads a different, but similar text about a megacity (a city with more than 10 million people). It's important to remind students to read only their text and to get information about the other texts via speaking.

The texts continue the theme of city living with a focus on three of the largest cities in the world. They have been chosen to review superlative forms and the language of describing a city. They also consolidate present and past tenses.

Tokyo The capital of modern Japan has developed into a megacity from a small fishing village. Prior to 1868, Tokyo was known as Edo. It became Japan's political centre in 1603 when the Emperor Tokugawa Ieyasu established his feudal government there. A few decades later, Edo had grown into one of the world's most populous cities. In 1868, the emperor and capital were moved from Kyoto to Edo, which was renamed Tokyo. Large parts of Tokyo were destroyed in the Great Kanto Earthquake of 1923 and in the air raids of 1945.

Shinto is the main religion of Japan, characterized by devotion to invisible spiritual beings and powers called *kami*. A shrine is a sacred place where *kami* live. Every village and town or district in Japan will have its own Shinto shrine, dedicated to the local *kami*.

Mumbai The capital of the Indian state of Maharashtra, Mumbai was formerly known as Bombay until it was renamed in 1995 for poitical reasons. The Hindu nationalist party Shiv Sena won elections in the state of Maharashtra and presided over a coalition that took control of the state assembly. After the election, the party announced that the port city had been renamed after the Hindu goddess Mumba Devi, the city's patron deity. They argued that *Bombay* was a corrupted English version of *Mumbai* and an unwanted legacy of British colonial rule.

Bollywood is the hugely successful Hindi film industry, located mainly in Mumbai. The name is said to derive from *Hollywood* and *Bombay*.

Mexico City The city now known as Mexico City was founded by the Amerindians Mexica, also called the Aztecs, in 1325. The city was originally built on an island of Lake Texcoco and called Tenochtitlan.

The Historic Centre has been declared a World Heritage Site by the UNESCO. Famous landmarks in the Historic Centre include the Plaza de la Constitución (Zócalo), the main central square, where Spanish-era buildings and an ancient Aztec temple are within a few steps of each other.

Encourage students to use the context to help them with new vocabulary and to pool knowledge with other students, or use a dictionary. With weaker classes or if you are short of time, ask students to check some of following vocabulary before the lesson:

Homework prior to the lesson

Tokyo: *to move fast, commuter, up-to-date, emperor, earthquake, Shinto shrine, humid, cherry blossom, huge, mysterious.*

Mumbai: *commercial centre, independence, snacks, headquarters, skyscraper, shopping mall, slums, running water, electricity, sanitation, sunrise/sunset, stone, crowded, poverty.*

Mexico City: *to invade, temple, colonial, handicrafts, high-class goods, valley, air quality.*

1 **T 9.10** **[CD 3: Track 11]** This exercise aims to generate some interest in the topic of megacities, and hopefully provide some motivation to read the texts.

Give students time to read the exercise and number the cities, working individually. Students then compare their answers in pairs and briefly justify their order.

Give students time to read the questions in exercise 1. Pre-teach/check *inhabitants* and *rural*. Then play the recording through once and check the answers to the order of the cities. If necessary, play the recording again and check the answers to the questions.

Answers and tapescript
[3] Mumbai [5] Shanghai [1] Tokyo [4] New York [2] Mexico City
A megacity is a city with more than ten million people.
In 2008, for the first time in the history of the world, more people on earth lived in cities than in rural areas.

T 9.10
A megacity is a city with more than ten million inhabitants.
The largest megacity is in fact Tokyo. The next biggest is Mexico City. Third is Mumbai. Fourth is New York, with about 22 million people. And last, the smallest is Shanghai, which has about 18.4 million.
Some time in 2008, for the first time in the history of the world, more people on earth lived in cities than in rural areas.

2 Focus attention on the photos and elicit a brief description of each city. Use this opportunity to feed in key words from the texts if your students didn't check vocabulary for homework (see *About the text* above), e.g. *Tokyo: to move fast, commuters, the latest fashions, Shinto shrine, cherry blossom; Mumbai: skyscraper, slums, running water, electricity, sanitation, sunrise/sunset, poverty; Mexico City: Aztec temple, skyscraper, colonial, air quality.*

Focus attention on the headings and elicit the answers to the questions in exercise 2.

Answers
Tokyo is very fast.
Mexico City has a mix of cultures.
Mumbai has a lot of poverty.

3 Put students into three groups, A, B, and C. (With larger classes, you may need to have multiple sets of the three groups.) Assign a text to each group and remind students to read only their text:

Group A – Tokyo

Group B – Mumbai

Group C – Mexico City

Get students to read their text quite quickly, asking others in their group for help with vocabulary if you didn't pre-teach the items listed in *About the text* or set them for homework. Monitor and help with any queries.

Check comprehension of the headings. Give students time to write down the headings to make recording their answers easier. You could ask students to choose one person to record their answers. Remind students to write their answers in note form. With weaker classes, demonstrate which words can be missed out by eliciting the notes for one of the headings (see *Answers*).

Get students to work in their groups and make notes. Monitor and help as necessary.

The answers for each group are provided below for reference but don't check the answers with the whole class at this stage.

Answers

Tokyo
The city and its people
largest and most expensive city in the world; one of the most exciting – everything moves fast; on east coast of Japan; huge but one of safest cities in the world; mysterious – difficult for foreigners to understand; 35 million people; wear latest fashions and have most up-to-date phones
Money and business
people earn highest salaries and spend most money
Buildings and history
not many old buildings – 1923 earthquake and Second World War; architecture very modern but also many Shinto shrines + public baths; originally small fishing village called Edo; name changed in 1868 when Emperor moved there
Climate
summers hot and humid; most beautiful time of year spring, when cherry blossom on trees
Transport
one of the biggest and busiest railway systems in world; 11 million commuters use it

Mumbai
The city and its people
India's largest city; both old and modern, rich and poor; on west coast; because of poverty can be difficult place to live, but experience unique; 22.8 million people; streets full of people doing business, selling snacks and clothes or just living; 60% live with no running water/electricity/sanitation
Money and business
India's most important commercial centre; most important businesses + banks have headquarters here; Bollywood film industry produces more films than Hollywood
Buildings and history
modern skyscrapers + new shopping malls next to slums; best at sunrise and sunset – colour of stone buildings changes; part of British Empire until independence in 1947; called Bombay until 1995; renamed after Hindu goddess Mumba Devi
Climate
wet season June to September; November to February a little cooler and dryer
Transport
cheapest and easiest transport by bus; trains crowded and dangerous

Mexico City
The city and its people
largest city in North and South America; offers variety of experiences; in valley in south central area, surrounded by mountains; air quality not good; visitors need to be careful, but city offers rich cultural mix; 23.4 million people; busy markets selling Mexican food + Indian handicrafts
Money and business
richest city in Latin America; elegant shops selling high-class goods, expensive restaurants, supercool bars; also many people in poor houses
Buildings and history
in main square, Spanish cathedral, Aztec temple, modern skyscraper; a lot of museums and theatres; European squares + colonial houses; Aztecs called it Tenochtitlan; already important city when Spanish invaded in 1521; country became independent in 1821
Climate
rainy season June to October; warmest months April and May
Transport
largest and cheapest subway system in Latin America; traffic slow – often faster to walk

4 Re-group the students, making sure there is an A, a B, and a C student in each group. Demonstrate the activity by getting a group of students to talk about their city. Encourage students to discuss the cities using comparative and superlative forms and *have/have got* where possible, e.g.

Tokyo has got the biggest population.

Mexico City is more multicultural than the other cities.

Mumbai has a film industry, but the other cities don't.

All three cities have got skyscrapers.

Students continue exchanging the information about their city. Remind them to use their notes, rather than read sections directly from their text. Monitor and help as necessary. Check for correct use of the present and past tenses, and for comparative and superlative forms. Note down any common errors but feed back on them at a later stage.

Bring the whole class together to conduct the feedback. Get information about all three cities, encouraging your students to compare and contrast. This way you might get some freer use of comparatives, superlatives, and *have got*, but don't force this; just be pleased if it happens! The aim of this feedback is to encourage some fluency practice. Finally, ask students which city they would/wouldn't like to live in and why.

Listening

5 **T 9.11** **[CD 3: Track 12]** Tell students they are going to hear three people talking about their city, first Makiko from Tokyo, then Vimahl from Mumbai, and finally Lourdes from Mexico City. Pre-teach/check *auto rickshaw, vendor, enthusiastic, smell* (n). Play the first paragraph of Makiko's description and elicit what she says. With weaker students, you could write prompts on the board to help students focus on the key information, e.g.

advantages of Tokyo – safe, _______, ________

favourite time of year?

exciting city – why?

Play the recording through without stopping. Students may tell you they didn't understand anything, but get them to pool their ideas in pairs or small groups before feeding back, as this will help build their confidence. Play the recording again if necessary to allow students to listen for any information they missed, but don't be tempted to keep repeating the recording. Students need to get used to picking out key information the first or second time they listen. Elicit answers to the questions from the class (see *Tapescript*).

Tapescript

Makiko from Tokyo

The first thing to say about Tokyo is that it is very safe. Women can walk everywhere anytime day or night. Little children walk to school. You can leave something on the table is a restaurant while you go out for a minute and nobody will take it.

Tokyo is also very clean, and it is very easy to travel around. All the trains and buses run on time.

Personally, my favourite time of year is spring, when it's dry and the cherry blossom is out.

Tokyo is a very exciting city, because there are always new things to do, new places to go, new things to eat. It changes very quickly!

Vimahl from Mumbai

I have two strong impressions of Mumbai. First, it is a city that is so full of activity! It is busy busy busy all day long and all night long! It's a city that doesn't sleep much. The day begins early because it is so hot. It's a noisy place. There are cars going beep beep, auto rickshaws by the thousand, fast trains rushing past, vendors shouting and trying to get you to buy their food, their drinks, their clothes. And people, people everywhere trying to get to work.

The second thing to say is that the people are very, very enthusiastic. Life isn't easy in Mumbai for a lot of people, but we really work hard and we really want to do our best. Every new day brings new possibilities! The future is exciting for us!

Lourdes from Mexico City

There are three things I like about living in Mexico City. First, the weather. It is warm and sunny most of the year. The second is the fresh fruit and vegetables – the markets are wonderful, the colours and smells are great! And the third is that I'm never bored because there is so much to see and do! We have museums, theatres, art exhibitions, parks, restaurants, bars … everything!

My favourite time of year in Mexico City is the end of December, from the 16th to the 31st. The city is full of lights, there are parties everywhere, and we eat and drink and give presents. Everyone's really happy! I love it!

EXTRA ACTIVITY

Students use the descriptions in **T 9.11** as a model for a description of their own town or city. Ask students to underline useful expressions from the script, e.g. *The first thing to say about … is …, My favourite time of year in … is …, I have (two) strong impressions of …, It's a city that …*, etc. Students work in small groups to describe their city. Encourage them to ask questions about each place.

Project

SUGGESTION

You can help students structure their presentation by preparing a handout with some key expressions:

Introduction

Good morning/afternoon/evening, everyone. Thank you for coming.

Starting the talk

I would like to start by …
Then, … Next, … After that, …
And finally, …

Main part of talk

So, let's begin with …
Moving on to …/Let's move on to …
My next point deals with …

Ending the talk

To sum up, …
In conclusion, you can see that …
Thank you for listening. Does anyone have any questions?

See *Note* at the start of this section. Ask students to use their notes in exercise 3 to help them do the research and organize their notes. If appropriate, encourage them to bring some visuals to support their presentation, e.g. a map and photos. If you have access to computers, students can give their talk with the support of a presentation program.

When students give their presentation, ask them to come to the front of the class (or stand up in front of their group in larger classes) and make sure the rest of the class is quiet and pays attention. Allow students to refer to their notes but don't let them read the information from a script. Encourage the class/groups to ask questions to the presenter. Be generous with praise after students have presented their talk, as it can be rather nerve-wracking, especially for weaker students.

VOCABULARY AND SPEAKING (SB p110)

Town and country

This section focuses on the objects and facilities typically found in urban and rural areas. Students match vocabulary to pictures and then use the key words in context. This also gives an opportunity to recycle comparative forms. Students then discuss how different places and facilities are used, and where they go in their town for leisure.

SUGGESTION

You could lead in to the topic by asking students to brainstorm the objects and places related to town life and country life. Write the headings TOWN and COUNTRY on the board and elicit suggestions as to which words belong where. Write up the words in the correct category or ask individual students to come up to the board to write the answers. Take the opportunity to review the alphabet by getting students to spell the words.

1 Focus attention on the pictures. Check the answer to the questions (*the picture at the top shows the town and the one at the bottom shows the village*).

2 Focus attention on the example and ask students to point to the square in the relevant picture. Students work in pairs and continue matching. They can use their dictionaries or they can ask you about words they don't know.

Check the answers, dealing with any pronunciation difficulties as you go. Make sure students understand the difference between a library (where you borrow books) and a bookshop (where you buy books).

Answers

6 square /skweə/	13 field
2 shopping centre	16 farm
7 statue /'stætʃuː/	23 wood
5 market	21 bridge
8 town hall	24 path
3 street	20 river
11 library /'laɪbri/	15 cottage /'kɒtɪdʒ/
9 car park	19 hill
12 cathedral /kə'θiːdrəl/	22 church
4 pavement	17 mountain /'maʊntɪn/
1 office block	14 pub
10 petrol station	18 lake

As an extension, you could elicit examples of what you usually find only in the country. Students may disagree here based on their own experience, so be prepared to accept a range of reasonable answers, e.g. *wood, farm, field, lake, mountain, cottage.*

3 This exercise aims to consolidate the town and country vocabulary and review comparative forms. Pre-teach/check *mayor* /meə/ and *pedestrian*. Focus attention on the example and then give students time to complete the sentences. Check the answers with the class.

Answers

1 A cathedral is bigger than a church.
2 A mountain is higher than a **hill**.
3 A **cottage** is smaller than a house.
4 A town is bigger than a **village**.
5 In my town, there's a **statue** of King Leopold II sitting on his horse. It's in the main **square**.
6 The mayor has an office in the **town hall**.
7 Cars drive on the **street**. Pedestrians walk on the **pavement**.

4 Focus attention on the example and put students in pairs/groups of three to discuss the other places. In multilingual classes, put students of different nationalities together so they can compare the function of the places listed.

Elicit a range of answers from the class.

Answers

These will vary according to students' own experience.
petrol station – buy petrol, check tyres/oil, buy maps and car equipment, buy snacks and drinks
library – read books/newspapers, borrow books/CDs/DVDs, do research, use a computer, find out local information
shopping centre – buy a lot of different things, e.g. clothes/gifts/CDs/food, etc., have lunch/a snack, go to the hairdresser's, book a holiday, go to the cinema
at a market – buy fruit and vegetables/meat/fish/cheese/bread, etc., sample local food and drinks, buy plants and flowers, buy local crafts/souvenirs/antiques
car park – park your car, have your car cleaned
farm – find out about animals, buy local food and drinks, stay at the farmhouse, go horse-riding, walk in the countryside

Your town

5 Check comprehension of *tourist sights* and elicit some examples of popular sights in the students' own country. Give examples of where you go to do the things listed.

Students then work in small groups to discuss their answers. Monitor and help as necessary.

Elicit a range of answers from the class. If appropriate, establish which places are the most popular with your class.

EXTRA ACTIVITY

If you would like to give more fluency practice on the topic of this section and review comparative adjectives, you can set up a debate on town vs country. Divide the students into two main groups *TOWN* and *COUNTRY*. Get students from each category to work together in pairs/groups of three to brainstorm the benefits of living in their area, e.g. *town – good transport, country – clean air.*

Then put students into groups of four, with two 'town' students and two 'country' students. Feed in useful language for the discussion stage, e.g. *Life in the (country) is better because … / Don't forget that (towns) have … / In the (country) you can … / You can't say that life in the (country) is … / That's true, but … / I know, but …* . Each pair gives arguments as to why their area is better and tries to persuade the other students that they are right.

Monitor and help as necessary. Check for accurate use of comparatives and acceptable pronunciation, especially of the /ə/ sound in comparatives.

ADDITIONAL MATERIAL

Teacher's Resource Disc

Communicative activity Unit 9 Town and country crossword

WRITING (SB p164)

Describing a place

Relative pronouns *which, who, where*

This section continues the focus on cities with a short descriptive writing task on the students' capital city. The language focus is the relative pronouns *which*, *who*, and *where*. Students will be familiar with these as question words and so should not have too much difficulty with the controlled practice. Exercise 2 consolidates the use of the relative pronouns in clauses and also serves as a model for students' own description of their capital city.

Exercise 3 contains examples of non-defining relative clauses, as well defining relative clauses. The punctuation needed for students to do the task is already in place, so do not go into an explanation of the difference between the two types of clause at this stage.

NOTE

The places mentioned in the description of London are:

Buckingham Palace, the official home of the British Royal Family.

the Houses of Parliament, the buildings in which the members of the British parliament meet. *Big Ben* is actually the large bell in the clock tower of the Houses of Parliament but the name is often used to refer to the clock itself.

Harrods, a large department store in the Knightsbridge area of London. It has the reputation of being able to source anything a customer wants.

the London Eye, the world's tallest observation wheel, located on the banks of the River Thames. It offers spectacular views of London and its famous landmarks such as Big Ben, Buckingham Palace and St Paul's Cathedral.

Hamleys, whose store in Regent Street is one of the biggest toy shops in the world and a very big tourist attraction.

The text also refers to the *Congestion Charge*, a fee for motorists travelling within areas of central London.

1 Work through the *Grammar Spot* with the class.

GRAMMAR SPOT (SB p164)

1 Read the examples with the whole class and elicit the answers.

Answers
1 things 2 places 3 people

Ask students which words are replaced by the relative pronoun in sentences 1 and 3 (1 *it*, 3 *she*). Point out that the reference to place in sentence 2 *in it* is replaced by *where* and so is not repeated.

2 Elicit the answer to number 1 and then get students to complete the task, working individually. Check the answers.

Answers
1 Jack wrote the letter which arrived this morning.
2 There's the park where we play football.
3 This is the hotel where I always stay.
4 Barbara's got a car which is faster than yours.
5 I met the man who lives in the house on the corner.

3 Get students to read through the text about London, ignoring the gaps, just to get an idea of the content. Check comprehension of *to land, to lie* (of a place, e.g. on a river), *to ride, traffic, pollution, air,* and *toy shop.*

Elicit the answer to number 1, pointing out the use of *ago* to help students choose the past tense to answer *where the Romans landed*. Give students time to complete the exercise, working in pairs. Encourage them to pool their knowledge of London. Check the answers.

Answers
1e 2c 3a 4h 5f 6d 7g 8b

SUGGESTION

If you think your students will need additional help in preparing for the writing task, build in a content planning stage. Brainstorm things to say about a capital city, e.g. population, history, buildings, tourist attractions, problems, etc. Elicit a few example statements from students about their capital or give some examples about yours. Give students time to make notes about their capital. Divide the class into pairs and get them to talk about their capital. Elicit any interesting facts/opinions in a short feedback session.

4 Read the instructions as a class. Focus attention on the paragraph plan and elicit possible answers to each of the questions. With weaker classes, draft a sample first paragraph on the board with the whole class.

Give students time to write their description in class or set it for homework. Point out that students should try to write four paragraphs of roughly equal length. If possible, display the descriptions on the classroom wall or noticeboard to allow students to read each other's work. When you check the students' descriptions, point out errors, but allow students to correct them themselves. Try to limit correction to major problems to avoid demoralizing the students.

EVERYDAY ENGLISH (SB p111)

Directions

The theme of city and country living provides an ideal context for the language of giving directions including prepositions of movement.

1 Focus attention on the map and ask students to give a brief description of Kingston, e.g. *There's a river in the centre. The town has got an old church, a modern hotel and a railway station,* etc.

Check pronunciation of the words in the box. Then get students to locate them on the map.

2 **T 9.12** **[CD 3: Track 13]** Briefly revise *left* and *right*. Get students to locate *YOU ARE HERE* and the A312 road to Dorchester at the top of the map. Focus attention on the example and give students time to read the directions and predict their answers.

Play the recording and get students to fill in the gaps. With weaker students, get them to mark the route across the map with a pencil when they first listen. Then play the recording again for them to write in their answers.

Check the answers with the class. Deal with any pronunciation difficulties as you go.

Answers and tapescript
Go along George Street, **past** the Bristol Hotel on your left, and **over** the bridge. At the roundabout, turn left and go **up** Park Avenue. Go **round** the corner, **through** the wood, and **down** the hill. Then go **under** the railway bridge and you are on the A312 to Dorchester.

3 **T 9.13** **[CD 3: Track 14]** Tell students they are going to hear three sets of directions, all starting from the *YOU ARE HERE* spot on the map. Pre-teach/check *castle* /ˈkɑːsl/ and check the pronunciation of *Sherwell* /ˈʃɜːwel/. With weaker students, give them time to look carefully at the map and name each of the places/features shown.

Play number 1 as an example and elicit the answer (*King's Castle*). Play the rest of the recording, pausing at the end of each set of directions. Allow students to check in pairs. If there is any disagreement, play the recording again and let students follow the route a second time.

Answers and tapescript
1 King's Castle 2 the church 3 the hotel

T 9.13
1 Go along George Street, past the hotel and over the River Sherwell. Go straight over the roundabout, and it's in front of you on the hill to your left.
2 Go straight past the hotel and over the bridge until you get to a roundabout. At the roundabout follow signs to the town centre. Go past a petrol station on your left, over a pedestrian crossing, and past a set of traffic lights. At the roundabout turn right. You're in ... Street.
3 Go over the bridge, the River Sherwell, and turn right into the town centre. Go straight on, past the traffic lights, and over a roundabout. When you are in the square, it's on the left-hand side, next to the museum, opposite the Town Hall.

4 Drill the pronunciation of the places in the list – *Appleby* /ˈæplbi/ and *Milbury* /ˈmɪlberi/. Point out that we say *the railway station* and *the Town Hall* (not *a* ...) as there is usually only one in each town.

Remind students of the fall/rise intonation used in polite requests (see exercise 3 on SB p63). Focus attention on the speech bubbles. Elicit complete examples, encouraging students to use the appropriate stress and intonation. Drill questions and answers in open pairs across the class.

Students continue to work in closed pairs. Monitor and check that students are using the key language correctly and attempting the polite intonation.

If appropriate, ask some of the pairs to act out their conversations for the rest of the class.

5 Demonstrate the activity by giving some directions to a few places near your school and getting students to call out when they think they know the answer.

Students continue working in pairs. Monitor and help as necessary.

Don't forget!

Grammar Reference (SB p190 and Teacher's Resource Disc)
Unit 9

Word list (SB p217 and Teacher's Resource Disc)
Unit 9

Test (Teacher's Resource Disc)
Unit test 9A
Unit test 9B

Video (DVD)
Unit 9 City living

10 Where on earth are you?

Present Continuous • *something/nothing* ... • Describing people • Social expressions (2)

This is the first unit where students meet the Present Continuous, in the context of 'Where are you and what are you doing?'. Students are already familiar with the Present Simple now and should be ready to compare and contrast the two present tenses. Further practice is provided in the context of describing people and what they are wearing. The unit also practises *something/nothing*, etc. The skills section includes reading and listening tasks on the International Space Station, and this provides further practice of the grammatical aims.

LANGUAGE INPUT

GRAMMAR

Present Continuous (SB p116)	• Understanding and practising the Present Continuous to talk about activities happening now and around now.
Present Simple or Continuous? (SB p118)	• Understanding and practising the difference between present tenses.
something/nothing ... (SB p119)	• Understanding and practising compounds with *some*, *any*, *every*, and *no*.

VOCABULARY

Describing people (SB p122)	• Understanding and practising adjectives and nouns to describe people.

EVERYDAY ENGLISH

Social expressions (2) (SB p123)	• Understanding and practising expressions in everyday situations.

SKILLS DEVELOPMENT

READING

The International Space Station (SB p120)	• An article about living in space.

LISTENING

Who's who? (SB p118)	• Listening and identifying people. **T 10.6** (SB p180/TRD)
An interview with an astronaut (SB p120)	• Listening for key information in an interview. **T 10.8** (SB p180/TRD)
Descriptions of people (SB p122)	• Listening and matching a description to a photo. **T 10.9** (SB p180/TRD)

SPEAKING

What can you see? (SB p117)	• Describing a scene through the classroom window.
Project (SB p120)	• Giving a presentation on an astronaut.
Describing someone in the room/in the news (SB p122)	• Giving descriptions of people.

WRITING

Comparing and contrasting – Linking words *but, however, although* (SB p165)	• Understanding linking words for expressing contrast, then writing a comparison of two people you know.

MORE MATERIALS

Photocopiable worksheets – Something's happening (TB p157/TRD), Describe and draw (TRD) **Test** (TRD) **Video** (DVD)

STARTER (SB p116)

This section reviews and extends the use of the prepositions *in/at/on* + place.

Focus attention on the examples and highlight the use of *at* and *in* + the different places. Ask *Where are you?* to the class and elicit one or two more examples. Put students in pairs to continue the task. Monitor and help as necessary.

Then check the answers with the class. Encourage students to record the answers in categories according to the preposition as in the *Answers* below.

Answers

in	a meeting/my car/bed/a café/my office/town/the pub/the kitchen
at	a party/work/home/the airport/the bus stop/school/university/Jenny's house
on	my way home/the train/holiday/the bus

Give a few examples of where your friends and family are now. Then let students continue sharing examples in pairs or small groups.

I'M SITTING ON THE TRAIN (SB p116)

Present Continuous

⚠ POSSIBLE PROBLEMS

The Present Continuous has no equivalent form in many other languages, which use the present tense to convey the two concepts of 'action which relates to all time' and 'activities happening now'. For example, in French, *il fume dix cigarettes par jour (he smokes ten cigarettes a day)* and *il fume en ce moment (he is smoking now)*, the present tense *fume* expresses both ideas.

Students not only confuse the two concepts of the Present Simple and the Present Continuous, they also confuse the forms. When they have seen the *am/is/are* in the Present Continuous, they tend to try to use it in the Present Simple.

Common mistakes

**She's come from Spain.*

**She's coming from Spain.*

**I'm come to school by bus.*

**What does he doing?*

**Does he coming to the party?*

The Present Continuous can also be used for activities happening in the near future. Examples of this use are included for recognition but there's no need to go into a detailed explanation at this stage, as it is covered more fully in Unit 11.

This presentation is carefully staged to help students get used to the form of the Present Continuous and understand its use. Students first identify where the key characters are, then focus on just the *I* form of the Present Continuous in simple sentences before moving on to a wider range of forms in short conversations. The use of the photos helps to support the context of 'activities happening now'.

1 **T 10.1** **[CD 3: Track 15]** Focus attention on the photo of Alice and Tony and then on Fiona and Tim. Tell students they are going to hear each character saying a line and they simply have to identify who is speaking. Pre-teach/check *laptop*. Play number 1 as an example and point to the photo of Fiona.

Play the rest of the recording and elicit the name of the character speaking. Play the recording again and get students to repeat chorally and individually. Make sure students can reproduce the /m/ of *I'm* /aɪm/.

Answers and tapescript

1 Fiona
2 Tony
3 Tim
4 Alice

T 10.1

1 I'm cooking.
2 I'm reading the paper.
3 I'm watching the football.
4 I'm working on my laptop.

2 **T 10.2** **[CD 3: Track 16]** Focus on the photos again. Ask *Who is on the phone?* (Tony and Fiona). Give students a few moments to read the gapped conversations through. Ask *Who is calling Tony?* (Nina) and *Who is calling Fiona?* (Pete). Ask *Who are Nina and Pete, do you think?* (a friend or relative).

Focus attention on the example and play the recording as far as *for the weekend*. Play the recording through to the end and let students fill in their answers. Play the recording again if necessary to let students check/complete their answers.

Put students in pairs to practise the conversations. If students have problems with pronunciation/intonation, play the recording again as a model and drill key lines chorally and individually.

Answers and tapescript

1 **Tony** Hello?
Nina Hi, Tony! It's Nina. Where are you?
Tony We're on the train. We're going to Birmingham for the weekend.
Nina Oh, great! How's the journey?
Tony Fine. I'**m reading** the paper, and Alice **is doing** something on her laptop ...

2 **Fiona** Hello?
Pete Fiona, hi! It's Pete. How are you? What **are** you **doing**?
Fiona Fine. We're at home. I'**m** just **cooking** some dinner.
Pete What'**s** Tim **doing**?
Fiona He'**s watching** the football. Can't you hear?
Pete Ah, right!

3 **T 10.3** **[CD 3: Track 17]** Focus attention on the example. Student ask and answer the question in open pairs. Students continue in closed pairs. Monitor and check for accurate formation of the questions and answers, and that students are including the correct contracted form of *to be* each time. With weaker students, drill some of the questions and answers chorally and individually and then let students continue in closed pairs.

Play the recording and let students check the questions and answers. If students need further practice, put them in new pairs to practise the exchanges again.

Answers and tapescript
1 What's Tony doing?
He's reading the paper.
2 What's Alice doing?
She's doing something on her laptop.
3 Where are Tony and Alice going?
They're going to Birmingham.
4 What's Fiona cooking?
She's cooking dinner.
5 What's Tim watching?
He's watching the football.

Negatives

This section continues the theme of 'Where are you?' and gives students the opportunity to practise the negative forms alongside the positive.

4 **T 10.4** **[CD 3: Track 18]** Pre-teach/check *to tell the truth*. Focus attention on the photo and read the instructions as a class. Ask students to identify Beth (*the girl with the phone*) and Ellie. Ask *Where are they?* (in the High Street/ in town).

Pre-teach/check *to shout* and *to look after*. Play the recording once and elicit the answer to the gist question *Is she telling the truth?* (No, she isn't.). Focus attention on the negative example and elicit as many other negative sentences as the students can remember. Play the recording again if necessary. With weaker students, you could write prompts on the board, e.g. *Internet*, *homework*, *Ellie's sister*.

Check the answers with the class, drilling the pronunciation chorally and individually. Make sure students can reproduce the negative forms accurately.

Answers and tapescript
They aren't sitting in Ellie's bedroom.
They aren't working on the Internet.
She isn't doing her homework.
They aren't looking after Ellie's sister.

T 10.4
Beth Oh, hi Dad! You OK?
Dad Yes. Fine. Are you all right? Where are you?
Beth Yeah, great! I'm … at Ellie's house. We're sitting in her bedroom.
Dad Ah, OK. And what are you doing at Ellie's house?
Beth We're er … working on the Internet.
Dad Oh, right. Is this school work?
Beth Yeah, I'm doing my homework.
Dad Who's that shouting?
Beth That's … Ellie's sister. We're looking after her.
Dad Hm. Really! OK. Well, see you later, then. Bye!
Beth I'll be home about 6.00, Dad. Bye!

5 **T 10.5** **[CD 3: Track 19]** Refer students back to the people on SB p116. Ask them to identify Alice, Tony, Fiona, Tim, Beth, and Ellie. Play sentence 1 and focus attention on the example. Ask students to identify the negative form (*isn't sleeping*) and the positive form (*'s working*).

Play the rest of the sentences, pausing after each one and getting students to correct the information. With weaker students, you could write the key words on the board as support, e.g. *Manchester/Birmingham*, *lunch/dinner*, etc.

Repeat the pairs of sentences until students can say them fluently, drilling chorally and individually. If necessary, highlight the contrastive stress in sentences with singular and plural forms:

Alice isn't sleeping! She's working on her laptop!

Alice and Tony aren't going to Manchester. They're going to Birmingham.

Answers and tapescript
1 Alice isn't sleeping! She's working on her laptop!
2 Alice and Tony aren't going to Manchester. They're going to Birmingham.
3 Fiona isn't cooking lunch. She's cooking dinner.
4 Tim isn't watching a film. He's watching the football.
5 Beth isn't doing her homework. She's shopping.
6 Beth and Ellie aren't sitting in Ellie's bedroom. They're sitting in the High Street.

T 10.5
1 Alice is sleeping.
2 Alice and Tony are going to Manchester.
3 Fiona's cooking lunch.
4 Tim's watching a film.
5 Beth's doing her homework.
6 Beth and Ellie are sitting in Ellie's bedroom.

GRAMMAR SPOT (SB p117)

1 Read the notes with the whole class. Elicit other examples by pointing to people in the class, e.g. *Yuko is sitting next to Adam, the teacher is standing at the front of the class*, etc.
2 Get students to complete the chart, using contracted and full forms. Check the answers with the whole class.

Answers

I	**'m (am)**	learning English. sitting in a classroom. listening to the teacher.
You	**'re (are)**	
He/She	**'s (is)**	
We	**'re (are)**	
They	**'re (are)**	

Name the tense and then get students to work out the negative and question forms. Get students to do this in pairs and then write up the answers on the board, or refer students to Grammar Reference 10.1 and 10.2 on SB p191.

Answers
Questions

Am	**I**	learning English? sitting in a classroom? listening to the teacher?
Are	**you**	
Is	**he/she**	
Are	**we**	
Are	**they**	

Negatives

I	**'m not**	learning English. sitting in a classroom. listening to the teacher.
You	**aren't**	
He/She	**isn't**	
We	**aren't**	
They	**aren't**	

3 Focus attention on the sentences. Get students to work out the difference between the two tenses. Make sure they understand that the Present Simple describes things that are always true, or true for a long time, and that the Present Continuous describes activities happening now and temporary activities. (At this stage, do not overload students by focusing on the use of the Present Continuous with future meaning. There are examples of this use included for recognition later in this unit and it is covered more fully in Unit 11.)

If students need more help, you could put further sentences on the board to discuss with the whole class, e.g.

Present Simple	**Present Continuous**
She usually wears jeans.	*She's wearing a dress today.*
He works in a bank.	*He's working in the garden today.*
They speak French.	*They're speaking English at the moment.*
I like music.	*Not usually possible: *I'm liking music.*

►► Read Grammar Reference 10.1 and 10.2 on SB p191 together in class, and/or ask students to read it at home. Encourage them to ask you questions about it.

PRACTICE (SB p117)

Questions and negatives

Exercises 1 and 2 give controlled practice in the question and negative forms, using a series of picture prompts.

1 Pre-teach/check *a romance* (= a romantic story). Ask two students to read the example question and answer across the class. Give students time to write the other five questions, using the base verb each time. With weaker students, focus on the answers in the speech bubbles and elicit the question words students need before they form the questions.

Check the answers by getting students to ask and answer across the class. Check students stress the questions correctly, with the auxiliary *are* unstressed and pronounced /ə/:

/ə/
What are you reading?

Answers
1 What are you reading? A romance.
2 What are you watching? The news.
3 Where are you going? To my bedroom.
4 Who are you talking to? My girlfriend.
5 What are you wearing? Jeans and a T-shirt.
6 Why are you crying? Because it's a sad film.

EXTRA ACTIVITY

If you want to give further practice of the Present Continuous *Wh-* and *Yes/No* question forms, you could write prompts on the board for questions about the pictures in exercise 1, e.g.

1 Where/she/sit? (by the fire); she/listen to music? (no)
2 Where/he/sit? (on the sofa); he/watch the news? (yes)
3 What/he/carry? (a rucksack); he/go upstairs? (yes)
4 Where/he/stand? (on the beach); he/use his mobile? (yes)
5 Where/she/wait? (at the station); she/sit/in a car? (no)
6 What/she/do? (watching a film); she/feel/happy? (no)

2 Pre-teach/check *romantic comedy*. Then focus on the example. Give students time to write their sentences, working individually. With weaker students, you could elicit the verb students will need in each negative sentence.

Check the answers with the class. You could get students to give a positive sentence to say what each person is doing as in the bracketed *Answers* below.

Answers
1 She isn't reading a detective story. (She's reading a romance.)
2 He isn't watching a film. (He's watching the news.)
3 He isn't going out with his friends. (He's going to his bedroom.)
4 He isn't talking to his mother. (He's talking to his girlfriend.)
5 She isn't wearing a dress. (She's wearing jeans and a T-shirt.)
6 She isn't watching a romantic comedy. (She's watching a sad film.)

Talking about you

3 This activity aims to practise the Present Continuous in a personalized way. Demonstrate the activity by giving two or three examples about yourself. Get students to work individually and write their answers.

Get students to work in pairs and exchange their answers. Monitor and check for correct use of the Present Continuous. If necessary, drill pronunciation before eliciting a range of answers from students.

Answers
1 I'm learning English.
2 We aren't learning Chinese.
3 I'm sitting next to a clever student.
4 It's raining./It isn't raining.
5 The teacher is talking to us./The teacher isn't talking to us.
6 The students are listening to the teacher./The students aren't listening to the teacher.

NOTE

If you have a large group, choose just three or four students at a time to do exercise 4. You could repeat the activity with different students in subsequent lessons. With a smaller group, you could do this as a pairwork activity, with Student A describing the scene and Student B with his/her back to the window and listening.

If you have a classroom with no windows, get students to imagine the scene.

4 This exercise gives students the opportunity to practise the Present Continuous in a connected way by describing a scene. Focus attention on the examples. Then look out of the window and give a brief description of the scenery and any actions people are doing, e.g. *I can see the street and a small park. Some people are talking and two children are eating ice-creams.*

Pre-teach the expression *I can see …* and get two confident students to look out of different windows if possible and give a description of the scene. Encourage them to be as detailed as possible (people/buildings/animals/traffic, etc.) and include colours and other adjectives in their description.

Monitor and check for accurate use of the Present Continuous. Point out any common errors and drill the corrections and pronunciation as necessary.

PRESENT SIMPLE OR CONTINUOUS? (SB p118)

Who's who?

This section contrasts the two present tenses and helps consolidate the different uses that students focused on in the *Grammar Spot* on SB p117. Exercises 1 and 2 are based on identifying and describing people in a listening task. Exercise 3 consolidates the two present tenses in questions and exercise 4 challenges students to complete sentences using the correct present tense.

1 **T 10.6** **[CD 3: Track 20]** This serves as a gist listening task in which students simply have to identify the people in the picture. Ask *Where are the people?* (in an art gallery). Read the instructions with the whole class. Explain that students don't need to understand every word to be able to do the task.

Play the recording through once. Students listen and write the names next to the correct people.

Check the answers, allowing students to share any additional information they understood.

Answers and tapescript

From left to right: Helena, Roger, Sam and Penny, Paul, Sophie

T 10.6

A Oh, dear! I don't know anybody. Who are they all?
B Don't worry. They're all very nice, I'll tell you who everybody is. Can you see that man over there?
A The man near the window?
B Yes. That's Paul. He's talking to Sophie. He's a banker. Very rich. And very funny. He works in New York.
A Wow! So he's Paul. OK. And that's Sophie next to him?
B Yes. She's laughing at Paul's jokes. She's lovely. She's a professor at Bristol University. She teaches business studies.
A And who's that woman on the left?
B That's Helena. She's drinking champagne. She's a writer. She writes stories for children. They're excellent. A very nice lady.
A And who's that man she's talking to?
B Helena's talking to Roger. Roger's eating crisps. He's an interesting man. He's an art dealer. He works for the British Museum.
A Really? Wow! What a job! So that's Paul and Sophie … Helena and Roger … Now there are two more. Who are they?
B They're Sam and Penny. They're looking at a photo on Sam's phone.
A And what do they do?
B They're designers. They make clothes for children.
A OK. So that's everybody. Thanks.
B That's all right.

2 **T 10.6** **[CD 3: Track 20]** This activity focuses on the detail in the recording and helps consolidate the difference between the two present tenses.

Pre-teach/check *banker, to laugh at, joke, professor, business studies, champagne, art dealer, designer* (n). Focus attention on the table and read out the questions at the top of each column. Remind students that *What's he/she doing?* refers to the activities in the gallery and that *What does he/she do?* refers to information about his/her job. Read out the names of the people in the table. Play the recording again as far as *He works in New York* and focus attention on the example for Paul.

Remind students to look at the picture in exercise 1 as they listen to help them understand who is talking to whom. Play the recording again and get students to complete the table. Get students to check their answers in pairs before checking with the whole class.

Answers

	What's he/she doing?	What does he/she do?
Paul	He's talking to Sophie.	He's a banker. He works in New York.
Sophie	She's laughing at Paul's jokes.	She's a professor at Bristol University. She teaches business studies.
Helena	She's drinking champagne.	She's a writer. She writes stories for children.
Roger	He's eating crisps.	He's an art dealer. He works for the British Museum.
Sam and Penny	They're looking at a photo on Sam's phone.	They're designers. They make clothes for children.

See exercise 1 for **T 10.6**

3 This exercise gives further practice of question forms in the two present tenses. Focus attention on the first pair of sentences. Ask *Which question refers to the activity in the gallery?* (Who's he talking to?) *Which talks about work and means 'for a long time'?* (Where does Paul work?).

Put students in pairs to continue asking and answering about the other people. Monitor and check for correct choice of tense and formation of the questions. Highlight and correct any errors carefully during the checking stage. If students have problems with the choice of tense, use the concept question again: *Happening in the gallery or true for a long time?*

Answers

1 Where does Paul work?
Who's he talking to?
2 Why **is** Sophie **laughing**?
Where **does** she **teach/work**?
3 What **is** Helena **drinking**?
What **does** she **write**?
4 Who **does** Roger **work** for?
What **is** he **eating**?
5 What **do** Sam and Penny **make**?
What **are** they **looking** at?

4 This final phase consolidates the practice by asking students to complete sentences with the verbs in the correct tense. Focus attention on the first pair of sentences and elicit the answer (*works*). Ask *Why Present Simple?* (because it's always true). Focus attention on the second sentence and elicit the answer (*'m working*). Ask *Why Present Continuous?* (because it's happening now – a temporary situation). Put students into pairs to complete the task. Check the answers with the class.

Answers

1 My father works in a bank.
2 **I'm working** very hard at the moment. I need the money.
3 Hi, Dave! Are you on the train? Where **are** you **going**?
4 I always **go** to the cinema every Friday.
5 Let's have lunch tomorrow. I usually **have** lunch at 1.00.
6 I'm sorry! **Are** you **having** lunch? I'll phone you back later.
7 Sh! **I'm doing** my homework. You**'re making** too much noise!
8 In my house, my mum usually **makes** the dinner, and my dad usually **does** the washing-up.

SUGGESTION

Students can get further practice by roleplaying the situation in exercise 1. Put students into groups of four and ask them to imagine they are at the art gallery. Allocate the roles of the people in exercise 1 to two of the students and let the other two play themselves. Briefly review the language of greeting and introducing people, *This is … . Hello, nice to meet you. Nice to meet you, too.* Feed in other possible questions to practise the Present Continuous, e.g.

Are you travelling a lot at the moment?

What are you writing just now?

Are you enjoying it?

What are you designing at the moment?

What's happening in the world of art?

Students introduce each other and then ask 'getting to know you' questions, using Present Simple and Present Continuous. Ask students to change roles and repeat, so that they all get the opportunity to play themselves. Monitor and check for correct use of the Present Simple and Present Continuous but wait until after the roleplay to feed back on any common errors.

SOMETHING'S HAPPENING (SB p119)

something/nothing . . .

⚠ POSSIBLE PROBLEMS

Students will have met words like *something, nothing, everybody*, etc. as lexical items in individual sentences but are unlikely to know that we can form a set of compounds by joining *some, any, every*, and *no* + *thing, body*, and *where*. As well as *…body*, compounds with *…one* can be used to refer to people. We have chosen to present just the *…body* compounds so as not to overload students, so try to stick to these through the presentation and practice. (As in Units 4 and 8, we do not suggest that you explore the use of *any* to mean 'it doesn't matter which', as in *Sit anywhere you like*.)

Students shouldn't have problems with meaning as the compounds are presented in context, but there may be confusion in the following areas:

- The difference between *something/somebody*, etc. and *anything/anybody*, etc. is the same as the difference between *some* and *any*, so you may need to review the general rules, especially with weaker students: *something/somebody*, etc. mainly in positive sentences, and *anything/anybody*, etc. mainly in negative sentences and questions.
- *Something/somebody*, etc. (not *any…*) is used in questions that are requests or offers, e.g. *Could I have something to drink? Would you like somebody to help you?*
- These compounds are singular, e.g. *Everywhere was closed. Something is wrong*, etc.
- Compounds with *no…* are used with a positive verb, e.g. *She said nothing* (NOT **She didn't say nothing.*) *Nobody answered my letter* (NOT **Nobody didn't answer my letter.*) Check for these double negatives and be prepared to correct them carefully.

1 Focus attention on the first photo and elicit the first answer as an example. Give students a few moments to complete the rest of the sentences. Students check in pairs before checking with the class.

Answers

1 something
2 anything
3 everything
4 Nothing

GRAMMAR SPOT (SB p119)

Focus attention on the chart and elicit the missing compound with *some* (*somewhere*). Put students in pairs to complete the chart. Monitor and help as necessary. Check the answers, asking students to spell each word. Make sure students stress the words correctly (*on the first syllable*). Also check the change in vowel sound in the compounds with *no...*:
nothing /ˈnʌθɪŋ/ *nobody* /ˈnəʊbədi/
nowhere /ˈnəʊweə/

Answers

some	any	every	no
something somebody **somewhere**	**anything** anybody anywhere	**everything** **everybody** everywhere	**nothing** nobody **nowhere**

▸▸ Read Grammar Reference 10.3 on SB p191 together in class, and/or ask students to read it at home. Encourage them to ask you questions about it.

2 This exercise highlights common mistakes. Focus attention on the example and ask *Why 'something' and not 'anything'?* (it's a positive sentence). Students choose the correct word in the other sentences, working individually.

Give students time to check in pairs before checking with the whole class. If students have problems, highlight the meaning of the prefix *every* and *no*, and review the difference in use between *some* and *any* (see *Possible problems*).

Answers
1 something
2 anywhere
3 Everybody's
4 anybody
5 Nobody's
6 everything

PRACTICE (SB p119)

Everything was too expensive!

1 **T 10.7** **[CD 3: Track 21]** This exercise practises each set of compounds according to the endings *...thing*, *...body*, and *...where*. Give students time to read the gapped conversations. Elicit what each one is about (*1 shopping, 2 a party, 3 going out on Saturday night*).

Focus attention on the example. Then give students time to complete the task, working individually.

Students check in pairs. Then play the recording as a final check.

Answers and tapescript

1 **A** Did you buy anything at the shops?
B No. Nothing.
A Why not?
B **Everything** was too expensive.
A What a pity!
B But I bought **something** for you. Happy birthday!

2 **C** Did you talk to **anybody** interesting at the party?
D No. **Nobody**.
C Why not?
D **Everybody** was dancing and the music was really loud!
C Oh!
D But I danced with **somebody** beautiful – a girl called Kate.

3 **E** Did you go **anywhere** on Saturday night?
F No. **Nowhere**.
E Why not?
F **Everywhere** was closed. There wasn't one club open.
E That's incredible!
F So next weekend I'm going **somewhere** more interesting.

2 Let the pairs of students choose two of the three conversations. Give them time to practise the conversations a few times to memorize them. Monitor and help as necessary. If students have problems with pronunciation, play selected lines of the recording again and drill chorally and individually. If students sound 'flat', encourage a wide voice range, drilling again as necessary.

Students act out their conversations to the class. Encourage them to prompt each other if they have problems remembering their lines. In larger classes, you may have to divide the class into groups for the acting stage or return to it in a later lesson.

Check it

3 This exercise covers the compounds from the previous section and also two examples of the Present Continuous. Focus attention on the first pair of sentences and elicit the answer (*Somebody is on the phone for you.*). Ask *Why 'somebody' and not 'anybody'?* (it's a positive sentence). Students choose the correct sentences, working individually.

Give students time to check in pairs before checking with the whole class.

Answers
1 Somebody is on the phone for you.
2 I don't have anything for your birthday.
3 I want to go somewhere hot for my holidays.
4 I'm learning English.
5 She isn't working hard.

Photocopiable Activity

UNIT 10 Something's happening TB p157/TRD

Materials: One copy of the worksheet with sentences 1–12 cut up and the key words chart left uncut for each pair/team of students. If you are short of time or with weaker students, the worksheet can also be used uncut so that the sentence halves appear in the correct order.

Procedure: Explain that students are going to do a language race to practise *something/nothing*, etc. Pre-teach/check *to pick up the phone*, *litter* (n), *designer shop*, and *in the corner*.

- Divide the students into pairs or teams of three students. Hand out copies of sentences 1–12 cut up and give a key words chart to each pair/team. Explain that students need to match the sentence halves and choose the correct word from the chart to complete the sentences. They should cross off the missing key words in the chart as they go, using pencil in case of mistakes! The first pair/team to complete the sentences accurately wins. (Alternatively, students can do an uncut version of the worksheet and just work as quickly as possibly to complete sentences 1–12, crossing off the key words as they go.)

- Students complete the task in their pairs/teams. Check the answers as the students finish. If students have made a mistake, get them to go back and check. Establish which pair/team is the winner.

Answers

1 I spent an hour looking for my car keys but I couldn't find them **anywhere**.
2 I called the police because **somebody** tried to steal my car.
3 I invited all of my friends for Sunday lunch but **everybody** was busy that weekend.
4 My old flat wasn't in a very nice area because there was litter **everywhere**.
5 The weather in the UK was awful last year so I decided to go **somewhere** warm this summer.
6 I had to stand on the train to work because there was **nowhere** to sit.
7 I didn't enjoy my French course very much because I didn't know **anybody** in the class.
8 I watched an old DVD because there was **nothing** interesting on TV.
9 I wanted to buy some new clothes but **everything** in the designer shop was too expensive.
10 I woke up suddenly because I heard **something** strange in the corner of the bedroom.
11 I picked up the phone and said 'hello' but there was **nobody** there.
12 I was so hungry when I got home but there wasn't **anything** in the fridge.

- As an extension, put students in new pairs/groups and ask them to use one of the complete sentences as the first line of a mini-story/anecdote.

READING AND LISTENING (SB p120)

The International Space Station

NOTE

At the end of this section, there is a project activity on the astronauts on the International Space Station. You will need to build in time for students to do some research on their chosen astronaut and make notes in order to give a short presentation. Students can also bring in pictures/visuals, if available.

ABOUT THE TEXT

This skills section picks up on the theme of space exploration first introduced in Unit 7, with a focus on the International Space Station (ISS). Fifteen countries participate in the ISS project, including the United States, Russia, European countries, Canada, and Japan.

The reading text gives a general description of the station and its aims, along with an insight into the everyday lives of the crew on board. The language has been simplified to make the text accessible to students and has also been chosen to consolidate the difference between Present Simple and Continuous. The use of a range of numbers in the texts provides for a number referencing task. The listening task is in the form of an interview with a Japanese astronaut. Although the language has been simplified, students may need help with the following references:

Mars – the fourth planet from the sun and the closest planet to Earth. Due to its relative proximity to Earth, a manned mission to Mars has often been the subject of science fiction and more recently has become a realistic aim for the 21st century.

Zero gravity – the condition in which the apparent effect of gravity is zero, as when a body is in free fall or in orbit.

There is an example of the Present Perfect in the section headed *The station*. This is for recognition only, as there is a full presentation and practice of this tense in Unit 12.

Encourage students to use the context to help them with new vocabulary and to pool knowledge with other students, or use a dictionary. With weaker classes or if you are short of time, ask students to check some of following vocabulary before the lesson:

Homework prior to the lesson

laboratory, to orbit, to develop, on board, supply ship, zero gravity, to do experiments, effect (n), *oxygen, the origin of the universe, weightlessness, muscle, bone, tin, to float away, spicy, sense of taste, compartment, attached, manned.*

1 Focus attention on the photos and ask students what they can see. Use this as an opportunity to feed in/review some of the key language (see *About the text* above) e.g. *the station orbiting the Earth, astronauts on board the station, astronauts in zero gravity/floating, a compartment of the station.*

2 Explain that students need to read just the introduction and the sections headed *The station* and *Aims*. Set a time limit of about two minutes to encourage students to read the first part of the text quickly. Get students to ask others in their group for help with vocabulary if you didn't pre-teach the items listed in *About the text* or set them for homework. Monitor and help with any queries.

Put students in pairs to answer the true/false questions.

Check the answers with the class, getting students to correct the false sentences. Ask students if they found any of the answers surprising.

Answers

1 True
2 False. It's orbiting the Earth at a distance of 360 kilometres.
3 True
4 False. New supplies arrive about eight times a year.
5 False. The space agencies from the different countries are working together.
6 True
7 False. They are studying the Earth's weather and geography.
8 False. They are looking at planets and stars to understand the origin of the universe.

3 Ask students to think about everyday life for the astronauts on the ISS. Focus attention on the prompts. Put students in pairs to form the questions. Then check the answers with the class.

Give students time to think of four or five additional questions of their own. Check they use the Present Simple, as the text focuses on the astronauts' routine.

Elicit a range of possible questions from the class.

Answers
Do you work every day?
What time do you wake up?
What do you do in your free time?
What do you eat?
Where do you sleep?
How do you wash?
What exercise do you do?

Possible additional questions
How can you eat in zero gravity?
Do you prepare your own food?
Do you work long hours?
What do you wear on board the station?

4 Give students time to read the second part of the article – *An astronaut's day, Food, Personal lives*, and *Future of the ISS*. Again, set a time limit of about two–three minutes to encourage students to read quickly. Get students to ask others in their group for help with vocabulary if you didn't pre-teach the items listed in *About the text* or set them for homework. Monitor and help with any queries.

Students read and find the answers to their questions in exercise 4, both those in the Student's Book and the ones they wrote themselves.

Check the answers with the class. Ask students if they found any of the answers surprising and if any of their questions weren't answered.

Answers
Do you work every day? **I work Monday to Saturday, but not Sunday.**
What time do you wake up? **We wake up at 6.00.**
What do you do in your free time? **I send emails home, read, and play games. What I like to do best is look out of the windows at Earth below.**
What do you eat? **All our food is in tins or packets. We have fresh fruit only when a supply ship comes. I like spicy food because in space the sense of taste isn't very strong.**
Where do you sleep on the station? **We have our own sleeping compartment. We sleep in bags attached to the wall and we sleep 'standing up'.**
How do you wash? **No information provided.**
What exercise do you do? **We do two hours' exercise every day.**

Possible additional questions
How can you eat in zero gravity? **We eat with a spoon. It is a good idea to have food with a sauce so that it stays on the spoon and doesn't float away!**
Do you prepare your own food? **No, we don't. There isn't a real kitchen. All our food is in tins or packets.**
Do you work long hours? **We work quite long hours during the week – 10 hours a day – and five hours on Saturday.**
What do you wear on board the station? **It's warm on board so we usually wear shorts and T-shirts.**

5 Refer students back to the final section of the article and check the answer to the question.

Answer
There will be a manned trip to Mars.

6 Elicit the reference for the first two numbers, *100 billion* and *1998* (see *Answers*.) Then give students time to complete the task, working in pairs. Monitor and help as necessary.

Check the answers with the class. making sure students can read out the numbers accurately as well as understand what they refer to.

Answer
100 billion – the cost of the station in dollars
1998 – the year the first part of the station went into space
six – the number of months the astronauts stay at a time
200 – the number of visitors there have been
15 – the number of different countries that visitors have come from
eight – the number of times supply ships arrive per year
zero – the number used in the expression zero gravity

Listening

7 **T 10.8** **[CD 3: Track 22]** Focus attention on the photo of Soichi /ˈsɔɪtʃi/ and ask where students think he is from. Pre-teach/check the following vocabulary from the recording: *aeronautical engineer, to do a space walk* (a period of physical activity by an astronaut outside a spacecraft), *to check the instruments, to make sure sth is working properly, crew, commander.*

Two space agencies are mentioned in the recording: *JAXA* (the Japan Aerospace Exploration Agency) and *Roscosmos* (the Russian Federal Space Agency) and two parts of Tokyo (*Yokohama* and *Kanagawa*). Write these proper nouns on the board and explain what they are to help students follow the recording.

Read the questions as a class. Get students to predict the types of words Soichi might use in the answers. Play the recording once without stopping. Get students to work in pairs and pool their information to answer the questions. With weaker students, you could play the recording in sections, pausing after set of information.

Play the recording again to allow students to check/complete their answers.

Check the answers with the class. You decide if you want students to give long answers, as shown in brackets below, or just the key information.

Answers and tapescript
1 He works for JAXA (the Japanese Aerospace Exploration Agency).
2 He studied aeronautical engineering at the University of Tokyo.
3 He's from Yokohama, Kanagawa, which is part of Tokyo. Yes, he's married, and he has three children.
4 He likes jogging, basketball, skiing, and camping with his kids.
5 He's part of the Russian crew. He's studying weather conditions in space, doing experiments with plants (to see how they grow in zero gravity), (he's) doing space walks, (going out into space,) and checking the instruments on the outside of the space station (to make sure they're working properly).
6 He spends a lot of time looking down at the Earth.

7 He thinks how lucky he is to be there, and he thinks that maybe people would stop fighting if they could see how beautiful our planet is.

T 10.8

I = Interviewer S = Soichi

I Soichi, what exactly is your job?
S I'm an aeronautical engineer, and I'm a JAXA astronaut.
I What is JAXA?
S JAXA is the Japan Aerospace Exploration Agency.
I What did you study at university?
S Well, I studied engineering, of course! Aeronautical engineering.
I Where did you study? Which university?
S I studied at the University of Tokyo, and I graduated in 1991.
I Which part of Japan are you from?
S I'm from Yokohama, Kanagawa, which is part of Tokyo.
I Are you married?
S Yes, and I have three children.
I What do you like doing when you're on Earth?
S Well, I guess my hobbies are jogging and basketball. And I like skiing and camping with my kids.
I What are you doing on the space station at the moment?
S I'm doing quite a few space walks. I'm going out into space, and I'm checking the instruments on the outside of the space station, to make sure they're working properly.
I You're part of the Russian crew. What does this mean?
S It means that my commander is Oleg Kotov, from Roscosmos, and I'm working in his team. We're studying weather conditions in space, and we're doing experiments with plants to see how they grow in zero gravity.
I What do you do when you aren't working?
S Well, I spend a lot of time just looking down at you on Earth! And I think how lucky I am to be here. And I wish that everyone could see the Earth from space. Maybe people would stop fighting if they could see how beautiful our planet is.

Project

See *Note* at the start of this section. Ask students to use the questions in exercise 7 to help them do the research and organize their notes. If appropriate, encourage them to bring in pictures/photos to support their presentation. If you have access to computers, students can give their talk with the support of a presentation program.

When students give their presentation, ask them to come to the front of the class (or stand up in front of their group in larger classes) and make sure the rest of the class is quiet and pays attention. Allow students to refer to their notes but don't let them read the information from a script. Encourage the class/groups to ask questions to the presenter. Be generous with praise after students have presented their talk, as it can be rather nerve-wracking, especially for weaker students.

EXTRA ACTIVITY

Students use the information they have researched in the *Project* section to roleplay an interview. Students work in pairs. Student A plays the interviewer and prepares a set of questions for the interview and Student B plays the astronaut. Students roleplay their interview and then change roles. If appropriate, get some pairs to act out their interview to the class.

VOCABULARY AND LISTENING (SB p122)

Describing people

This section revises structures students have already met in the context of describing people – *be* + adjective, *have got* + colour/style of hair/colour of eyes, and Present Continuous: *be wearing* + clothes.

1 **T 10.9** **[CD 3: Track 23]** Focus attention on the photos. Briefly revise the key vocabulary for the clothes and colours shown in the photos. Use the photos to teach *striped* and *checked*. Check students can pronounce the vowel sounds in the following words correctly:

shirt	/ʃɜːt/
trousers	/ˈtraʊzəz/
boots	/buːts/
suit	/suːt/
tie	/taɪ/

Play the recording through and let students choose the correct person. Allow students to check in pairs before checking with the class.

Answers and tapescript

1 Tanya 2 Simon 3 Stephanie 4 Giles

T 10.9

1 She's got dark brown hair and she's quite pretty. She's wearing boots, and a hat, and a red scarf, and she's jumping in the air. She looks really happy!
2 He's got short dark hair. He's wearing trainers, and a purple T-shirt, and he's carrying a ball. He isn't very tall.
3 She's wearing a scarf. She's pretty, and she's got long, blond hair, and blue eyes. She isn't smiling. She doesn't look very friendly.
4 He doesn't look very happy. Perhaps he's a businessman. He's wearing a white shirt and a striped tie. He's also wearing black glasses.

2 Pre-teach/check *pretty* and check students understand the difference between *good-looking* (general), *handsome* (for men), and *pretty* (for girls/women).

Focus attention on the photo of Mark and elicit a description. (*He's tall and good-looking. He's wearing jeans and trainers, and he's wearing a scarf.*) Elicit one or two other descriptions from the whole class, drilling the sentences as necessary. Students continue in pairs.

Possible answers

Ruby isn't very tall. She's about seven or eight years old. She's wearing a black and grey dress with a pink bow. She's wearing pink shoes and a big hat. She looks very happy.
Amy is quite short. She's got short dark hair and she's quite pretty. She's wearing boots, jeans, and a checked coat. She's smiling and she looks friendly.
Cheryl has got long red hair and brown eyes. She's very pretty. She's wearing a black coat, a red scarf, and a hat.
Matt is very tall and he's got short dark hair. He's wearing a purple T-shirt, white shorts, and trainers. He's carrying a ball and he isn't smiling.

3 Choose a photo on SB p122 and give a description of the person. Get the class to guess who you are describing. Put students into groups of three or four to continue the guessing game. Monitor and check for accurate use of *have got* and the Present Continuous. Highlight and correct any common mistakes after the game.

4 Students now personalize the game by describing their classmates. Focus attention on the examples. Ask a confident student to choose a classmate without saying who it is. Ask *Yes/No* questions, e.g.

Is it a girl?

Yes, it is.

Is she sitting near the door?

No, she isn't.

Elicit other questions, drilling the pronunciation chorally and individually if necessary, until students guess the correct person.

Continue the game with the whole class. Remind them to use only *Yes/No* questions and not to ask questions that are too personal! Monitor and check for accurate formation of *Yes/No* questions and short answers. Highlight and correct any common mistakes after the game.

The famous person game!

5 Focus attention on the examples in the Student's Book. Choose someone in the news and describe them in the same way. Get students to guess who it is. Students then continue in pairs/small groups. Monitor and check for correct use of *be* + adjective, *have got*, and the tenses. Highlight and correct any common mistakes after the activity.

ADDITIONAL MATERIAL

Teacher's Resource Disc

Communicative activity Unit 10 Describe and draw

WRITING (SB p165)

Comparing and contrasting

Linking words *but*, *however*, *although*

The writing syllabus continues with a focus on three linkers of contrast – *but*, *however*, and *although* – and how they can be used to join sentences. This builds on the practice of linkers students studied in Units 4 and 6. Students do a sentence joining task and complete a gapped description of two people before going on to write a short comparison of two people in their family.

1 Read the notes with the class. Ask what the linking words express (*contrast*). Check students understand that the sentences show three ways of saying the same thing. Highlight the position of each linker in the examples. Point out that we cannot use *but* in the same way as *although*, i.e. we can't say **But I love travel, I don't like flying – I prefer the train.*

Elicit which sentences are the most formal.

Answers
I love travel. **However**, I don't like flying – I prefer the train.
Although I love travel, I don't like flying – I prefer the train.

2 This exercise checks students know how to use each of the linkers to join sentences. Elicit the answers to number 1 as an example. Students then join the sentences in 2 and 3 in three ways.

Allow students to check in pairs before checking with the whole class. Ask students to give the punctuation in each sentence.

Answers
1 I like Peter, **but** I don't love him.
I like Peter. **However**, I don't love him.
Although I like Peter, I don't love him.
2 My flat has a balcony, **but** it doesn't have a garden.
My flat has a balcony. **However**, it doesn't have a garden.
Although my flat has a balcony, it doesn't have a garden.
3 My brother's older than me, **but** he's smaller than me.
My brother's older than me. **However**, he's smaller than me.
Although my brother's older than me, he's smaller than me.

3 This task covers the linkers from this section and also reviews those from earlier units. Focus attention on the photo and elicit a brief description of the two brothers. Pre-teach/check *twins* and *identical twins*. Get students to read the text through quickly to get an idea of the content. Encourage them to use the context to help them understand new vocabulary, or let them use a dictionary. With weaker students or if you are short of time, pre-teach/check *to look alike*, *to dress alike*, *individual* (n), *to have sth in common*, *IT (information technology)*, *personality*.

Elicit the answer to number 1 as an example and then get students to continue the task, working individually. Remind them to read all the text around the gap and to use the punctuation to help them choose the correct linker. Students check in pairs before checking with the class.

Answers

1 although	7 However
2 because	8 so/and
3 However	9 but
4 because	10 Although
5 when	11 but
6 when	12 However

SUGGESTION

It can be helpful to get students to talk about the content of a writing task as part of the planning stage. In this case, give students a few moments to choose the two people for their description. Then divide the class into pairs to talk about the people and their appearance, personality, and likes and dislikes. Students can make brief notes at this stage if it helps them.

4 Give a brief example by describing the similarities and differences between two people you know. Briefly review key structures, e.g. *My (brother and sister) both (have blue eyes); My (mum) likes (classical music), but my (dad) prefers (jazz); Although my (sister) is sometimes (annoying), I love (her) very much.*

Before getting students to write their own comparison, focus attention on the highlighted expressions in the model text. Check their use by asking the following questions: Which expression:

- introduces the first comparison? (*For a start …*)
- introduces another comparison? (*Something else …, Another thing is that …*)
- gives an example? (*For example, …*).
- introduces the last point/paragraph? (*Finally, …*)

Focus attention on the writing plan and elicit possible sentences for each bullet point. Get students to write brief notes for each section, if they didn't do so earlier (see *Suggestion* above). Remind students to write paragraphs of roughly equal length.

Give students time to write their description in class or set it for homework. If possible, display the descriptions on the classroom wall or noticeboard to allow students to read each other's work. If appropriate, get them to vote for the most interesting description. When you check the students' work, point out errors but allow students to correct them themselves. Try to limit correction to major problems to avoid demoralizing students.

EVERYDAY ENGLISH (SB p123)

Social expressions (2)

This is the second focus on social expressions, building on the language students practised in Unit 3.

NOTE

This exercise introduces the use of the Present Continuous to refer to arrangements in the near future. At this stage, this is intended for recognition, rather than active production. Students are introduced to the *going to* future in Unit 11 and the use of Present Continuous with future meaning is also covered there. The conversations also include examples of *will* for spontaneous decisions. These are also for recognition, so there's no need to go into a full presentation of this use of *will* at this stage. The area of future forms and the concepts that they express in English is very complex, and we do not suggest that you explore it in detail at this level.

1 Focus attention on the photos and elicit who and where the people are in each one (*1 friends in a restaurant, 2 customer and shop assistant in a shoe shop, 3 customer and mechanic at a garage, 4 friends in town, 5 a little boy and a man next to a vending machine, 6 a secretary in an office, 7 friends in a park, 8 friends in a car saying goodbye.*)

Focus attention on the example. Elicit a possible reply for number 2. Then get students to continue the activity, working in pairs. Monitor and help as necessary.

Elicit a range of possible replies in a short feedback section.

2 **T 10.10** **[CD 3: Track 24]** Focus attention on photo 1 again and ask two students to read the lines that go with it. Then elicit the correct line from the box for photo 2. Students continue matching the lines from the box to complete the task, working in pairs.

Play the recording and get students to check. Remind students that *I'm afraid* in the answer to number 6 means *I'm sorry*. Also check comprehension of *What a pity!* (= that's too bad) and *Never mind!* (= don't worry) in the answer to number 7.

Play the recording again and let students focus on the extra lines. Elicit some of the wording in a short feedback session.

Answers and tapescript

1 A Patrick and I are getting married.
B Wow! That's fantastic! Congratulations!
A Thanks. We're both very excited. And a bit nervous.
2 C Can I help you?
D **No, I'm just looking, thanks.**
C Just tell me if you need anything.
D That's very kind.
3 E Don't forget it's a bank holiday on Monday.
F **Sorry, what does that mean?**
E It means it's a national holiday. The garage is closed – most places are closed.
4 G We're going to the cinema tonight.
H **Oh, lovely! Well, I hope you enjoy the film!**
G Thanks. I'll tell you all about it.
H Great!
5 I Excuse me! This machine isn't working!
J **I'm sorry. Let me have a look. Ah! It isn't switched on. That's why!**
I Oh, great! Thank you very much.
J No problem.
6 K Hi. Can I speak to Dave, please?
L **I'm afraid he isn't here at the moment. Can I take a message?**
K Yes. Could you ask him to phone Kevin?
L Sure. I'll do that.
7 M Thanks for the invitation to your party, but I'm afraid I can't come.
N **What a pity! Never mind!**
M I'm going away that weekend.
N It's OK. Another time.
8 O/P Bye! Have a safe journey!
Q/R **Thanks. We'll see you in a couple of days.**
O/P I hope you have a good time.
Q/R We'll try!

3 Put students in pairs to practise the conversations. Weaker students can refer to **T 10.10** on SB p180, though encourage students to work from memory as much as they can. Monitor and help as necessary. If students have pronunciation problems, play sections of the recording again. Students listen and repeat, paying special attention to stress patterns and intonation, following the model as closely as possible.

If you have time, students can learn one or two of the conversations by heart to act out for the rest of the class.

SUGGESTIONS

As with the first section on *Social expressions*, students can do the following activities:

- Students can think of other situations when these expressions would be useful and write or act out parallel conversations.
- Encourage students to use the expressions in class whenever appropriate, e.g. talking about plans for the evening/weekend, saying congratulations, wishing someone a good journey, etc. You could put key phrases on a classroom poster.

Don't forget!

Grammar Reference (SB p191 and Teacher's Resource Disc)
Unit 10

Word list (SB p219 and Teacher's Resource Disc)
Unit 10

Test (Teacher's Resource Disc)
Unit test 10A
Unit test 10B

Video (DVD)
Unit 10 Camden

11 Going far

going to future • Infinitive of purpose • What's the weather like? • Making suggestions

The theme of this unit is planning the future, including travel plans. We focus on the *going to* future for plans and intentions, and for predictions from what you can see now. We do not at the same time introduce and contrast the Future Simple with *will* (this rather complex distinction is for a later stage of learning), but in the *Everyday English* section *will* for spontaneous decisions is included for recognition. The second presentation in the unit is the infinitive of purpose, which is relatively simple to operate in English but is often realized differently in other languages. The skills work includes an article about three young men who are walking around Britain and singing! This continues the theme of travel and adventure, and provides opportunities to revise the grammar not only of this unit but also of previous units (Present Simple and Past Simple).

LANGUAGE INPUT

GRAMMAR	
going to (SB p128)	• Understanding and practising *going to* for future plans and predictions.
Infinitive of purpose (SB p131)	• Understanding and practising the infinitive to answer the question *Why …?*
VOCABULARY	
What's the weather like? (SB p134)	• Understanding and practising language to talk about the weather.
EVERYDAY ENGLISH	
Making suggestions (SB p135)	• Understanding and practising expressions to make and respond to suggestions.

SKILLS DEVELOPMENT

READING	
Meet Ed, Will, and Ginger (SB p132)	• An article about a group of young men with an unusual lifestyle.
LISTENING	
Two people talk about travel plans (SB p131)	• Listening to hear the order of countries on a trip. **T 11.6** (SB p181/TRD)
A weather forecast (SB p134)	• Listening for key information in a weather forecast. **T 11.9** (SB p181/TRD)
SPEAKING	
Talking about you (SB p129)	• Asking and answering questions about plans.
When …? Why …? (SB p131)	• Asking and answering questions about where you went and why.
Roleplay (SB p132)	• Roleplaying an interview between a journalist and a singer.
WRITING	
Describing a holiday – Writing a postcard (SB p166)	• Understanding adjectives to describe a holiday, then writing a holiday postcard.

MORE MATERIALS

Photocopiable worksheets – Making suggestions (TB p158/TRD), Life plans information gap (TRD) **Test** (TRD) **Video** (DVD)

STARTER (SB p128)

1 Read out *I'm going to India* and *I went to India*. Establish what time they refer to by asking *Past, present, or future?* about each one. Students should recognize *went* as the past of *go* but make sure that they realize *going to* refers to the future. (Do not go into a full presentation of the tense at this stage.)

Pre-teach/check the meaning of *retire*. Students work in pairs and make sentences using the time references in the second column. Check the answers with the whole class.

Answers
I'm going to India soon/next month/in a year's time/when I retire.
I went to India when I was a student/two years ago.

PLANNING MY FUTURE (SB p128)

going to

⚠ POSSIBLE PROBLEMS

The *going to* future is made easier by the fact that students already know the present forms of the verb *to be*, both on its own and as part of the Present Continuous, which they met in Unit 10. These are, of course, intrinsic parts of this structure. Also, this is the first main future form students have encountered, apart from the Present Continuous with future meaning, which was included in Unit 10 for recognition and is revisited in this unit. The problem of when to use *going to* in relation to other future forms (always an area of difficulty for students) is deferred to later levels of the course, so that students can simply concentrate on *going to*. The two uses of *going to* are introduced in the unit: plans and intentions, such as *I'm going to be a photographer*; and making predictions based on present evidence, such as *It's going to rain./He's going to fall.*

Students may need help with the following aspects of the presentation:

- With the verbs *go* and *come* we often avoid using the full *going to* future form, and just use the Present Continuous.

  She's going to go to Rome next week. → *She's going to Rome next week.*

- The Present Continuous can be used for future arrangements and is often interchangeable with the *going to* future. This is not such a leap for students, even though in their own language this concept may be expressed by the equivalent of the Present Simple.

  I'm going to see the doctor tomorrow./I'm seeing the doctor tomorrow.

- To express an arrangement in the near future, the Present Continuous usually needs a future time reference, e.g.

  I'm doing my homework. (= now)
  I'm doing my homework tonight.

- The *when* clauses in exercises 1 and 2 use the Present Simple. Sometimes students find it strange that the Present Simple is used to talk about future events; they might want to say **When I will get home …*, etc. You can correct individual mistakes if necessary but don't try to give a detailed explanation of this point at this stage.

The context for the presentation of *going to* is the plans of a range of people in different situations. These show the use of *going to* for short-term plans, e.g. *When I get home …*, and longer-term plans, e.g. *When I retire …*.

There is a reference to Koh Samui Island in one of the examples. This is an island on the south-east coast of Thailand, popular with tourists for its beaches and scenery.

1 Focus attention on the photos of the people and check pronunciation of *Leila* /ˈleɪlə/ and *Ayesha* /ˈaɪʃə/. Pre-teach/check *get a pay rise* and *grow up*. Focus attention on the thought bubbles and explain that each person is thinking about their future. This can be something happening soon, e.g. their evening, or further in the future, e.g. their career.

Ask *What is Alan doing? What is he thinking about?* as an example (He's going home. He's thinking about his evening after work.) Then put students in pairs to talk about the other people. Monitor and help as necessary.

Check the answers with the class.

Answers
Alan is going home. He's thinking about his evening after work.
Brendan is sitting at his desk at work. He's thinking about money.
Jason is playing in his bedroom. He's thinking about his future job.
George is teaching a class. He's thinking about his retirement.
Leila is sitting on a plane. She's thinking about her holiday.
Yvonne is looking after her children. She's thinking about her evening after the children's bedtime.
Ayesha is sitting at her desk at school. She's thinking about her plans for after the lesson/school.

2 **T 11.1** **[CD 3: Track 25]** This is the first time that students see *going to*. Allow them to focus on the context to help convey the meaning but if students query *going to*, just explain that we use it to talk about future plans.

Pre-teach/check *racing driver* and *ring* (n). Give students time to read the sentences quickly and deal with any other vocabulary queries. Focus attention on sentences 1–3 and on the example. Then ask students to continue matching just the names, working in pairs. Check the answers.

Focus attention on the prompt for sentence 4 and elicit the complete sentence (*I'm going to buy my girlfriend a ring.*) Give students time to complete the plans in sentences 5–7, working in pairs. Monitor and check for correct use of *going to*. If students have a lot of problems, correct common errors carefully and drill one or two example sentences before letting students continue the pairwork.

Play the recording and let students check their answers.

Answers and tapescript
1 Alan
2 Jason
3 Yvonne
4 I'm going to buy my girlfriend a ring. – Brendan
5 I'm going to lie on the beach. – Leila
6 I'm going to learn to play golf. – George
7 I'm going to meet my friends for coffee. – Ayesha

T 11.1
1 When I get home, I'm going to relax with my wife.
2 When I grow up, I'm going to be a racing driver.
3 When the kids are in bed, I'm going to sit down and have a glass of wine.
4 When I get a pay rise, I'm going to buy my girlfriend a ring.
5 When I arrive on Koh Samui island, I'm going to lie on the beach.
6 When I retire, I'm going to learn to play golf.
7 When this lesson ends, I'm going to meet my friends for coffee.

3 **T 11.2** **[CD 3: Track 26]** Draw a large question mark on the board to signal that you are going to introduce the question form. The formation and pronunciation of the question should not cause students too much difficulty because they are already familiar with the Present Continuous. With weaker students, you could highlight the change from first person to third person (*I'm going to – Alan is going to*) before focusing on the question forms.

Give students time to read the examples. Then play the recording. Focus on the weak pronunciation of *to* in *going to*: /ˈgəʊɪŋtə/. Practise it in isolation first, and then as part of a full sentence, drilling the examples in the book. If students have problems, get them to focus on the main stresses and then repeat the questions and answers in open pairs.

What's Alan going to do? *He's going to relax.*

You could also drill a few questions and answers about different people in exercise 1 to provide additional support.

Put students in pairs to practise the questions and answers. Monitor and check for correct question forms and pronunciation. If students have a lot of problems, correct common errors carefully and drill one or two more examples before letting students continue the pairwork.

Answers
What's Alan going to do? He's going to relax.
What's Jason going to do? He's going to be a racing driver.
What's Brendan going to do? He's going to buy his girlfriend a ring.
What's George going to do? He's going to learn to play golf.
What's Leila going to do? She's going to lie on the beach.
What's Yvonne going to do? She's going to sit down and have a glass of wine.
What's Ayesha going to do? She's going to meet her friends for coffee.

T 11.2 See the first two answers above.

4 **T 11.3** **[CD 3: Track 27]** Explain that this exercise practises the negative. Tell students the recordings are in the same order as the speakers in exercise 2. Focus attention on the example about Alan and play number 1 on the recording. With weaker students, you could highlight the negative form at this stage.

Pre-teach/check *do the washing.* Play the rest of the recording and get students to focus on the negative forms in each set of sentences. With weaker students, you could write the key verbs for what each speaker isn't going to do in random order on the board as additional support.

Give students time to talk about each of the speakers. Monitor and check for correct use of *going to*, both positive and negative forms. If students have a lot of problems, correct common errors carefully and drill one or two example sentences before letting students continue the pairwork.

Tapescript
1 When I get home, I'm going to relax with my wife. I'm not going to talk about work.
2 When I grow up, I'm going to be a racing driver. I'm not going to work in an office like my dad.
3 When the kids are in bed, I'm going to sit down and have a glass of wine. I'm not going to do the washing.
4 When I get a pay rise, I'm going to buy my girlfriend a ring. I'm not going to buy a new car.
5 When I arrive on Koh Samui island, I'm going to lie on the beach. I'm not going to check emails for a week.
6 When I retire, I'm going to learn to play golf. I'm not going to stay at home and do nothing.
7 When this lesson ends, I'm going to meet my friends for coffee. I'm not going to do my homework.

Talking about you

5 Now we move away from the people in the Student's Book and get students to talk about themselves in an exercise practising *Yes/No* questions.

Drill the example in the Student's Book individually and chorally. Get one or two students to demonstrate the second question in open pairs. Then get students to work in closed pairs, asking and answering the rest of the questions. Monitor and check as they do this, checking for correct use of the *Yes/No* questions. Pay attention to all aspects of pronunciation – sounds, stress, and intonation.

6 Focus attention on the examples. Highlight the use of *both* for plans that students have in common. Ask students to tell the class about themselves and their partner. This provides practice in the third person singular and first person singular and plural.

GRAMMAR SPOT (SB p129)

Demonstrate that the form of *going to* builds on what students already know by getting the class to chorus first the positive and then the negative forms of the verb *to be*. (Conjugating verbs may be deemed old-fashioned in these communicative days, but it is an effective way of consolidating grammatical forms!)

1 Read the notes with the whole class and then get students to complete the chart, using contracted forms. Check the answers with the whole class.

Answers

I	'm	going to cook tonight.
He/She	's	
You/We/They	're	

2 Get students to work out the question and negative forms in pairs, and then write the answers on the board, or refer students to the Grammar Reference on SB p192.

Answers
Questions

Am	**I**	going to cook tonight?
Is	**he/she**	
Are	**you/we/they**	

Answers
Negatives

I	**'m not**	going to cook tonight.
He/She	**isn't**	
You/We/They	**aren't**	

3 Focus attention on the uses of the Present Continuous for the future and *going to*. Establish that there is little difference between the two sentences.

▶▶ Read Grammar Reference 11.1 and 11.2 on SB p 192 together in class, and/or ask students to read it at home. Encourage them to ask you questions about it.

ADDITIONAL MATERIAL

Teacher's Resource Disc

Communicative activity Unit 11 Life plans information gap

PRACTICE (SB p130)

Careful! You're going to drop it!

Here we introduce the second use of *going to*, when we can see now that something is sure to happen in the future. Students should understand this concept from the pictures and contexts, but with weaker students be prepared to refer to the note on this use at the start of the section.

1 **T 11.4** **[CD 3: Track 28]** Focus attention on picture 1 and the example. Students then write a sentence for each picture, using *going to* and the correct verb in the box. If students have access to dictionaries, get them to look up new words, or they can ask you. Students can work in pairs so that they can help each other with vocabulary. With weaker students, you could match the verbs to each picture before students write the sentences.

Read through the note about the use of *going to* as a class if you didn't do so at the start of the section.

Play the recording and get students to check their answers.

Answers and tapescript
1 What a pity! It's going to rain. He can't play tennis.
2 Look at the time. He's going to be late for his meeting.
3 Come on! Come on! She's going to win. Fantastic!
4 Oh no! Jack's on top of the wall! He's going to fall.
5 Careful! She's going to drop the vase. Too late!
6 They're so excited. They're going to have a baby. It's due in July.
7 There's my sister and her boyfriend! Yuk! They're going to kiss.
8 He's going to sneeze. 'Aaattishooo!' 'Bless you!'

2 There are some useful little expressions included in the sentences: *What a pity! Look at the time. Bless you!* Illustrate the meaning of these when you go through the exercise and get the class to repeat them. It can also be interesting and fun to discuss what is said in the students' own language(s) when someone sneezes.

Students then practise saying the sentences with a partner and have fun practising the stress and intonation in the expressions.

Check it

3 Elicit the answer to number 1 as an example. Students work in pairs and complete the exercise.

Answers
1 He's going to watch the football.
2 We're going to the cinema tonight.
3 She isn't going to cook.
4 Is it going to rain?
5 When are they going to get married?
6 I'm going to the pub.

WE'RE OFF TO SEE THE WORLD! (SB p131)

Infinitive of purpose

⚠ POSSIBLE PROBLEMS

The infinitive of purpose answers the question *why*, replacing *because I wanted to*, e.g. *Why did you go to the shops? Because I wanted to buy a newspaper./To buy a newspaper.*

There is often a problem for learners when they attempt to translate this item from their own language and insert *for*, which is wrong in English.

Common mistakes

**I went to the shops for to buy a newspaper.*

**I went to the shops for buy a newspaper.*

**I went to the shops for buying a newspaper.*

ABOUT THE TEXT

If students query some of the places in exercise 1, the following notes may be helpful.

- **Mount Kilimanjaro** /kɪlɪmən'dʒɑːrəʊ/, at 5,895m is the highest mountain in Africa. There are six official routes up the mountain, and although not an easy climb, it has become an increasingly popular activity with tourists.
- **Ayers** /eəz/ **Rock** is a very large red rock in the Northern Territory, Australia. Known in the Aboriginal language as *Uluru*, it is a very popular tourist site because it changes colour in different lights.
- **Machu Picchu** /mætʃuː 'piːʃuː/ is an ancient ruined city high in the Andes mountain in Peru. It was built by the Incas, a native people of South America in about 1500 AD. The site with its terraces and buildings is a must-see for tourists for all over the world.
- **Yellowstone Park** is a large national park in Wyoming, in north-west USA. It is known for its hot springs and geysers (natural springs of hot water that rise suddenly into the air). They are fuelled by heat from a large reservoir of partially molten rock from one of the world's largest volcanic systems.
- **Angkor** is one of the most important archaeological sites in south-east Asia. Angkor Archaeological Park contains the magnificent remains of the different capitals of the Khmer Empire, from the 9th to the 15th century. They include the famous Temple of Angkor Wat.

1 The aim of this activity is to set the scene and check the vocabulary needed for the presentation dialogue in exercise 2.

First ask your students to look at the photos and ask them which places they recognize. The photos will also help to check some of the vocabulary needed for the matching exercise. Briefly check the pronunciation of the names of the places, focusing on *Tanzania* /tænzən'iːə/, *Peru* /pə'ruː/, *Antarctica* /æn'tɑːktɪkə/, *Egypt* /'iːdʒɪpt/, and *Cambodia* /kæm'bəʊdiə/ in particular.

Elicit the activity for Australia as an example (*take photos of Ayers Rock at sunset*). Ask students to point to the correct photo. Students work in pairs to match the places with the activities and also the photos.

Check the answers with the class, correcting pronunciation as you go. If necessary, point out the silent letter in *climb* /klaɪm/ and the vowel sound in *cruise* /kruːz/.

Ask students if they have visited any of the places in the list, and which place and activity they would like to try.

Answers
a Australia – take photos of Ayers Rock at sunset
b Cambodia – visit the temples of Angkor Wat
c Peru – visit Machu Picchu
d India – go on a tiger safari
e Tanzania – climb Mount Kilimanjaro
f The US – see the supervolcano at Yellowstone Park
g Egypt – take a cruise down the River Nile
h Antarctica – fly over the coldest place on earth

SUGGESTION

Rob and Becky's conversation with their friend incorporates revision of *going to* and also highlights the fact that with the verb *go* we do not usually say *going to go*, but simply use the Present Continuous. The notes in the *Grammar Spot* spell this out in more detail. You could read this with your students either after they first read the conversation, or after they have listened to check the answer.

2 **T 11.5** **[CD 3: Track 29]** Focus attention on the photo and ask students to point to Rob and Becky. Explain that they are talking to a friend about their world trip. Go through the conversation with the whole class, asking three students to take the role of the characters, read the lines, and complete the missing words.

Play the recording for your students, not only to check the answers, but also to familiarize them with the stress and intonation patterns in the conversation. Students then practise the conversation in pairs.

Answers and tapescript
R = Rob F = Friend B = Becky
R First we're going to Egypt.
F Why? To see the pyramids?
B Well, yes, but also we want to **take a cruise** down the Nile.
F Fantastic! Where are you going after that?
R Well, then we're going to Tanzania to …
F Wow! You're going to **climb Kilimanjaro**!

GRAMMAR SPOT (SB p131)

1 Read through the notes with the class (if you have not done so earlier) and point out the use of *going/coming* rather than *going to go/going to come.*

2 Focus attention on the sentences and get students to decide if they mean the same.

Answer
Yes, the sentences do mean the same.

Explain that the infinitive can be used in answer to a *Why … ?* question.

►► Read Grammar Reference 11.3 on SB p192 together in class, and/or ask students to read it at home. Encourage them to ask you questions about it.

PRACTICE (SB p131)

Listening and speaking

1 **T 11.6** **[CD 3: Track 30]** Tell students they are going to hear Rob and Becky continuing their description of their trip.

Ask students *What is one of the main tourist attractions in Egypt?* (the pyramids). *And in India?* (the Taj Mahal). Pre-teach/check *a day trip* and *grizzly bear.*

Focus attention on the examples and play the recording as far as … *climb Kilimanjaro.* Tell students that one of the countries needs to appear twice. Play the rest of the recording without stopping and get students to write the rest of the countries on the itinerary.

Check the answers and then let students pool any additional information they understood.

Answers and tapescript
Egypt, Tanzania, India, Cambodia, Australia, Antarctica, Australia, Peru, the US

T 11.6

R = Rob **F** = Friend **B** = Becky

R First we're going to Egypt.
F Why? To see the pyramids?
B Well, yes, but also we want to take a cruise down the Nile.
F Fantastic! Where are you going after that?
R Well, then we're going to Tanzania to …
F Wow! You're going to climb Kilimanjaro.
R Yes, and then we're flying to India.
F Are you going to visit the Taj Mahal?
B Of course, but we're also going on a tiger safari.
F You're going to see tigers!
R Well, we hope so. Then we're going to Cambodia to visit the temples of Angkor Wat and …
B … then to Australia to see Ayers Rock. We want to take photographs of it at sunset. Did you know it turns from pink to purple at sunset?
F Really! And are you going to Sydney?
R Oh, yes we're taking a flight from Sydney to Antarctica.
B Yeah, it's a day trip to see the coldest place on earth.
F I can't believe this. How many more places?
R Two. We're flying from Sydney to Peru to …
F … to see Machu Picchu of course.
R Yes and then from Peru to the US to Yellowstone Park to see the supervolcano and perhaps some grizzly bears.
B Then home!
F Amazing. What a trip! How long is it going to take?
R Nine months to a year – we think.

2 Focus attention on the example and get a student to read the first sentence aloud. Elicit the continuation (*Then, they're going to Tanzania to climb Kilimanjaro.*)

Put students into groups of four so that the activity can be completed quite quickly. Ask them to take turns to tell part of Rob and Becky's planned journey. Remind them to use the adverbs *first*, *then*, *next*, *after that*, and *finally*.

Sample answer
Student 1: First they're going to Egypt to see the pyramids and to take a cruise down the Nile. Then they're going to Tanzania to climb Kilimanjaro.
Student 2: Next they're going to India to visit the Taj Mahal and to go on a tiger safari. Then they're going to Cambodia to visit the temples of Angkor Wat.
Student 3: After that they're going to Australia to take photos of Ayers Rock at sunset. Then they're going to Antarctica to see the coldest place on earth.
Student 4: Next they're going from Sydney to Peru to see Machu Picchu. Finally, they're going to the US to Yellowstone Park to see the supervolcano and perhaps some grizzly bears.

EXTRA ACTIVITY

Students work in groups of four to plan their own round-the-world trip. Write the following headings on the board and elicit possible examples:

Place	**Reason**
China	*walk along the Great Wall*
Japan	*visit Mount Fuji*

Ask students to plan seven or eight countries and activities for their trip, and decide on the order of travel. Students then change groups to talk about their trip, using language from exercise 2. With smaller classes, students can present their plans to the whole class. If appropriate, ask students to vote for the most exciting trip.

When …? Why …?

3 This activity personalizes the infinitive of purpose. It also moves away from practising the structure with *going to*, and revises the Past Simple.

You could introduce the activity by just going through the examples in the Student's Book, but it is much more interesting if you say some names of places you visited in the past and then get students to ask you why you went there and when, for example:

Teacher I went to Milan.
Student(s) When did you go to Milan?
Teacher Eighteen months ago.
Student(s) Why did you go?
Teacher To visit a friend and to practise my Italian.

Model the highlighted stress patterns in the examples, drilling as necessary.

Ask students to write down the names of some places they visited in the past – countries, cities, villages, or any places of interest. Then put them into pairs to ask each other questions about the places. Let this go on for as long as students are interested if you have time.

Round the activity off by asking students to give feedback to the class about their partner.

SUGGESTION

If you think your students need more practice with the infinitive of purpose, you can follow the same procedure as exercise 3, but focus on the future. Remind students of the expressions of future time that they can use, e.g. *soon, next week/month/year, in a few weeks' time,* etc. Give an example about a place you are going to visit, e.g.

Teacher I'm going to New York.
Student(s) When are you going to New York?
Teacher Next Christmas.
Student(s) Why are you going?
Teacher To do some sightseeing and to go shopping.

Students work in pairs and ask each other questions about the places. Ask one or two individuals to give feedback to the class about their partner.

WRITING (SB p166)

Describing a holiday

Writing a postcard

This unit of the writing syllabus gives students the opportunity to write a holiday postcard. It is an ideal way to practise the weather vocabulary covered in the unit and also gives further practice in a range of tenses.

1 Read the instructions as a class. Pre-teach/check *hired car* and then give students time to read the information in the chart.

2 **T 11.7** **[CD 3: Track 31]** Focus attention on the example. With weaker classes, you could focus on the *Grammar Spot* before students complete the questions.

Give students time to write the questions, using the prompts in the *Questions* column of the chart. Monitor and help as necessary.

Then put students in pairs to ask and answer about Luke and Tina's holiday. Monitor and check for accurate question formation and use of Present Continuous and *going to*.

Play the recording and let students check their answers. Ask *Why 'going to' and not Present Continuous in number 6?* (Present continuous would mean '*now*'.)

Answers and tapescript

1 Where are they going?
To the South of France.
2 When are they going?
On May the 21st.
3 How are they travelling?
By plane and hired car.
4 How long are they staying?
For ten days.
5 Where are they staying?
In a house in a village.
6 What are they going to do?
They're going to swim, go shopping in the markets, read and relax, and eat in good restaurants.
They're going to have a great time, aren't they?
Yes, they really are!

GRAMMAR SPOT (SB p166)

Read the notes and examples as a class. Elicit examples of what students are doing after class, e.g. *We're going for a coffee. I'm meeting my friend for dinner,* etc.

►► Read Grammar Reference 11.2 on SB p192 together in class, and/or ask students to read it at home. Encourage them to ask you questions about it.

3 As a lead-in to the writing section, ask what information people typically include in a postcard (*weather, accommodation, food, activities, places to visit*).

Get students to read the postcard quickly and ask *Who is on holiday?* (Luke and Tina), *Where are they?* (in the South of France), *Who is the postcard to?* (their friends, Toby and Mel).

Pre-teach/check *loud* and *peaceful*. With weaker students, go through the adjectives in the box first and elicit a possible context for each one. Point out that *warmer* is in the comparative form.

Students then read the postcard again and fill in the gaps with the missing adjectives. Remind them to use each adjective only once. It's a good idea if they use pencil so that they can change any answers they get wrong earlier in the task.

Check the answers with the class.

Answers

1 wonderful
2 old
3 beautiful
4 hot
5 warmer
6 huge
7 loud
8 frightened
9 sunny
10 colourful
11 expensive
12 delicious
13 peaceful
14 relaxed
15 busy

4 Divide the class into pairs and get them to discuss the questions, giving examples where possible. Elicit any interesting examples in a short feedback session. You could ask students to feed back on their partner's examples.

5 Focus attention on the writing plan and elicit possible ideas for each point. Check students use the correct tense for things they do often/most of the time (Present Simple), things they did yesterday (Past Simple), and things they are going to do tomorrow (*going to*/Present Continuous).

If possible, bring in real postcards for students to write on to add authenticity and encourage them to base their ideas on a real holiday if appropriate. Remind them to use adjectives like those in exercise 3 to make their writing interesting.

Give students time to write their postcard in class or set it for homework. Students then take it in turns to read their postcard aloud to a partner.

If possible, display the postcards on the classroom wall or noticeboard to allow students to read each other's work. If appropriate, you could get students to vote for the best/worst holiday described in the postcards. When you check the students' work, point out errors but allow students to correct them themselves. Try to limit correction to major problems to avoid demoralizing the students.

READING AND SPEAKING (SB p132)

Meet Ed, Will, and Ginger

NOTE

At the end of this section, there is a project activity on traditional songs and music. You will need to build in time for students to do some research and make notes on their favourites, probably for homework. Students then give a short presentation about their chosen songs/music to the class. In larger groups, you may need to stage the presentations across a series of lessons or get students to give their presentations in groups.

ABOUT THE TEXT

The reading section continues the theme of travel and adventure with an article on three young Englishmen who have an unusual lifestyle – they are walking around Britain and singing traditional folk songs to local people. Exercise 1 of the section gives an example of the type of music.

The text describes the trio and what happens when they arrive in a place and start singing. It also sets out their reasons for doing their walk. It has been chosen to review a range of structures from this and recent units. It also consolidates present and past tenses.

The people/places mentioned in the text are:

Robin Hood and his Merry Men In traditional English stories, Robin Hood was a man who lived in Sherwood Forest in central England with a group of followers – his Merry Men. They are said to have robbed the rich to help the poor.

Petersfield Set in a beautiful range of hills called the South Downs, Petersfield is an ancient market town dating from the 11th century. The town has a vibrant musical and artistic scene.

Canterbury Located in south-east England, Canterbury is a small city famous for its impressive 11th century cathedral.

The expression used in the title *sing for your supper* fits with the men's traditional lifestyle. It is an old-fashioned expression meaning to do something for someone in order to receive something in return, especially food.

Encourage students to use the context to help them with new vocabulary and to pool knowledge with other students, or use a dictionary. With weaker classes or if you are short of time, ask students to check some of following vocabulary before the lesson:

Homework prior to the lesson

backpack, walking stick, passer-by, supper, to smile, to sing in perfect harmony, folk /fəʊk/ *songs, comfortable, hospitality, freedom, simple, stressful, podcast.*

1 **T 11.8** **[CD 3: Track 32]** This recording is to set the scene and give an example of the type of song that Ed, Will, and Ginger perform on their travels. There's no need to go into the vocabulary in the song in any detail.

Ask *What type of music is folk?* (traditional music) *What are folk songs often about?* (the countryside and country people). Read the instructions and then play the recording. Just let students listen to the song and pick out what words they can.

Elicit a few examples of words students remembered. Then ask them if they enjoyed the song and elicit why/why not.

Tapescript

Oats and beans and barley grow
As you and I and everyone knows,
Oats and beans and barley grows
As you and I and everyone knows,
A-waiting for a partner.

First the farmer sows his seeds,
Then he stands and takes his ease,
Stamps his feet and claps his hands
And turns around to view his lands
A-waiting for a partner.

Now you're married you must obey,
Must be true in all you say,
Must be kind and must be good
And help your wife to chop the wood,
A-waiting for a partner.

Oats and beans and barley grow
As you and I and everyone knows,
Oats and beans and barley grows
As you and I and everyone knows,
A-waiting for a partner.

2 Focus attention on the photos. Explain that they are called Ed, Will, and Ginger (the one with red hair!) Elicit the answer to *Where are they?* in each photo (SB p132: in a town; SB p133: on top of a hill; on a country road). Check the difference between *wear* and *carry* with simple mimes.

Put students in pairs to answer the rest of the questions. Then check the answers with the class. Ask students what they think the three men are doing and why. Elicit a range of possible ideas but don't confirm or reject answers at this stage.

Answers

SB p132: They are in a town; SB p133: They are on top of a hill and on a country road.
They're wearing trousers, green/brown shirts or jackets, hats, and walking boots.
SB p132: They're standing in the doorway of a church and waiting for people to give them money; SB p133: They're standing on top of a hill and singing; they're walking along a country road.
They're carrying backpacks, walking sticks, and walking/camping equipment.

3 This exercise focuses on the first part of the article as far as … *look and feel happier*. Get students to read this part of the text quite quickly, asking others for help with vocabulary if you didn't pre-teach the items listed in *About the text* or set them for homework. Monitor and help with any queries.

Elicit the correction to sentence 1. Then let students continue the task, working in pairs.

Check the answers with the class.

Answers

1 It isn't a rainy Sunday morning. It's a sunny Saturday afternoon.
2 They aren't carrying suitcases and wearing suits and ties. They're carrying backpacks and walking sticks. They're wearing green and brown jackets, hats, and boots.
3 They don't start singing pop songs. They start singing folk songs.
4 The people of Petersfield are interested. They stop to listen and smile.
5 They do give the men some money. The hat is soon full.

4 Explain that students are going to read the second part of the text – *Meet the singers* and *Why are they doing this?* Set a time limit of about two–three minutes to encourage students to read quickly.

Students read and find the answers to the questions in exercise 4, working in pairs. Encourage them to ask other students for help with vocabulary if you didn't pre-teach the items listed in *About the text* or set them for homework. Monitor and help with any queries.

Check the answers with the class. Ask students if the predictions they made about Ed, Will, and Ginger before reading the text were correct.

Answers

1 Ed is 27, Ginger is 25, and Will is 26.
2 Ed and Ginger are brothers.
3 They walk in good and bad weather, and in all seasons.
4 They sleep anywhere they can find, in woods, fields, and sometimes houses.
5 They met when they were all at school together in Canterbury.
6 Ed became an artist, Ginger became a gardener, and Will a bookseller.
7 They sing in streets, pubs, and market squares.
8 Their families worry about their futures.
9 Last year they started a website and they made a CD of 16 of their songs.
10 This year they are going to make podcasts to tell more stories of their walks and they're going to make another CD. They also plan to start a charity to help traditional country activities.

What do you think?

Put students into groups of three or four to discuss their answers. Monitor and help as necessary but don't interrupt or over-correct as this is primarily a fluency task.

Allow the discussion to continue for as long as students' interest is held, and exchanges are taking place mainly in English! Elicit a range of opinions in a feedback session.

Possible answers

They are walking around Britain to have fun/to teach folk songs to local people/to stop folk songs from disappearing/to help protect the countryside.
Simple human activities include: walking/singing/talking/spending time with friends/eating local food/drinking water/sleeping/being healthy.
Less simple human activities include: working long hours, travelling long distances to school/work, not spending time with family and friends, eating junk food, trying to find a job, being competitive at school/work.

Roleplay

5 This gives students the opportunity to transfer the information in the text to a speaking activity. Put students into A/B pairs and assign the role of journalist to the A students and the role of one of the singers to the B students.

Give students time to prepare their roles. The A students can use the questions in exercise 4 as a starting point but encourage them to think of their own questions too. The B students can look back at the text and make notes of the key information. Encourage them to use their imagination to add details about the singers' way of life and philosophy.

Demonstrate the activity by getting two students to ask and answer the questions from the prompts in the Students Book. Students continue the roleplay in their pairs. (If you want to do the *Extra Activity* below, get the journalist in each pair to note down any interesting information to use in their report.) Monitor and help as necessary. Note down any common errors but don't correct these until after the roleplay.

SUGGESTION

You can ask pairs of students to act out their interview to the whole class. If you have access to recording equipment, it would be a great idea to record some of the roleplays and play them back to the whole class for them to comment on and correct. Students often find this very productive and satisfying.

EXTRA ACTIVITY

Students follow up their roleplay with a written task. The A students (journalists) write up the notes from the interview into a report for their newspaper. The B students (one of the singers) write the text for a podcast, telling the story of one of their walks.

Project

See *Note* at the start of this section. Ask students to use some of the following headings to help them do the research and organize their notes:

Country and region

Type of music

Musicians, singers, and instruments

Favourite song(s)

Story in the song(s)

If appropriate, encourage them to bring some visuals/recordings to support their presentation, e.g. a map and photos, an MP3 or recording on CD. If you have access to computers, students can give their talk with the support of a presentation program.

When students give their presentation, ask students to come to the front of the class (or stand up in front of their group in larger classes) and make sure the rest of the class is quiet and pays attention. Allow students to refer to their notes but don't let them read the information from a script. Encourage the class/groups to ask questions to the presenter. Be generous with praise after students have presented their talk, as it can be rather nerve-wracking, especially for weaker students.

VOCABULARY AND LISTENING (SB p134)

What's the weather like?

NOTE

The last task in this section asks students to write a short weather forecast for the coming weekend. If possible, get students to research the weather for the country they are studying in ahead of the lesson.

The British are well known for their interest in the weather and students may well have their own ideas about weather conditions in the UK. A few points to note:

- Weather is often the initial topic in any conversation in Britain. Students can be encouraged to talk about the weather as a 'safe' opening topic, particularly with people they don't know.
- Despite London's reputation, the last big fog/smog (smoke + fog) was in 1957 when the Clean Air Act was passed!
- There are lots of jokes about British weather. Can your students understand this one?

  If you don't like English weather, wait ten minutes!

⚠ POSSIBLE PROBLEMS

What … like? for descriptions always creates some difficulty because of the different use of *like*. Be prepared to make these two points clear to your students:

1 It has nothing to do with the verb *like*. The note on *What … like?* will help you do this.

2 The answer does not contain the word *like*.
What's the weather like? It's sunny. NOT **It's like sunny.*

1 **T 11.9** **[CD 3: Track 33]** Focus attention on the photo and ask *What's her job?* (She's a weather forecaster.) Then focus on the map. Point to the following areas/countries and elicit the names, checking pronunciation as you go: the UK, Scandinavia, Poland, Germany, Norway, Hungary, Russia, Italy, Turkey, Greece, Portugal, Spain, and France. Also check the pronunciation of the cities Warsaw and Nice.

Explain that students are going to hear a weather forecast for Europe. They don't need to understand every word, but just listen for the temperatures to add to the map and for the correct season.

Play the recording as far as *20 degrees celsius* and elicit the temperature for the cities of Berlin and Warsaw – 20°C. Point out that for some temperatures students will here the name of a country, not a city. Play the rest of the recording without stopping. Let students check their answers in pairs. Play the recording again if necessary to let students check/complete their answers.

Check the answers with the class.

Answers and tapescript

Berlin/Warsaw 20°C
London 19°C
Oslo 17°C
Budapest 23°C
Moscow 15°C
Rome 24°C
Istanbul 21°C
Athens 28°C
Madrid/Lisbon 32°C
Paris 20°C
Nice 29°C

The season is late summer.

T 11.9

Presenter Here's Fiona with the weather for Europe for the next 24 hours.

Fiona Hello there. Here's the forecast for Europe today. At the moment there's some wet and windy weather over the UK and Scandinavia, and this is going to move south and east over Poland and Germany. Temperatures in Berlin and Warsaw are now about 20°C but it's cooler in London, 19°C, and cooler still in Oslo, 17°C. To the south it's a bit warmer, in Budapest, 23°C, but to the east, cool and cloudy in Moscow, where the temperature is a welcome 15°C after all that extreme summer heat. Moving south it's getting warmer, 24°C in Rome, but it's going to be cloudy and showery across much of Italy and also over northern Turkey, with heavy rain in Istanbul and a temperature of 21°C. Most other Mediterranean countries are going to be warm and dry. Greece will be hot and sunny with a lot of late summer sunshine, 28°C in Athens and warmer still in Portugal and Spain with temperatures up to 32°C. France is going to be cool and cloudy in the north, 20°C in Paris, and hot and stormy in the south with a high of 29°C in Nice. And that's your European weather for today. I'll be back at lunchtime with an update.

Presenter Thank you Fiona, and now …

2 Ask students to look at the weather symbols on the map. Elicit words for symbols students already know and then get them to continue working in pairs to match the remaining symbols and words. If students have access to dictionaries, get them to look up words they don't know.

Go through the answers with the class.

Answers

sunny = 
rainy = 
windy = 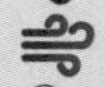
cloudy = 
stormy = 

snowy and foggy are not in the forecast

3 This exercise is to practise which pairs of adjectives commonly go together to describe weather. This will vary in different countries according to the climate, for example it can be warm and windy in many climates but is only rarely so in Britain.

Lead in to the topic by asking students for their ideas about British weather. (Everyone always has something to say about British weather!)

Focus attention on the examples. Then get students to continue making sentences working in pairs. Monitor and help as necessary.

Sample answers (for Britain)

cool and cloudy	cold and windy
cool and rainy	warm and sunny
cool and windy	hot and sunny
cold and cloudy	cold and foggy
dry and cloudy	cold and rainy
wet and windy	cold and snowy

Also you often hear the pairs *warm and dry*, *cold and wet* together.

SUGGESTION

If you have time, you could have a mini-discussion comparing which pairs of words go together to describe the climate in Britain and which for the climate of their own country.

T 11.10 **[CD 3: Track 34]** Draw a large question mark on the board to signal that you are going to introduce a question form.

Play the recording and get students to repeat chorally and individually. Read the note on *What ... like*? with students (See *Possible problems* above).

4 Practise the question and elicit possible answers about where you are and about other places that students know. Encourage students to use some of the sentences from exercise 3. Drill the pronunciation as necessary.

5 **T 11.11** **[CD 3: Track 35]** Give students a few moments to read the gapped conversation. Play the recording and get students to write in the weather for today, yesterday, and tomorrow. Check the answers.

Students practise the questions and answers about the weather where you are in open and then closed pairs. Monitor and check for correct tense use.

Answers and tapescript

A What's the weather like today?
B It's **cool** and **cloudy**.
A What was it like yesterday?
B Oh, it was **wet** and **windy**.
A And what's it going to be like tomorrow?
B I think it's going to be **warm** and **sunny**.

6 This is an information-gap activity. Divide the class into A/B pairs. If possible, get students to sit opposite each other so they can't see each other's books. Tell Student A to look at the world weather information on SB p195 of the Student's Book and Student B at the information on SB p198.

Briefly check the pronunciation of the cities, focusing in particular on *Edinburgh* /ˈedɪnbrə/ and *Reykjavik* /ˈreɪkjəvɪk/.

Demonstrate the activity by doing the first question and answer about Berlin across the class. This is a good time to feed in the modifier *quite*, if you feel your students can cope with it. Make sure they realize that this is tomorrow's weather and therefore they need to use *going to* in the questions and answers.

Get students to continue the activity in closed pairs. Monitor and check as they do it.

Check the answers with the whole class. Get students to read out their answers as complete sentences, e.g. *It's going to be rainy and (quite) cold in Berlin tomorrow. 7 degrees.*

Answers

World weather: tomorrow

		°C	It's going to be:
Berlin	R	7	wet/rainy and cold
Boston	Fg	6	foggy and cold
Cairo	S	18	sunny and warm
Edinburgh	C	5	cloudy and cold
Hong Kong	S	29	sunny and hot
London	R	10	wet/rainy and cool
Luxor	S	40	sunny and very hot
Milan	Fg	9	foggy and cool
Moscow	Sn	-1	snowy and very cold
Mumbai	C	18	cloudy and warm
Prague	R	4	wet/rainy and cold
Reykjavik	Sn	-4	snowy and very cold
Rio de Janeiro	R	24	wet/rainy and hot
Sydney	C	22	cloudy and warm

S = sunny C = cloudy Fg = foggy R = rainy Sn = snowy

7 Elicit/pre-teach the points of the compass (*north, south, east, west*). Also pre-teach/check other useful vocabulary to referring to regions of a country, e.g. *in/over the mountains, on the coast*, etc. Get students to think about different areas of the country where they are studying and make notes about the weather for the coming weekend. Students can use the information they researched before the lesson (see *Notes* above) or base their forecast on recent weather conditions.

Give students time to write their forecast. Monitor and help as necessary. Students read their forecast to a partner and compare the details for each area.

EVERYDAY ENGLISH (SB p135)

Making suggestions

NOTE

In order not to overload students, we have restricted the functional content to two of the most common expressions for asking for and making suggestions:

- *shall* to ask for suggestions and make suggestions, e.g. *What shall we do?/Shall we go out for dinner?*
- *Let's* to make a suggestion for everyone, e.g. *Let's go to the cinema.*

Will for spontaneous decisions is also included, but just for recognition.

1 Focus attention on the headings in the chart and the two examples. Then elicit a few more activities for good weather (*go for a walk, play tennis, do gardening,* etc.) and some for bad weather (*read a book, do a jigsaw, play chess,* etc.) Students continue the two lists, working individually and then compare their lists with a partner.

Elicit examples from the whole class and build more lists on the board. Tell students that they will need their lists later in the lesson.

2 **T 11.12** **[CD 3: Track 36]** Tell students that they are going to hear two conversations, one for good weather and one for bad. Ask them to read the gapped conversations quickly. With weaker students, get them to predict possible words for each gap.

Play the recording and get students to complete the conversations.

Check the answers. Then get students to listen and repeat in chorus. First focus on the question, and then practise the answer. Encourage good stress and intonation.

What shall we do? /wɒt ʃəl wi duː/

Let's go for a walk. /lets gəʊ fərə wɔːk/

Ask students to practise the conversations in pairs.

Answers and tapescript

1 **A** What a lovely day?
B Yeah! It's really **warm** and **sunny**. What shall we do?
A Let's **go for a walk**!

2 **A** What an awful day! It's raining again.
B I know. It's so **cold** and **wet**! What shall we do?
A Let's **stay in** and **watch a DVD**.

Read through the notes on *Shall we* and *Let's* with the whole class. In a monolingual class, you could ask students to translate the sentences.

3 **T 11.13** **[CD 3: Track 37]** Ask your students to work in pairs. Ask them first to find the 'good weather' lines and then the 'bad weather' lines. Then ask them to put each set in order to complete the conversations from exercise 2.

Play the recording and get students to listen and check their answers.

Students work in their pairs to practise the conversation. Monitor and check. If students have problems with pronunciation, play key lines of the recording again, drilling chorally and individually. Then let students continue practising the conversation in closed pairs.

Answers and tapescript

T 11.13

1 **A** What a lovely day!
B Yeah! It's really warm and sunny. What shall we do?
A Let's go for a walk!
B Oh no! It's too hot to walk.
A OK, let's go to the beach.
B Good idea! Why don't we take a picnic?

2 **A** What an awful day! It's raining again.
B I know. It's so cold and wet! What shall we do?
A Let's stay in and watch a DVD.
B Oh no, that's boring! We did that last night.
A OK then, shall we go out for a coffee?
B Great! I'll get my coat and an umbrella!

4 Students continue to work in pairs, changing partner if appropriate. Ask them to look at the lists they made in exercise 1. Demonstrate the activity by asking for examples of a good weather and a bad weather activity and building the conversations with the whole class. Get students to continue in pairs, using the activities in their lists. Monitor and check. Note down any common errors but don't feed back on these until after the activity.

SUGGESTION

To round off the activity in exercise 4, you could either ask a couple of pairs to act out their conversations for the whole class, or record a few conversations and play them for the class to correct any mistakes in the language and the pronunciation.

Photocopiable Activity

UNIT 11 Making suggestions TB p158/TRD

Note: This activity is best used in a later lesson as consolidation and not straight after finishing SB p135.

Materials: One copy of the worksheet for each student.

Procedure: Explain that students are going to do a worksheet to practise making suggestions. Lead in to the topic by asking *What's the weather like today? What activities could we do?* Elicit a range of possible answers.

- Hand out a copy of the worksheet to each student. Elicit an example of a good and a bad weather activity for exercise 1. Students complete the task, working in pairs. Check the answers.

Answers

Good weather	Bad weather
go to the beach	go to a gallery
have a picnic	play cards
go for a walk	go to the cinema
go fishing	update our blog
play golf	make a cake
do some gardening	watch a DVD

- Focus attention on the flow diagram in exercise 2. Elicit possible lines in an example conversation with the whole class. If students have problems with pronunciation, drill key lines as necessary. Encourage a lively delivery with a good voice range. With weaker classes, write the conversation on the board to provide added support.
- Put students in pairs and give them time to build their conversation, using the prompts in brackets. Monitor and help as necessary.
- Students work with a new partner and make another conversation. Encourage them to choose a different type of weather and so different activities. Students act out their conversation(s) for the rest of the class.
- As an extension, divide the class into groups of three and get them to plan an evening out for the class. They need to make suggestions on when/where to meet and what activities to do. Students present their ideas to the class and then vote for the idea they like best.

Don't forget!

Grammar Reference (SB p192 and Teacher's Resource Disc)
Unit 11

Word list (SB p221 and Teacher's Resource Disc)
Unit 11

Test (Teacher's Resource Disc)
Unit test 11A
Unit test 11B

Video (DVD)
Unit 11 A charity expedition

12 Never ever!

Present Perfect • *ever, never, yet,* and *just* • *take* and *get* • Transport and travel

This unit introduces one of the most difficult tenses for students of English. The Present Perfect is one of the most commonly used tenses in English, especially spoken English, but its presentation has been left until Unit 12. This is because until students have understood the concept that the Past Simple refers to the definite past, they will not be able to grasp the idea that the Present Perfect refers to the indefinite past. The second grammar section brings together all the key tenses students have covered in this level.

The theme of this unit is 'in my life', and various people's experiences in life and travel are explored. The skills section focuses on experiences at the Glastonbury Music Festival. The *Everyday English* section further develops the travel theme with a focus on transport by bus, train, and plane.

LANGUAGE INPUT

GRAMMAR

Present Perfect + *ever* and *never* (SB p140)	• Understanding and practising the Present Perfect to talk about experiences.
Present Perfect + *yet* and *just* (SB p142)	• Understanding and practising the Present Perfect with the adverbs *yet* and *just*.

VOCABULARY

take and *get* (SB p146)	• Understanding and practising words and expressions that go with *take* and *get*.

EVERYDAY ENGLISH

Transport and travel (SB p147)	• Understanding and practising useful words and expressions in travel situations.

SKILLS DEVELOPMENT

READING

The Glastonbury festival (SB p144)	• An article about the Glastonbury Music Festival.

LISTENING

Two people talk about experiences at a music festival (SB p145)	• Listening for key information in two anecdotes about a music festival. T 12.8 (SB p182/TRD)

SPEAKING

Talking about you (SB p142)	• Asking and answering questions about experiences.
What do you think? (SB p145)	• Discussing the Glastonbury Music Festival.
Talking about you (SB p146)	• Asking and answering questions to practise words and expressions that go with *take* and *get*.

WRITING

A poem – Choosing the right word (SB p167)	• Choosing words to complete a poem, then writing additional verses.

MORE MATERIALS

Photocopiable worksheets – Have you ever …? (TB p159/TRD), Challenge! (TRD) **Tests** (TRD) **Video** (DVD)

STARTER (SB p140)

This section is a fun way of getting students into the topic of places people have visited.

1 Focus attention on the first two flags and elicit the names of the corresponding countries and their capitals. Students continue the task, working in pairs/small groups.

Check the answers with the whole class. If students have problems with the pronunciation of the countries, drill them chorally and individually.

Answers

a Italy – Rome	g Australia – Canberra
b Switzerland – Bern	h Brazil – Brasília
c Spain – Madrid	i China – Beijing
d Egypt – Cairo	j Japan – Tokyo
e Great Britain – London	k The US – Washington D.C.
f Greece – Athens	l Hungary – Budapest

2 Tell students the countries you have been to. Students then tick (✓) the countries they have visited. Elicit a range of examples from the class.

BEEN THERE! DONE THAT! (SB p140)

Present Perfect + *ever* and *never*

⚠ POSSIBLE PROBLEMS

In this unit, the coverage of the Present Perfect is staged across the two presentations. In this first section, we introduce one of the main uses of the Present Perfect – to refer to an experience at some time in your life. On SB p142, we focus on another use – to refer to the present result of a past action – with the adverbs *yet* and *just*. We do not introduce at all the third main use of the Present Perfect, which is to refer to unfinished past (*I have been a teacher for ten years*), nor do we teach the Present Perfect Continuous.

The aim of this unit is to provide an introduction to the Present Perfect, but do not expect your students to master it quickly! It takes a long time (and a lot of mistakes, correction, and re-teaching) before students feel confident with this tense.

The following aspects of the tense often present problems:

- A similar form of auxiliary verb *have* + past participle exists in many European languages, but it is used in a very different way. In English, the Present Perfect expresses the concept of an action happening at an indefinite time before now, and so it cannot be used when a definite time is given.
- Students find the difference between *He's gone to Paris.* and *He's been to Paris.* quite confusing. We do not suggest that you attempt to sort this out at this stage of the presentation.
- Students have already seen a Present Perfect form with the structure *have got*, but we do not suggest that you mention this at all. It would be very confusing for students, as *have got* expresses an essentially present-time concept.

Common mistakes

**I have seen him last week.*
**When have you been to the States?*
**Did you ever try Chinese food?*
**In my life I went to most countries in Europe.*

1 **T 12.1** **[CD 3: Track 38]** Focus attention on the photo and read the instructions. Ask students to identify Kyle and Lara. Ask *What nationality are they?* (Australian) and *Where are they?* (In a camping/travel shop).

Read the questions as a class. Then play the conversation and elicit the answers.

Answers and tapescript

They are talking about Lara and Mel's trip to Europe.
Mel is Lara's friend.
Lara wants to end the conversation because Mel is waiting for her and they've got a lot to do.

T 12.1

K = Kyle **L** = Lara

K Hi Lara! Are you and Mel ready for your trip?
L Yeah, nearly, we leave next Monday for Rome.
K Ah, Rome, I've been to Rome many times.
L Well, I've never been there. It's my first time in Europe.
K Really? What about your friend, Mel?
L She's been to London and Paris, but she hasn't been to Rome.
K Ah, London and Paris. I've been there, too. I studied in Paris for a year before I went to work in New York. Have you ever been to the US?
L No, I haven't, I haven't travelled much at all, so I'm really excited.
K Oh, I've been to North *and* South America so many times and I've …
L I'm sure you have, Kyle. Oh dear, look at the time! Mel's waiting for me. We've got so much to do. Bye Kyle, we'll send you a postcard.

2 **T 12.2** **[CD 3: Track 39]** Ask students to do this task from memory. With weaker students, you could ask *Who has travelled a lot?* (Kyle) *Who hasn't visited many countries?* (Lara) but don't give an explanation of the Present Perfect at this stage.

Focus attention on the example. Give students time to complete the task and check in pairs before checking with the class.

Play the recording of the sentences and get students to repeat chorally and individually. Check students can reproduce the contracted forms in each sentence. Correct any mistakes carefully.

Remember that students will probably never have seen the Present Perfect tense before, and *been* will be unfamiliar. If students query the tense, explain, using L1 if possible, that *have been* is an example of the Present Perfect tense. Don't try to do a full presentation at this stage, but just explain that the sentences refer to the idea of 'some time in your life'. Focus attention on the highlighted contracted forms. Also elicit the full form of *hasn't* (*has not*) and *haven't* (*have not*).

Answers and tapescript

1 I've been to Rome many times. **(Kyle)**
2 I've never been there. **(Lara)**
3 She's been to London and Paris. **(Mel)**
4 She hasn't been to Rome. **(Mel)**
5 I haven't travelled much at all. **(Lara)**
6 I've been to North and South America. **(Kyle)**

3 Demonstrate the activity yourself with information about the countries you have and haven't visited. Ask students to read the examples in the Student's Book aloud. Then ask students to make similar sentences, saying which countries they have/haven't been to. Elicit examples from a range of students, so you can check students' accuracy in the use and pronunciation of the structure.

Students then continue the activity in groups. Monitor and check. Correct any mistakes carefully with the class after the groupwork.

4 **T 12.3** **[CD 3: Track 40]** This activity introduces the question form and covers the 'experience' use of the Present Perfect in contrast to the Past Simple.

Give students a few moments to read the gapped conversation through. Then play the recording and let students complete the replies.

Get students to read the conversation across the class. If necessary, highlight the main stresses in the Present Perfect questions and short answers:

Have you ever been to Greece?

No, I haven't.

Play the recording again or model the sentences yourself and get students to repeat.

Focus attention on the question form of the Present Perfect and name the tense. Then focus on *When did you go? Where did you go?* and *Did you have a good time?* Ask *What tense this is?* (Past Simple). Just name the tenses at this stage and do not try to explain the different uses. (These are given in the *Grammar Spot* below.)

Get students to ask you questions about countries you have been to, following the model in exercise 4. Encourage them to ask *When did you go? Where did you go?* and *Did you have a good time?* and give appropriate answers.

Students continue in open pairs asking and answering about countries they have been to, when and where, and if they had a good time. This might sound repetitive, but remember you are introducing students to a very new concept with the Present Perfect tense and they need practice with forming questions, answers, and negatives.

Answers and tapescript
A Have you ever been to Greece?
B No, I **haven't**.
A Have you ever been to Italy?
B Yes, I **have**.
A When did you go?
B Two years **ago**.
A Where did you go?
B Rome, Florence, and Venice.
A Fantastic! Did you have a good time?
B Yes, I **did**. It was great!

5 Students write down the names of two countries or cities and make similar conversations, working in pairs. Monitor and check for accuracy in the use and pronunciation of the two tenses. Highlight and correct any mistakes carefully.

6 This practises the third person singular in a personalized way. Students will need to make the change from *have/haven't* to *has/hasn't*. Focus attention on the examples and elicit the full form of *Maria's* (*Maria has*). Drill the examples chorally and individually. Then elicit examples from a range of students about their partner.

GRAMMAR SPOT (SB p141)

1 Read the notes with the whole class. Point out the use of *ever* with the Present Perfect in the question form to mean 'at any time in your life'. Stress that we do not use *ever* in the answer.

2 Read the notes with the whole class. Focus attention on the use of the Past Simple to say exactly when something happened. Elicit other past time references that can be used with the Past Simple, e.g. *last month*, *a long time ago*, *yesterday*, etc.

3 Read the notes with the whole class and get students to complete the charts. Check the answers.

Answers

	Positive	Negative	
I/You/We/They	**have**	**haven't**	been to Paris.
He/She	**has**	**hasn't**	

4 Students complete the sentences with *ever* or *never*. Check the answers.

Answers
Has he **ever** been to London?
He's **never** been to Paris.

►► Read Grammar Reference 12.1 and 12.2 on SB p192 together in class, and/or ask students to read it at home. Encourage them to ask you questions about it.

SUGGESTION

If your students have a similar tense form in their language, you might like to make a brief comparison in L1 between the way L1 and English use the auxiliary verb *have* + past participle. Be careful, however! Keep it short, and as simple as possible, because it would be very easy to overload students with too much information at this early stage of their exposure to the Present Perfect.

7 This exercise presents the past participle of a range of high-frequency verbs. Many of them are used in exercises that come later in this unit and they are very common verbs when talking about experiences.

Remind students of the terms *past participle* and *infinitive* and elicit examples for *been (be/go)* and *lived (live)*. Tell students that they will often be able to guess which infinitive a past participle comes from.

Students write in the infinitives for the rest of the verbs. Get students to check in pairs before checking with the whole class. Elicit which two verbs are regular.

Answers

been	be/go	failed	fail	given	give
lived	live	seen	see	made	make
flown	fly	slept	sleep	had	have
met	meet	run	run	taken	take
eaten	eat	bought	buy	done	do

The two regular verbs are *live* and *fail*.

8 Elicit the Past Simple forms of *be (was/were)* and *live (lived)* and get students to continue the list in pairs.

▶▶ Refer students to the list of irregular verbs on SB p202 and get them to check their answers.

9 Focus attention on the examples. Say a few more verbs in the infinitive and elicit the Past Simple and past participle. Students continue the task in pairs, taking it in turns to test each other. Encourage students to get faster and faster as they do the task.

PRACTICE (SB p142)

Talking about you

This section consolidates the use of Present Perfect to ask about experiences and the Past Simple to talk about exactly when/how something happened.

1 Focus attention on the bulleted list and pre-teach/check the following vocabulary: *foreign* /ˈfɒrən/, *rise*, *jumbo jet*, *tent*, and *marathon*.

Ask students to go through the list and tick the things they have done.

SUGGESTION

With weaker classes or if you want to give students additional practice before the groupwork in exercise 2, you could get students to ask you the questions in the bulleted list. Make sure they remember to include *ever* in the Present Perfect questions and to use the Past Simple in the follow-up questions.

2 Put students into groups of three or four to ask and answer the questions in the list. Focus attention on the example exchanges in the Student's Book. With weaker students, you could go through other possible follow-up questions for some of the prompts, e.g. *Have you ever worked through the night? Why did you do that? How did you feel? What time did you go to bed?*

Get students to ask and answer the questions, giving true answers. If necessary, highlight the contrastive stress in the third speech bubble:

Well, I have.

Give students time to work through the list, encouraging a reasonably fast pace so that students don't stay on the same question for too long. Monitor and check for correct formation of the questions and short answers, both Present Perfect and Past Simple, and for accurate pronunciation. If students have problems, drill key forms chorally and individually and then get students to repeat the groupwork.

3 Focus attention on the example. Students tell the class about people in their group. Make sure they give follow-up information in the Past Simple where appropriate, e.g. *Kati has flown in a jumbo jet. She flew from London to New York five years ago.*

Photocopiable Activity

UNIT 12 Have you ever ...? TB p159/TRD

Materials: If you have ten students or fewer, cut up one copy of the worksheet into cue cards. If you have a larger group, divide up two copies to create two parallel mingling activities.

Procedure: Explain that students are going to do a mingling activity to practise the Present Perfect and Past Simple.

- Briefly review the use of the Present Perfect with *ever* to mean 'at some time in your life' and the use of the Past Simple to ask about a specific time in the past, e.g. *Have you ever had a phone conversation in English? Who did you speak to?*
- Hand out a question card to each student. If you have fewer than ten students, give the stronger students more than one card. Check students understand the questions on their card and that they understand they will need to ask a question of their own to get more information. Demonstrate the activity by getting two students to ask and answer sample questions in open pairs. Point out that if someone answers *No, I haven't* to the first question, the student asking the question should just say *OK, thank you* and move on to the next person.
- Get the students to stand up and do the mingling activity, encouraging them to ask their question to as many other students as possible and to modify their follow-up questions as appropriate. Monitor and check for correct question formation, but don't correct errors until after the activity.
- If you have time and/or if you think your students need more practice, get students to think of their own *Have you ever ...?* and follow-up question. You could write a range of past participles on the board to help them with ideas, e.g. *ridden*, *flown*, *run*, *made*, etc.
- Elicit any interesting information from the class in a short feedback session. Remind students to use the Past Simple if they say exactly when someone did something. Then check any common errors, encouraging students to self-correct.

GETTING READY TO GO! (SB p142)

Present Perfect + *yet* and *just*

⚠ POSSIBLE PROBLEMS

The concepts expressed by *yet* and *just* are very subtle and they are realized by different structures in different languages. We do not ask any questions in the *Grammar Spot* that test concept (only form), because the language required would be more complex than the target items themselves. Students should be able to get the meaning through context and use, but you need to make sure, probably via translation into L1 if possible, that students have understood them. Explain that *(not) yet* means '(not) before now' whereas *just* means 'a short time before now'. Use examples from the text and/or put additional examples on the board.

Note that American English can use the Past Simple with *just* and *yet*.

Did you do your homework yet? I just did it.

SUGGESTION

- Be prepared to prompt and help with the questions in the *Grammar Spot*, as students may find them hard.

1 **T 12.4** **[CD 3: Track 41]** Focus attention on the photo of Lara. Elicit information about her (*She's Australian. She's planning a trip to Europe.*) Ask *Who is the other girl?* (Mel, Lara's friend.) *Is she going to Europe with Lara?* (Yes, she is.)

Focus attention on the 'Things to do' list and ask students to locate it in the photo. Read the list as a class, referring to the photo to add support, and check comprehension of *packing*, *print e-tickets* (= electronic tickets), and *check in online*. With weaker students, elicit the past participle for each verb in the 'Things to do list' (*bought*, *finished*, *collected*, *emailed*, *found*, *printed*, *checked*).

Read the instructions for exercise 1 as a class. Play the recording as far as *we did that a while ago* and focus attention on the example. Students listen to the rest of the recording and put a tick next to the things Lara and Mel have done. They can put a cross (✗) next to the things they haven't done. Only play the recording a second time if students had problems doing the task.

Check the answers.

Answers and tapescript
Things to do …
1 buy new backpacks ✓
2 finish packing ✗
3 collect euros from bank ✓
4 email Mel's aunt in London ✓
5 find out weather forecast for Rome ✓
6 print e-tickets ✓
7 check in online ✗

T 12.4
L = Lara M = Mel

L Where's the list?
M I've got it. OK let's check through. Er- we've bought new backpacks, we did that a while ago.
L They look quite big. I hope we can carry them.
M No worries. I haven't finished packing mine yet. Have you?
L Not yet, just one or two more things to go in. Oh, have you collected the euros from the bank?
M Yup. I've just collected five hundred for you and five hundred for me.
L All our savings. I hope it's enough!
M No worries. We can stay with my aunt in London.
L Have you emailed her yet?
M Yeah, she's just emailed back. She's going to meet us at the airport when we fly in to London from Rome.
L Fantastic. Hey, look, I've just found out the weather in Rome for next week. Hot and sunny!
M Yeah, it's going to be so good. We're going to leave winter here, and arrive in the middle of summer in Europe.
L What about the tickets?
M I think we only need passports, but I've printed e-tickets just in case, but I haven't checked in online yet. You can only do that 24 hours before the flight.
L Oh Mel! I am so excited. I can't wait.

2 **T 12.4** **[CD 3: Track 41]** Refer students back to the 'Things to do' list. If you didn't do so in exercise 1, elicit the past participle of each of the verbs in the list (*bought*, *finished*, *collected*, *emailed*, *found*, *printed*, *checked*). Drill the examples in the Student's Book and elicit one or two more examples. If students query the use of *yet*, just explain it means 'before now'.

Students continue working in pairs, saying what Lara and Mel have and haven't done. Monitor and check for the correct form of the Present Perfect and the correct position of *yet*.

Play the recording again so that students can check their answers. Then check the answers with the whole class.

Refer students to **T 12.4** on SB p182. Get them to practise the conversation in pairs. If students have problems with pronunciation, drill key lines chorally and individually and then get students to repeat the pairwork.

Answers
1 They've bought new backpacks.
2 They haven't finished packing yet.
3 They've collected euros from the bank.
4 They've emailed Mel's aunt in London.
5 They've found out the weather forecast for Rome.
6 They've printed e-tickets.
7 They haven't checked in online yet.

See exercise 1 for **T 12.4**.

GRAMMAR SPOT (SB p142)

Look at the questions in the *Grammar Spot* as a class.

1 Get students to think about which form of *have* they need to complete the gapped sentences. Allow students to check in pairs before checking with the class. Focus on the use of *yet* and *just* in the sentences, and check comprehension (see *Possible problems*).

Answers
1 They **haven't** finished packing yet.
2 **Have** you emailed your aunt yet?
3 She**'s** just emailed back.

2 Elicit the answers to the questions about the position of *yet* and *just*.

Answers
yet comes at the end of a sentence
just comes before the past participle

3 Allow students time to work out the rules for the use of *yet*. Check the answer.

Answer
We can use *yet* only in questions and negative sentences, not in positive sentences.

▸▸ Read Grammar Reference 12.3 on SB p192 together in class, and/or ask students to read it at home. Encourage them to ask you questions about it.

PRACTICE (SB p143)

Tense revision

Exercises 1 and 2 help to review and consolidate the tenses students have covered in this level – Present Simple and Present Continuous, Past Simple and Present Perfect, and *going to*. Exercise 1 covers positive and negative forms, and exercise 2 *Wh*-question forms in a range of tenses.

NOTE
The places mentioned in Lara's description are:

Bali An island in Indonesia, which is a popular place for tourists because of its beaches and ancient traditions.

Perth The largest city in south-west Australia, located on the Swan River 20 km inland from the Indian Ocean.

Cairns A city and port on the north-east coast of Australia, in the state of Queensland.

Great Barrier Reef The largest coral reef in the world (about 2000 km long), located off the north-east coast of Australia.

A **747** refers to the Boeing passenger plane, often used for long-distance flights.

1 **T 12.5** **[CD 3: Track 42]** Tell students they are going to hear Lara talking about travelling and her trip to Europe. Pre-teach/check *to scuba dive*. Read the first sentence with the class and elicit the answer to number 1 (*haven't travelled*).

Put students in pairs to continue the task. With weaker students, you could write the range of tenses covered in the text on the board (see the note at the start of this section). Ask students to underline any answers that they are unsure about or can't agree on.

Elicit the numbers of the answers that students had problems with and write them on the board. Play the recording and let students check their answers. Go back to the 'problem' sentences on the board and confirm the correct answers. Ask students to explain the answers as best they can. If necessary, refer them back to the Grammar Reference at the end of the Student's Book.

Answers and tapescript
I'm really excited about my trip to Europe. I **haven't travelled** much outside Australia before. Just once, two years ago, I **went** on holiday to Bali with my family, but I**'ve never been** to Europe or the US. I often **travel** inside Australia. Last year I **flew** to Perth to visit my cousin, who **lives** there. It's a five-hour flight from Sydney, where I **live**. Australia's a big country! Also, I**'ve been** up to Cairns in the north three times. I **learned** to scuba dive there on the Great Barrier Reef. We**'ve just finished** packing, and now we**'re waiting** for the taxi to take us to the airport. I**'ve never flown** on a 747 before. It's a very long flight. It **takes** 20 hours to get to Rome. I**'m going to watch** films all the way. I can't wait!

2 Get students to ask and answer question 1 across the class as an example. Students then answer the questions, working individually. Monitor and help as necessary.

Put students in pairs to ask and answer the questions. Encourage students to give full answers so that they practise statement forms too. Monitor and check for correct question formation and verbs forms in the answers.

Students ask and answer the questions in open pairs to check with the whole class. Highlight and correct mistakes carefully.

Answers
1 She's excited about her trip to Europe.
2 Yes, she has, just once. She went to Bali two years ago.
3 Yes, she does. She often travels inside Australia.
4 She went to Perth to visit her cousin.
5 She lives in Sydney.
6 She's been to Cairns three times.
7 She learned to scuba dive.
8 They're going to the airport by taxi.
9 It takes 20 hours.
10 She's going to watch films all the way.

No, not yet!

3 **T 12.6** **[CD 3: Track 43]** Focus attention on the examples. Drill the question and possible answers, encouraging students to imitate the intonation and main stresses. Students give one or two more examples in open pairs. Remind them that they will need to use different pronouns in their answers (*it*/*him*/*her*) and that they should try to use *not yet* or *just* where possible.

Students continue working in closed pairs. Monitor and check for correct question formation and use of *yet* and *just*.

Play the recording and let students compare their answers. If you think students need further practice, put them in new pairs and get them to practise the questions and answers from **T 12.6** in closed pairs.

Tapescript

1 **A** Have you checked your emails yet?
  B Yes, I've just checked them but there wasn't one from you.
2 **A** Have you done the shopping?
  B No, I haven't. I'm too tired to go out.
3 **A** Have you washed your hair?
  B Yes, I've just washed it.
4 **A** Have you cleaned the car yet?
  B Yes, I've just cleaned your car and mine!
5 **A** Mum, have you made the dinner yet?
  B Yes, dinner's ready. Go and wash your hands.
6 **A** Have you done the washing-up yet?
  B No. I did it last night. It's your turn!
7 **A** Have you met the new student yet?
  B Yes, I have. I met her on the way to school this morning.
8 **A** Have you finished the exercise?
  B Yes, I've just finished it. Thank goodness!

Check it

4 This exercise revises the grammar just covered in the unit and also consolidates the main tenses covered in the course.

Students work in pairs to choose the correct sentence. Then check the answers with the whole class.

Answers

1 I saw Kyle yesterday.
2 Have you ever met my cousin?
3 When did she go to Bali?
4 What are you going to do in Rome?
5 He doesn't like flying.
6 Has Lara finished packing yet?
7 Have you ever been to a rock concert?

READING AND LISTENING (SB p144)

The Glastonbury festival

This skills section continues the theme of experiences with a focus on the Glastonbury Music Festival – considered a must-do experience by fans of contemporary music from all over the world.

NOTE

The following artists and bands are mentioned in the article on Glastonbury: Paul McCartney, Bruce Springsteen, Robbie Williams, rapper Jay Z, and soul singer Amy Winehouse, REM, Radiohead, Coldplay, Arctic Monkeys, and Sigur Ros (an experimental rock band from Iceland). Students are likely to be familiar with a good many of the artists but if you would like your students to hear examples of their music, you could bring in short extracts or ask your students to provide some of them.

ABOUT THE TEXT

Glastonbury /ˈglæstənbri/, known as *Glasto* for short, is one of the largest open-air music and performing arts festivals in the world. It is best known for its contemporary music, but also features dance, comedy, theatre, circus, and cabaret. Since the first festival in 1970, the event has grown in scope and popularity, with a number of different stages/performance areas dedicated to different styles of music and acts. Since 1981, the festival has been organized by local farmer and site owner Michael Eavis. Much of the profit from the festival is donated to local and international charities. The 2012 festival was cancelled because all the portable toilets were used at the Olympics. The highlight of the 2013 festival was the performance by the Rolling Stones.

Exercise 2 has an extract from a song by Turin Brakes, a folk-rock duo from London. They performed the song *They Can't Buy The Sunshine* at Glastonbury. See the above *Note* about other performers/bands mentioned in the article.

Sonar is an annual three-day music festival held in Barcelona, Spain.

Encourage students to use the context to help them with new vocabulary and to pool knowledge with other students, or use a dictionary. With weaker classes or if you are short of time, ask students to check some of following vocabulary before the lesson:

Homework prior to the lesson

acre /ˈeɪkə/, *farmland, act* (n), *to attend, slogan, mud, knee, to be great fun, highlight, rubbish* (adj), *complaint, atmosphere, toddler, crowd.*

1 Lead in to the topic by asking students *What's your favourite type of music?* and list different styles on the board. Ask *Do you prefer to listen to music on a CD/an iPod or hear music live?*

Then ask and answer the questions in exercise 1 with the class, eliciting a range of experiences and opinions. Elicit what students know about the Glastonbury Music Festival. If they haven't heard of it, focus on the photos and elicit impressions of the event and the people who attend it.

2 **T 12.7** **[CD 3: Track 44]** Tell students they are going to hear an extract from a song that was played at Glastonbury (see *About the text* above). Play the recording and elicit students' opinion of the song.

3 Get students to read the facts about Glastonbury quite quickly, asking others for help with vocabulary if you didn't pre-teach the items listed in *About the text* or set them for homework.

Students read and find the answers to the questions, working in pairs. Monitor and help with any queries.

Check the answers with the class. If appropriate, play extracts of music by the performers listed in the article (see *Note* above) and ask students for their opinions.

Elicit students' reactions to the facts about Glastonbury in a short feedback session.

Answers
1 It takes place in 1,000 acres of farmland in south-west England, in June. It lasts four days.
2 There are 21 hours of music every day.
3 In 1970, 1,500 people attended the first festival people. They paid £1 a ticket. Last year, 190,000 people attended. They paid £200 for a ticket.
4 Students' own answers.
5 In 2009, Michael Jackson died during the festival and T-shirts with the slogan 'I was at Glastonbury when Michael Jackson died' went on sale.
6 In 2005, it rained every day and people danced in the mud. It is a good song because the festival is famous for its rain.

4 This exercise focuses on the second part of the article and the experiences of people who have been to Glastonbury. The aim of the task is to get students to scan the paragraphs for the information they need to match the names to the questions. Stress that students don't need to understand every word to be able to do the task and that they may need more than one name for each question.

Focus attention on the photos of the four people and say each of their names. Set a time limit of about two minutes to ensure that students don't spend too long on the details in the article. If appropriate, you could set the task up as a race, with students working in pairs.

Students read quickly to find the correct names to match the questions. Check the names, eliciting the lines from the article that gave students the answers.

Answers
1 Marina (I've now been six times!)
2 Dave (my first time …), Izzi (This was my first year at Glastonbury.)
3 Marina (I loved it!), Len (We loved everything.), Izzi (It was amazing. Long live Glastonbury!)
4 Dave – mobile phones (Only one complaint – there were so many mobile phones.)
5 Len (I've taken my kids to Glastonbury twice. We watched Radiohead with my 11-year-old son.)
6 Izzi (I travelled 10,000 miles to be there.)

5 This exercise allows students to read the second part of the article again, this time more slowly so that they can process the information to answer the true/false questions.

Elicit the answer to number 1 as an example. Then put students in pairs to answer the other true/false questions. Get students to ask others in their group for help with vocabulary if you didn't pre-teach the items listed in *About the text* or set them for homework. Monitor and help with any queries.

Check the answers with the class, getting students to correct the false sentences.

Answers
1 False. She took off her shoes and danced in the mud up to her knees.
2 True
3 True
4 False. He thought there were too many mobile phones.
5 True
6 False. The crowds all moved back so his son could see better.
7 False. She's been to other festivals in Australia and Europe. She went to the Sonar Festival in Barcelona two years ago.
8 False. She travelled from New Zealand to be there.

Listening

6 **T 12.8** **[CD 3: Track 45]** Read the instructions to exercise 6 as a class. Pre-teach/check *highlights*, *pear cider*, *sausages*, *House music* (a type of modern electronic music that developed in the 1980s), *rubbish* (adj), *message board*. With weaker students, you could play the recording through once and elicit who had the best experience (*Daniel*) and then play it again and ask students to focus on the detail.

Write the headings *food*, *drink*, *music*, and *people* on the board. Tell students to listen for the information for each category. Point out that Daniel doesn't say anything about food or drink.

Play the recording of both Elsa and David and get students to make notes for each person. Students check their answers in pairs. Play the recording again to allow students to check/complete their answers.

Check the key information with the class and elicit who had the best experience.

Answers and tapescript
Elsa
Food: the best sausages and chips ever
Drink: pear cider
Music: disappointed with the music on Saturday night. DJs played House music all night but it was rubbish.
People: went back to her tent to finish a bottle of pear cider with friends.
Daniel
Music: brilliant
People: 100,000 friendly people – can have good conversations with people at Glastonbury.
Daniel had the best experience.

T 12.8
1 **Elsa from Birmingham, England**
OK, I've been to Glastonbury five times now. My highlights this year were: pear cider to drink, and the American diner van with the best sausages and chips ever. However, I was very disappointed with the music on Saturday night. DJs played House music all night. I love House but this was rubbish. I got really bored, so I went back to my tent to finish a bottle of pear cider with friends!
2 **Daniel Evans from Wales**
Last Wednesday at 2.30 in the afternoon, I decided that I wanted to go to Glastonbury. I was lucky! I found a ticket on the Glastonbury message boards. I'm so glad I went. The music was brilliant. Sometimes it took a long time to get to the stages. The queues were long but always friendly. In the busy 'real world' it's difficult to have good conversations with people. At Glastonbury you can do this. It's a great festival, with a great crowd of people. What more could you want? 100,000 friendly people. I wish the rest of life was the same! Four days out of 365 is a good start!

What do you think?

Discuss the questions as a class. Encourage students to give reasons for their answers. Establish how many students would/wouldn't like to go to Glastonbury and why.

EXTRA ACTIVITY

Students work in small groups to plan their own one-day music festival for an international audience of different ages. Tell them they need to plan who will perform on stage, the order of acts, and what facilities they want to offer to the public, e.g. food, things to buy, other entertainment, parking, etc. Also ask them to decide the timings, pricing of tickets, and also the name of a charity which will benefit from some of the profits.

Give students time to discuss their plans, making notes on their final choices. Students present their ideas to the rest of the class, who in turn ask questions/give opinions on each of the planned festivals. Students then vote for the one they like best.

VOCABULARY AND SPEAKING (SB p146)

take and *get*

The last vocabulary section in this level highlights an important feature of English – the use of high-frequency verbs like *take* and *get* that change their meaning according to the noun or expression that follows, e.g. ***take*** *photos/a break/a lot time/it easy*, etc.

1 Lead in to this section by writing on the board: *photos, married, a seat,* and *up in the morning*. Elicit which two examples go with *take* (*photos/a seat*) and which two with *get* (*married/up in the morning*).

Read the instructions to exercise 1 as a class. Then give students time to look at the sentences. Elicit the infinitive form of the expressions with *take* (*take place/take off/take a long time*) and *get* (*get on well/get bored*).

2 **T 12.9** **[CD 3: Track 46]** Elicit the answer to number 1 as an example. With weaker students, you could elicit the expressions students need to use in each conversation in the infinitive form and get students to put them into the correct tense.

Play the recording and let students check their answers. Then put students into pairs to practise the conversations. Monitor and check. If students have problems with pronunciation, drill key lines chorally and individually and then get students to repeat the pairwork.

Answers and tapescript

1 **A** Ugh! It's really hot in here.
B Why don't you **take off** your jumper?
2 **A** Is your office near where you live?
B No, it **takes a long** time to **get to** work
3 **A** What are your work colleagues like?
B Great! We all **get on** really **well**.
4 **A** How often are there exhibitions in the museum?
B They **take place** regularly, every two months.
5 **A** Do you like learning English?
B It's OK, but sometimes I **get** really **bored**!

3 Focus attention on the example. Then ask students to work in their pairs to categorize the words and expressions according to the verb.

Check the answers with the class. If appropriate, point out that *get* is often followed by an adjective to express the idea of 'become', e.g. *get ready/wet*.

Answers

take		get	
a test	it easy	home late	a lot of emails
photos	a taxi	on/off the bus	better soon
a long time		married	very wet
		ready	

4 **T 12.10** **[CD 3: Track 47]** Elicit the answer to number 1 as an example. With weaker students, you could elicit the tenses students need to use in each sentence as a class and then get students to write the correct forms.

Give students time to complete the sentences, working individually. Students then take it in turns to read the sentences aloud. Ask them to note down any differences in their answers.

Play the recording as a final check. Be prepared to explain the tense use if students had problems.

Answers and tapescript

1 The best way to **get** to the airport is to **take** a taxi.
2 How long **does** it **take** if you go by train?
3 I haven't **got** a camera. I **take** photos with my iPhone.
4 Sue **has taken** her driving test three times, and she's failed every time.
5 Are you still **getting** ready? We're going to be so late!
6 The doctor told me to **take** it easy if I want to **get** better soon.
7 It rained on the day we **got** married. We **got** very wet, but still had a great day.
8 You can't **get** on the bus with that big dog. Please, **get** off!

Talking about you

5 Tell students that they need to use a range of tenses in this exercise, as in exercise 4. Elicit the answer to number 1, then get students to complete the sentences, using the correct form of *take* or *get*. Monitor and help as necessary. With weaker classes, check students have completed the sentences correctly before they do the pairwork.

Put students in pairs to ask and answer the questions in closed pairs. If necessary, get students to ask and answer across the class as a final check.

Answers

1 How long does it **take** you to **get** to school?
2 What time do you **get** back home after school/work?
3 What time do you usually **get** up in the morning.
4 Have you **taken** any exams recently?
5 Does it **take** you a long time to **get** ready before you go out?
6 Are you **getting** tired of this exercise?

EXTRA ACTIVITY

Ask students to write some more personalized questions, using the expressions in this section, e.g. *Do you like taking photos? Do you get a lot of emails every day? Who do you get on well with at work/school?*, etc. Students work in new pairs/small groups to ask and answer the questions. Then ask students to report back about their partner/group in a short feedback session.

SUGGESTION

Students will meet more expressions with *take* and *get* and other verbs that have a lot of collocations as they continue their learning. It's a good idea to help them with organizing their vocabulary learning by suggesting they allocate a page for each of the verbs *take, get, have, make*, and *do*. They can add words/expressions to the relevant page as they come across them and add an example sentence and a translation into L1.

EVERYDAY ENGLISH (SB p147)

Transport and travel

This final *Everyday English* section continues the travel theme with a focus on the situational language used when travelling by bus, train, and plane.

1 Lead in to this section by asking students *When did you last travel by bus, train, or plane? Were there any problems?* Elicit a range of examples, writing up any relevant vocabulary on the board.

Focus attention on the chart and elicit an example for the *bus* column. Students work in pairs to complete the task.

Check the answers with the class, dealing with any pronunciation difficulties as you go. If necessary, remind students that the first part of compound nouns have greater stress, e.g. *airport, return ticket, bus stop.*

Answers

bus	train	plane
return ticket ticket office bus stop	return ticket arrivals railway station ticket office platform departures	airport return ticket arrivals boarding pass customs security check hand luggage flight departures

2 **T 12.11** [**CD 3: Track 48**] Tell students they are going to hear three travel announcements. They need to listen for the key words to match them to *bus, train*, or *plane*.

Play the recording and let students compare in pairs before checking with the class.

Answers and tapescript

1 train 2 bus 3 plane

T 12.11

1 The 11.55 for Newcastle stopping at Peterborough, York, and Darlington is now ready to board on Platform Ten. There is a buffet car on this train. Please check that you have all your luggage with you.
2 This is the number 22 for Piccadilly Circus. Next stop Green Park. Stand back from the doors, please.
3 Flight BA1536 to New York is now ready for boarding at Gate 58. Will passengers in rows 12 to 20 please board first. Passengers are reminded to keep their hand luggage with them at all times.

3 **T 12.11** [**CD 3: Track 48**] Pre-teach/check *gate* (the place in an airport where you get on/off a plane) and *row* /rəʊ/ (a line of seats in a plane). Play announcement 1 again and elicit the numbers and what they refer to (11.55 – the train time, 10 – the platform number).

Play the rest of the recording and get students to write down the numbers in announcements 2 and 3. Allow students to check in pairs before checking with the class.

Elicit any places in the announcements that students can remember. Play sections of the recording again as necessary.

Answers

See exercise 2 for **T 12.11**.

1 Numbers: 11.55 – the train time, ten – the platform number
Places: Newcastle, Peterborough, York, Darlington (cities on the route to the north-east of England)
2 Numbers: 22 – the bus number
Places: Piccadilly Circus, Green Park (places in London)
3 Numbers: BA1536 – the flight number, 58 – the gate number, 12 to 20 – the number of the rows
Places: New York

4 This exercise helps to prepare students for exercises 5 and 6, as the lines are taken from the conversations in those tasks.

Elicit the answer for sentence 1. Get students to complete the task in pairs. Then check with the class.

Answers

1 bus 2 train 3 bus 4 plane 5 plane 6 train

5 **T 12.12** [**CD 3: Track 49**] Explain that exercise 5 contains the lines from conversations 1 and 2 in jumbled order. The lines for speaker A and speaker B appear in separate columns of the charts.

Focus attention on the example for conversation 1 and then elicit the next line (*A day return to Oxford, please.*) Put students in pairs to continue working out the correct order for each conversation. With weaker students, you could order all of the lines in conversation 1 as a class activity and then let students do conversation 2 in pairs. Monitor and help as necessary.

Play the recording and let students check they have ordered the lines correctly. Ask them to practise the conversations in their pairs.

Answers and tapescript

Conversation 1

A	B
5 At 9.55. The platform number has just gone up on the departures board. 1 Next, please! 7 Have a good journey! 3 That's £12.70.	6 Oh, yes. I can see. Thank you very much. 2 A day return to Oxford, please. 4 Thank you. What time does the next train leave?

Conversation 2

A	B
5 Oh, thanks for your help. 3 Where can I get it? 1 Excuse me, does the number 24 go to the Natural History Museum?	4 From that bus stop over there. 6 Don't mention it. 2 No, it doesn't. You need the 360.

T 12.12

Conversation 1

A Next, please!
B A day return to Oxford, please.
A That's £12.70.
B Thank you. What time does the next train leave?
A At 9.55. The platform number has just gone up on the departures board.
B Oh, yes. I can see. Thank you very much.
A Have a good journey!

Conversation 2

A Excuse me, does the number 24 go to the Natural History Museum?
B No, it doesn't. You need the 360.
A Where can I get it?
B From that bus stop over there.
A Oh, thanks for your help.
B Don't mention it.

6 **T 12.13** **[CD 3: Track 50]** Focus attention on the photo of Mel and Lara. Ask students what they can remember about them. (*They are friends from Australia. They are planning a trip to Europe.*)

Check students understand that A in the conversation stands for *Assistant*. Pre-teach/check *scales*. With weaker classes, give students time to read the conversation through before playing the recording.

Play the recording and get students to complete the conversation. Elicit where Lara and Mel are and check the missing words in the conversation.

Answers and tapescript

Lara and Mel are at the airport.

T 12.13

A = Assistant M = Mel L = Lara

A Have you **checked in** online?
M Yes, we have.
A Fine. How many **suitcases** have you got?
L We haven't got **suitcases**, just **backpacks**.
A Oh, yes. Can you put them on the scales?
M Here you are …
A They're fine. And how many pieces of **hand luggage**?
L Just these **bags**.
A They're fine, too. You **board** from Gate Nine at 10.20.
L Where do we go now?
A To the departure gate and **security check**. They're over there. Have a nice **flight**!
M Thanks very much. Goodbye.

7 Give students time to practise the conversations in their pairs. Monitor and check. If students have problems with pronunciation, drill key lines chorally and individually and then get students to repeat the pairwork.

Students choose one or two conversations and rehearse them a few times to help them memorize the lines. Monitor and help. Students act out their conversation(s) to the class.

EXTRA ACTIVITY

Students review the language of travelling by plane by ordering the key stages of getting a flight. Dictate the following sentences *in jumbled order* and then get students to number them in the correct order. (This is based on a passenger with just hand luggage.)

1 You check in online.
2 You print your boarding pass.
3 You arrive at the airport.
4 You show the assistant your boarding pass and hand luggage.
5 You go through passport control and the security check.
6 You wait in the departure lounge.
7 You hear the announcement for the gate number for your flight.
8 You go to the gate and board the plane.

Students can then personalize the language by telling a true anecdote or imagining a story about an experience they had when waiting to board a flight.

ADDITIONAL MATERIAL

Teacher's Resource Disc

Communicative activity Unit 12 Challenge!

WRITING (SB p167)

A poem

Choosing the right word

The final unit in the writing syllabus appeals to students' creative side with a guided task on writing verses of a poem. The model poem *Why did you leave?* sits well with the unit theme of travel and moving on, but is also open to interpretation, allowing students to use their imagination in discussing the poem and writing their own verses.

1 This task reviews question words and prepares students for the question and answer format of the poem.

Elicit the matching answer to *What …? (A suitcase)*. Check students understand that *Whose …?* asks about possession, e.g. *Whose mobile is that? It's Mike's.* Then put students in pairs to continue the task. Check the answers.

Elicit a possible complete answer for the *What …?* question, e.g. *What are you taking on holiday?* Students then continue the task, working in their pairs.

Elicit a range of possible answers in a brief checking stage. Different tenses are possible in some of the questions but make sure students use the Past Simple in questions for *Last September* and *Because I needed a holiday*.

Answers
What …? A suitcase.
Where …? Spain.
When …? Last September.
Why …? Because I needed a holiday.
Who …? Nobody.
How …? By boat.
Which …? The small brown one.
Whose …? It's mine.

Possible complete questions
What are you taking on holiday? A suitcase.
Where are you going on holiday? Spain.
When did you go to the US? Last September.
Why did you go to Italy? Because I needed a holiday.
Who are you travelling with? Nobody.
How are you going to travel? By boat.
Which backpack is yours? The small brown one.
Whose suitcase is this? It's mine.

2 Focus attention on the title and give students time to read the poem. Tell them not to worry about the missing words for now. Explain that there are no 'right' answers to the questions in exercise 2. Give students a few moments to think about their answers and then put them in pairs/ small groups to compare their ideas.

Elicit a range of ideas from the class, encouraging students to give reasons for their answers.

3 Focus attention on the pairs of words for each gapped line of the poem and deal with any vocabulary queries. Students work in their pairs/small groups to discuss the words they think fit best. With weaker classes, you could give students time to choose the words independently first and then move on to the discussion stage. Again, explain that there are no 'right' answers to the choice of words, but encourage students to justify their ideas as best they can.

Ask a student from each pair/group to read out a verse of their version of the poem. Establish if most of the class have made similar or very different choices.

4 **T 12.14** **[CD 3: Track 51]** Tell students they are going to hear a version of the poem. Play the recording and get students to circle the word chosen each time.

Students then compare their version with the recording. Ask which they think is better and why.

Answers
Verse 1: morning, asleep
Verse 2: huge, place
Verse 3: mobile phone, memories
Verse 4: taxi, plane, always
Verse 5: the world, me
Verse 6: known, say
Verse 7: somebody

5 Focus attention on the framework for the next verses in the poem. Point out the repetition in the questions and that students need to write a different answer each time. With weaker students, elicit the type of language that can complete each answer and write examples on the board, e.g.

I met	*a wise old man/a young child/a happy traveller*
	someone sitting on the beach/someone walking in the hills/someone travelling the world
You	*can listen to my story/give me food and water/ offer me a place to sleep*
I've learned	*to be patient/not to judge people*

Give students time to write their verses in class or set the task for homework.

Students take it in turns to read out their verses, either later in the same lesson or in a subsequent class. Let students compare the different versions and choose which they find most interesting.

If possible, display the poems on the classroom wall or noticeboard. When you check the students' work, point out errors but allow students to correct them themselves. Try to limit correction to major problems to avoid demoralizing the students.

SUGGESTION

If your students enjoyed the poem-writing task, you could get them to bring along an illustration that they feel fits with the words. This can be a photo of their own, an image taken from a magazine, or for the artistic ones, a drawing/painting they have done themselves. These can be displayed on the wall/noticeboard with the students' poems.

Don't forget!

Grammar Reference (SB p192 and Teacher's Resource Disc)
Unit 12

Word list (SB p221 and Teacher's Resource Disc)
Unit 12

Tests (Teacher's Resource Disc)
Unit test 12A
Unit test 12B
Stop and check 3 (Units 9–12)
Progress test 2 (Units 7–12)
Skills test 4 (Units 9–12)
Skills test 5 (Units 1–12)
Exit test 1
Exit test 2

Video (DVD)
Unit 12 Experiences

Student A

1 Read the conversations with a partner. Find out the missing words.

Conversation 1

A Thank goodness it's Friday! Bye, Harry.
B ____________________
A Thanks. Same to you.
B ____________________

Conversation 2

C Hello, Mr Harrison. How are you?
D ____________________
C Very well, thanks.

Conversation 3

E Good morning!
F ____________________
E Yes, of course! Anything else?
F ____________________

Conversation 4

G ____________________
H No, thank you. I'm just looking.
G ____________________

2 Work with a new partner. Practise the conversations.

Student B

1 Read the conversations with a partner. Find out the missing words.

Conversation 1

A ____________________
B Bye, Tessa. Have a good weekend.
A ____________________
B See you on Monday.

Conversation 2

C ____________________
D Fine, thank you. And you?
C ____________________

Conversation 3

E ____________________
F Good morning! Can I have a coffee, an espresso, please?
E ____________________
F No, thank you.

Conversation 4

G Good afternoon! Can I help you?
H ____________________
G That's OK.

2 Work with a new partner. Practise the conversations.

START	**About you** my age ▶	**Make a question** Your teacher = married?	**What's the job?** He looks after people's teeth. ▼
Make a question Where / your favourite actor come from? ▼	**Opposites** the opposite of *cheap*	**Make a question** What / your phone number?	**What's the job?** She works with money. ◀
Make a question Where / your best friend work? ▶	**What's the job?** She designs buildings.	**About you** my job	**What's the job?** He cuts hair. ▼
Make a question Where / your teacher live? ▼	**Make a question** What / your best friend's job?	**What's the job?** She writes news stories.	**Opposites** the opposite of *nice* ◀
Make a question What time / now? ▶	**About you** I like ...	**Opposites** the opposite of *old*	**Make a question** Your teacher = speak Italian? ▼
FINISH	**Make a question** What / your best friend like doing?	**About you** I / married.	**Make a question** How / spell your surname? ◀

		Question	Answer
1	go to the gym	______	______
2	play cards	______	______
3	read a book	______	______
4	cook for friends	______	______
5	go skiing	______	______
6	listen to music	______	______
7	go swimming	______	______
8	go to the cinema	______	______
9		______	______
10		______	______

1 Write questions for 1–8. Use your own ideas for 9 and 10.

2 Work in pairs. Ask and answer the questions. Write your partner's answers.

3 Work in groups of four. Talk about your answers and find ...

- an activity your group does every day
- an activity your group never does.

1 Do the numbers quiz. Then compare your answers with a partner.

Numbers

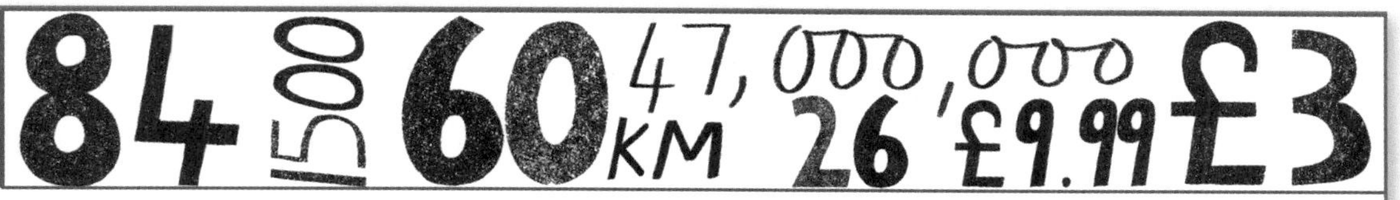

1	How many players are there in a hockey team?	a 9	b 10	c 11
2	How many letters are there in the English alphabet?	a 24	b 26	c 30
3	How many seconds are there in an hour?	a 3600	b 3000	c 36,000
4	How many keys are there on a piano?	a 66	b 77	c 88
5	At what age can you vote in the UK?	a 16	b 18	c 21
6	Which of these are coins in the UK?	a 20p, 50p, £5	b 50p, £1, £5	c 50p, £1, £2
7	What's the speed limit on motorways in the UK?	a 113km an hour	b 133km an hour	c 153km an hour
8	What will the population of the UK be by 2018?	a about 63,000,000	b about 65,000,000	c about 70,000,000

2 How much are these things in your country and in the UK? If you are not sure, guess.

Prices

	Your country	the UK
a day travel-card in the capital city		
a coffee and a daily newspaper		
a cinema ticket for an adult		
a week's food shopping for two adults		
dinner in a 3-star restaurant		
a top-20 CD		
a litre of petrol		
a month's rent in a small flat in the capital city		

3 Compare your answers to exercise 2 in small groups. What things are expensive in your country? And in the UK?

me a hand with the washing-up?	Can you ride	a motorbike?	Do you live
on the third floor?	How often do you look	after the children?	Can I try
on these jeans?	Do you send	a lot of text messages?	How many languages
can you speak?	Could you tell	me the time, please?	Do you like listening
to music?	Can I have	a black coffee, please?	Do you earn
a lot of money?	Could I speak	to you for a minute?	Can I borrow
your pen, please?	Do you watch	television a lot?	Do you wear
a suit and tie for work?	Can you lend	me €20 till next week, please?	Can you play
the guitar?	Could you post	this letter for me?	Can you give

1 Read the sentences and circle the correct adjectives in *italics* (*-ed* or *-ing*).

2 Change the underlined information in the sentences to make them true for you.

3 Compare your answers in pairs or small groups.

1. The most *tiring/tired* part of my week is commuting to work.
2. As a child, I was *frightening/frightened* of dogs.
3. I'm always *annoying/annoyed* when people use their mobile in a restaurant.
4. I was really *embarrassing/embarrassed* when I fell over in the street.
5. My best friend's most *irritating/irritated* habit is talking all the time.
6. My most *interesting/interested* teacher at school taught French.
7. I was really *boring/bored* when I saw the film Avatar.
8. I was a bit *worrying/worried* before my driving test.
9. The most *exciting/excited* sport is football.
10. I was very *surprised/surprising* when my brother got married.

close the door … quietly		ride a motorbike … carefully	
drive … badly		go to sleep … quickly	
play the piano … well		study … hard	
skateboard … slowly		arrive … late	
breathe … deeply		do the housework … happily	
get up … early		drink tea … noisily	
eat an ice-cream … quickly		sit down … carefully	

Student A

1 Answer Student B's questions about your recipe.

Aromatic chicken

Ingredients
- 1 tbsp oil
- 2 onions, chopped
- 3 cloves garlic, chopped
- 1 tsp ginger
- 500g chicken, chopped
- 300ml chicken stock
- 200g dried apricots
- 25g almonds, chopped

1 Heat the oil in a medium saucepan. Fry the onion and garlic until soft.

2 Add the chicken and the ginger. Cook for about 5 minutes. Then add the stock.

3 Boil, then cover the pan with a lid and cook on a low heat for about 15 minutes.

4 Take off the lid and add the apricots. Mix well and cook for another 10 minutes until the sauce is thick and the chicken is cooked.

5 Sprinkle the almonds on top of the chicken. Serve with couscous and a green salad.

2 Ask Student B about his/her recipe. Complete the information.

Fresh tuna with tomatoes

Ingredients
- ______ tuna steaks
- ______ tbsp olive oil
- ______ small onion, chopped
- ______ clove garlic, chopped
- ______g tomatoes, peeled and chopped
- ______ml dry white wine
- ______g anchovies, mashed
- ______g black olives

1 Heat the oil in a frying pan. Fry the tuna for about ______ minute until brown on both sides. Move the fish to a warm plate.

2 Add the onions and ______ and fry until soft. Mix in the ______, tomatoes, and anchovies.

3 ______, then cover the pan and cook on a low heat for about ______ minutes.

4 Put the fish back in the pan and cook for another ______ minutes.

5 Add the ______ and mix gently. Serve with crusty ______ and a green salad.

3 Which recipe would you like to try? What was the last thing you cooked at home?

Student B

1 Ask Student A about his/her recipe. Complete the information.

Aromatic chicken

Ingredients
- _____ tbsp oil
- _____ onions, chopped
- _____ cloves garlic, chopped
- _____ tsp ginger
- _____g chicken, chopped
- _____ml chicken stock
- _____g dried apricots
- _____g almonds, chopped

1 Heat the oil in a medium saucepan. Fry the _____ and _____ until soft.

2 Add the chicken and the _____. Cook for about _____ minutes. Then add the stock.

3 Boil, then cover the pan with a lid and cook on a low heat for about _____ minutes.

4 Take off the lid and add the _____. Mix well and cook for another _____ minutes until the sauce is thick and the chicken is cooked.

5 Sprinkle the _____ on top of the chicken. Serve with couscous and a green salad.

2 Answer Student A's questions about your recipe.

Fresh tuna with tomatoes

Ingredients
- 4 tuna steaks
- 3 tbsp olive oil
- 1 small onion, chopped
- 1 clove garlic, chopped
- 750g tomatoes, peeled and chopped
- 75ml dry white wine
- 25g anchovies, mashed
- 50g black olives

1 Heat the oil in a frying pan. Fry the tuna for about 1 minute until brown on both sides. Move the fish to a warm plate.

2 Add the onions and garlic and fry until soft. Mix in the wine, tomatoes, and anchovies.

3 Boil, then cover the pan with a lid and cook on a low heat for about 10 minutes.

4 Put the fish back in the pan and cook for another 8 minutes.

5 Add the olives and mix gently. Serve with crusty bread and a green salad.

3 Which recipe would you like to try? What was the last thing you cooked at home?

Unit 9 The best place to live TB p103

1 Complete the questions with the superlative form of the adjectives. Then write the answers for your country. Don't always choose your own city / region!

Where's the best place to live?		Answers
1	Which city has the biggest (BIG) population?	__________
2	Which city has __________ (bad) architecture?	__________
3	Where is __________ (beautiful) countryside?	__________
4	Which region has __________ (good) reputation for food?	__________
5	Where are __________ (interesting) tourist attractions?	__________
6	Which airport is __________ (busy)?	__________
7	Which region is __________ (expensive)?	__________
8	Who are __________ (friendly) people?	__________
9	Which city is __________ (dangerous)?	__________
10	Which region has __________ (modern) public transport?	__________

2 Work in groups and discuss your answers. Give reasons for your answers.

3 Work as a class. Tell your classmates about the best region / city in your country. Try to persuade them to live there!

Unit 10 Something's happening TB p116

1 I spent an hour looking for my car keys but	I couldn't find them __________.
2 I called the police because	__________ tried to steal my car.
3 I invited all of my friends for Sunday lunch but	__________ was busy that weekend.
4 My old flat wasn't in a very nice area because	there was litter __________.
5 The weather in the UK was awful last year so	I decided to go __________ warm this summer.
6 I had to stand on the train to work because	there was __________ to sit.
7 I didn't enjoy my French course very much because	I didn't know __________ in the class.
8 I watched an old DVD because	there was __________ interesting on TV.
9 I wanted to buy some new clothes but	__________ in the designer shop was too expensive.
10 I woke up suddenly because	I heard __________ strange in the corner of the bedroom.
11 I picked up the phone and said 'hello' but	there was __________ there.
12 I was so hungry when I got home but	there wasn't __________ in the fridge.

Key words

everything	**nobody**	**somewhere**
nothing	**anybody**	**everywhere**
anything	**somebody**	**anywhere**
something	**everybody**	**nowhere**

Unit 11 Making suggestions TB p134

1 Write the activities in the correct column.

go to the beach **go to a gallery**
have a picnic **play cards**
go to the cinema **go for a walk**
go fishing **update our blog**
play golf **make a cake**
watch a DVD **do some gardening**

Good weather	Bad weather

2 Work with a partner. Have a conversation. Talk about the weather and make suggestions about what to do.

A (Talk about the weather, good or bad.)
What ...!

B (Agree about the weather. Ask for a suggestion.)
Yeah!/I know. It's ... . What ...?

A (Make a suggestion.)
Let's ...!/Shall we ...?

B (Disagree with the suggestion. Give a reason.)
Oh no! I/We/It's ...

A (Make a different suggestion.)
OK, then, let's ... /shall we ...?

B (Agree with the suggestion. Say what you will do.)
Great!/Good idea! I'll ...

3 Work with a new partner. Make another conversation.

1 Have you ever bought anything on the Internet ? Yes/No
What did you buy?
____
(your own question)
____

2 Have you ever written a blog ? Yes/No
How many people read it?
____
(your own question)
____

3 Have you ever won a competition ? Yes/No
What did you win?
____
(your own question)
____

4 Have you ever broken a bone ? Yes/No
How did it happen?
____
(your own question)
____

5 Have you ever eaten Mexican food ? Yes/No
What was it like?
____
(your own question)
____

6 Have you ever been to South America ? Yes/No
Where did you go?
____
(your own question)
____

7 Have you ever lost something important ? Yes/No
What was it?
____
(your own question)
____

8 Have you ever slept on the beach ? Yes/No
Why did you do that?
____
(your own question)
____

9 Have you ever seen an accident ? Yes/No
What did you do?
____
(your own question)
____

10 Have you ever done anything for charity? Yes/No
What did you do?
____
(your own question)
____

OXFORD
UNIVERSITY PRESS

Great Clarendon Street, Oxford, OX2 6DP, United Kingdom

Oxford University Press is a department of the University of Oxford. It furthers the University's objective of excellence in research, scholarship, and education by publishing worldwide. Oxford is a registered trade mark of Oxford University Press in the UK and in certain other countries

First published in 2014
2018 2017 2016 2015 2014
10 9 8 7 6 5 4 3 2

ISBN: 978 0 19 474132 3 Teacher's Pack
ISBN: 978 0 19 474127 9 Teacher's Book
ISBN: 978 0 19 474133 0 Teacher's Resource Disc
ISBN: 978 0 19 474130 9 Class Audio CDs

Printed in China

This book is printed on paper from certified and well-managed sources.

ACKNOWLEDGEMENTS

The authors and publisher are grateful to those who have given permission to reproduce the following extracts and adaptations of copyright material:

p.24 *Babur Ali* The direct quotations in this story have been adapted to assist understanding.

pp.57–58 adapted from 'Relative Values: Nicola Benedetti and her father, Gio' by Beverly D'Silva, *The Sunday Times Magazine*, 30 September 2007. © Beverley D'Silva/The Sunday Times Magazine/nisyndication.com. Reproduced by permission.

p.67 This interview with Ben Way is fictitious and is based on factual information from a number of sources.

p.79 *1909 The first air journey* The direct quotations in this story have been adapted to assist understanding.

p.119 This interview with Soichi Noguchi is fictitious and is based on factual information from a number of sources.

p.130 Recording of 'Oats and Beans' used by kind permission of Walk Around Britain Ltd. www.awalkaroundbritain.com.

Illustrations by: Gill Button p.150, p.153, p.158; Debbie Powell p.151, p.156; Harry Venning p.154

Although every effort has been made to trace and contact copyright holders before publication, this has not been possible in some cases. We apologise for any apparent infringement of copyright and, if notified, the publisher will be pleased to rectify any errors or omissions at the earliest possible opportunity.